A Cloistered War

Behind the Convent Walls during the Japanese Occupation

A CLOISTERED WAR is a coming-of-age memoir set in Malaya before and after World War II. Maisie Duncan brings us back to the delightful times of curry tiffins, porcelain dolls, Cantonese amahs, and (not-so-delightful) castor-oil Saturdays. This happy state of affairs changes dramatically when the author's mother dies and her father remarries. Maisie and her siblings are sent away from the family home to CHIJ institutions and Christian Brothers' schools.

The two girls spend the next fourteen years of their youth traversing Malaya as boarders in these cloistered worlds. Having witnessed the first air raid over Singapore, the sisters survive a number of perilous events, including a convent invasion by Japanese troops looking for 'comfort women'. Throughout the Occupation, they lived under the watchful eyes of the convent nuns — a varied lot fleshed out by Maisie's sharp, humorous and often poignant recollections.

An unusual feature of this book is the even-handed account of Japanese behaviour towards their captive civilian population. Graphic descriptions of Japanese brutality are juxtaposed with incidents of kindness and humanity displayed by the occupying forces.

This first-time author, granddaughter of Captain Vaz, a well-known Penang identity, offers some memorable insights into an important slice of Malayan history.

Maisie Duncan

A CLOISTERED WAR

Behind the Convent Walls during the Japanese Occupation

TIMES EDITIONS

Cover design and map (page xii) by Benson Tan.

Aerial view of CHIJ convent (cover) and photographs (in pages 104 & 105) published with permission from CHIJMES Investment Pte Ltd.

Illustration of CHIJ convent gate (title page) published with permission from CHIJMES Investment Pte Ltd and the Sisters of the Infant Jesus (Singapore).

Japanese 'banana' note on page 106 courtesy of the National Archives of Singapore.

Many thanks to Sister Carmel of St Maur International School, Yokohama, Japan for her permission to publish the extract on page 60.

Published by Times Editions – Marshall Cavendish
An imprint of Marshall Cavendish International (Asia) Private Limited
A member of Times Publishing Limited
Times Centre, 1 New Industrial Road, Singapore 536196
Tel: (65) 6213 9288 Fax: (65) 6285 4871
E-mail: te@sg.marshallcavendish.com
Online Bookstore: http://www.timesone.com.sg/te

Malaysian Office:
Federal Publications Sdn Berhad
(General & Reference Publishing) (3024-D)
Times Subang
Lot 46, Persiaran Teknologi Subang
Subang Hi-Tech Industrial Park
Batu Tiga, 40000 Shah Alam
Selangor Darul Ehsan, Malaysia
Tel: (603) 5635 2191 Fax: (603) 5635 2706
E-mail: cchong@tpg.com.my

National Library Board (Singapore) Cataloguing in Publication Data

Duncan, Maisie, 1931-
A cloistered war : behind the convent walls during the Japanese occupation / Maisie Duncan. – Singapore : Times Editions, 2004.
p. cm.
ISBN : 981-232-814-9

1. Duncan, Maisie, 1931- 2. Convent of the Holy Infant Jesus (Singapore) – History. 3. World War, 1939-1945 – Personal narratives. 4. Young women – Malaya – Biography. 5. Malaya – History – Japanese occupation, 1942-1945. 6. Singapore – History – Japanese occupation, 1942-1945. I. Title.

D811.5 940.5425092 — dc21 SLS2004016948

Printed in Singapore

For 'Big Sister' Olga

in appreciation of your enduring devotion and loyalty

Contents

Author's Note

Everyone has a story to tell, but for a variety of reasons many people remain silent. My memoir is the result of two major stimuli — family curiosity on the one hand and friendly encouragement from my fellow teachers at Brisbane Girls' Grammar School on the other.

Many years ago my children were attending a primary school on Brisbane's northside. Usually, as soon as they got home, they'd ask for something to eat. But on one occasion they asked, out of the blue, 'Mum, where were we born? Our teacher wants to know.'

At the time I was busy in the kitchen, so I gave them a short answer — 'Batu Gajah, a small town in Malaya.'

They looked bewildered.

'Your father worked there as a tin miner and you were all born at the local hospital … I'll tell you about it one day.'

The other stimulus occurred in the BGGS staffroom, during the less frenzied working climate of the 70s and 80s. The leisurely lunch periods allowed time for teachers to recharge their batteries and exchange anecdotes from their widely-diverging backgrounds. As the newly-appointed teacher of Japanese, my tales of World War II Japanese Occupation of Malaya always received a good hearing. My listeners were intrigued to discover that I first studied Japanese as a compulsory subject in Singapore, way back in 1942.

The collective wisdom of my peers could be expressed in one sentence: 'Write it all down, Maisie — do it now, before you forget what happened.'

My response invariably was, 'Yes, of course I will, but I'm too busy now. I'll get round to it sometime.'

In writing my memoir, I have obviously ignored the famous exhortation by John Cleese in *Fawlty Towers*: 'DON'T MENTION THE WAR!' For those of us who lived through it, avoiding the subject altogether was extremely difficult. We are all aware that the actor did not follow his own advice. For my part, I did mention the war frequently. As one might expect, the 'W' word was the dominant influence, but scores of other important words made their presence felt and demanded serious attention: the 'D' word for Death, the 'R' Word for Religion, Romance and Racial Prejudice, while the 'H' word for Humour kept popping up on occasion to maintain the balance between tears and laughter.

I discovered that the mere physical act of putting pen to paper released a flood of long-submerged memories. My memoir grew apace and it became a question of what to exclude instead of what to include if I was ever to complete the work and redeem my promise.

So here is my story — nearly thirty years later!

Special thanks to …

I would like to make the following acknowledgments:

To my cousin Billy Coules, for undertaking the daunting task of finding me a publisher and cleverly knocking on the door of Marshall Cavendish.

To the hardworking and helpful team at Marshall Cavendish, who listened to my suggestions and requests and attempted, where possible, to carry them out.

To Chijmes Investment Pte Ltd, especially Esther Yong and Tanya Fum, for their generous sponsorship in connection with the book launch.

To my old and valued friends, Mary and Doris Liew, for their enthusiastic support of this venture.

To my former colleague Svyetlana Hadgraft, for acting as my BGGS in-house publicity agent, and to Roberta King, for aiding and abetting her.

To my daughter-in-law Jan for capably handling all the email traffic between me and my contacts in Singapore.

And to my wonderful family and friends, for their continuing support and encouragement.

Maisie Duncan
Helensvale, Queensland
Australia

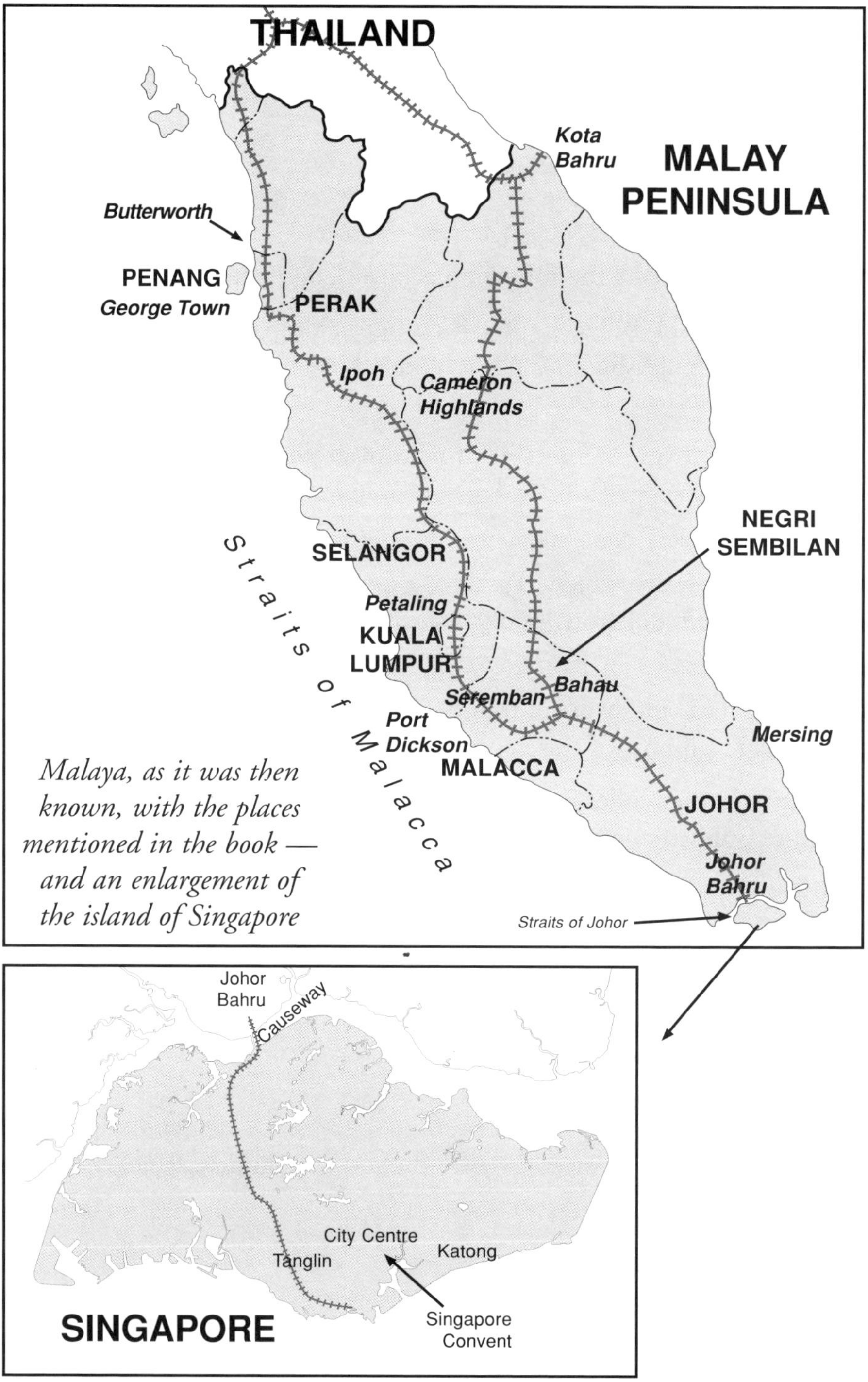

Malaya, as it was then known, with the places mentioned in the book — and an enlargement of the island of Singapore

1

THE IMPREGNABLE FORTRESS

August 1941: Katong Beach

Wash of warm wavelets on the gritty sand
Bathing-capped nuns' heads bobbing up and down in the shallows
Muffled drumbeats rising to a crescendo
as khaki-clad, sinewy 'drumsticks' pound their way past the front fence
and round the corner towards the boarders' dormitory.
Its heavy-shuttered windows crash open
as if on cue to reveal a cloud of disembodied balloon faces
shadowy against the interior gloom, straining towards the exterior
sunlight and the jetstream of turbulence
raised by the wild marching feet on the gravelled laneway below.
Hoots of laughter, wolf whistles and snatches of song
greet the dramatic window-stage appearance of the faces.
A current of excitement builds up
between the pale, cloistered, curiosity-filled girls above
and the sunburnt, devil-may-care, slouch-hatted warriors below.

'Girls! Girls!' the stern voice of authority breaks the spell. 'Close the shutters at once!' The duty nun claps her hands hard and repeatedly as she patrols the fence 'Close them NOW!' The order is obeyed — but not immediately, not before those inside have overheard and savoured several cheeky retorts. 'Girls worrying you, Sister? We'll look after them for you! Promise!' Followed by a loud chorus: 'Oh, Sister, please!'

And an older, apologetic voice — 'Don't mind the lads, Sister, they're all keyed up.'

The marching men moved on, the laneway was quiet once more, then footsteps were heard on the staircase and we knew before Madame uttered a word that we were all in trouble.

Mine was the face at the base of the balloon cloud. I was ten years old, the youngest and smallest of the group, and had joined in enthusiastically as we cheered and waved to the passing parade. Carried away in the excitement of the moment, we had acted in an unladylike manner. My thirteen year-old sister had been equally unrestrained, but we knew that the older members of the group would be considered the most culpable, because wisdom was supposed to come with age. Two years in the convent had taught us how the system worked. There were two or three twenty-year-olds and even one 'venerable' twenty-one year-old in our group. They were all barred from swimming that afternoon as a punishment, and the rest of us were warned that a similar fate would befall us if we behaved like brazen young hussies instead of conducting ourselves as well-bred young ladies. 'Nice young ladies,' we were informed, 'do not wave and call out to strange young men, especially not to soldiers.'

'They weren't English soldiers, were they?' I asked.

'They were Australians!' came the answer — and no further explanations were required.

I wanted to ask, 'What's a hussy?' but I wasn't game; however, I did know why Madame had used that scornful dismissive tone when she said 'Australians'. We'd all heard of 'the Aussies'. They hadn't been in our part of the world for very long, but already they were notorious. The local press frequently printed accounts of their escapades, accurately or grossly exaggerated and word of mouth did the rest.

The boarders were not allowed to read the papers but day girls could be coaxed or bribed to sneak in the juicy items for our secret perusal. So we had some idea, however lopsided, of the 'goings-on' outside the high walls topped by broken glass.

According to local gossip, the Aussies behaved like a bunch of overgrown schoolboys let loose on an orderly, law-abiding community. They indulged in public pranks such as taking rickshaw drivers for a spin in their own rickshaws, taking over from traffic policemen at busy intersections and attempting to direct the traffic themselves, relieving travelling hawkers of their shoulder-borne mobile stalls and collecting headgear of all descriptions from the local people: songkoks from the

Malays, conical straw hats from the Chinese, turbans from the Sikhs (the last group of locals were not susceptible to snatch-and-grab attempts, as the lads soon discovered). Oh yes, we'd heard about the Australians!

No wonder we'd stared down at the men pounding the gravelled laneway below with a more than usual intensity. Columns of marching troops had become quite commonplace in Singapore in 1941. The island city had turned into a garrison town and people joked that soon there would be one soldier per citizen.

Generally speaking, the white middle-class establishment tended to look down on the crass, unruly Diggers who, they believed, were letting down the tone of mannered, colonial society. But the very things the upper echelons found objectionable were the qualities that endeared them to us; young would-be rebels who found the strict, perhaps repressive convent discipline very irksome at times.

The Diggers were unlike the neat and orderly British troops. There was a laxity about the way they interpreted their military dress code. The carelessly-buttoned khaki shirts topped-off by the jaunty set of the slouch hat proclaimed 'Yes, we are soldiers, but make no mistake about it, we are also free spirits!'

Late that evening, we girls sat around after dinner engaging in one of our most popular pastimes: the search for 'Mr Right'. It began, 'When I grow up, I'll marry a — '

'Your turn, Maisie, what's it to be? Butcher, baker, soldier, sailor … ?'

I announced with quiet conviction: 'I'll marry an Australian.'

December 1941

The brash young men we'd seen in late August did not have to wait long for the big adventure. The air was heavy with discussion about the course of the war in Europe and rumours of an impending attack on Malaya. Even in a protected environment like ours, news filtered through and the nuns no longer attempted to silence the war talk that boarders indulged in freely. We sat our end-of-year exams early that year and began to take part in air-raid drills directed by newly appointed air-raid wardens. They recommended that, in the absence of proper air-raid shelters, we should take cover under the many concrete or wooden staircases in the imposing main school buildings, smack in the heart of Singapore's business district. Crouched or kneeling in their makeshift shelters, some of the older nuns, survivors of World War I in Europe, shared their experiences with their young, inquisitive charges. After every gripping anecdote the narrator would conclude, 'Pray for Peace, children, pray very hard. War is terrible!'

Quietly subversive, I thought, 'War is exciting! I want to experience it — just for a little while, so that I'll be able to tell my children I have lived through a war.' I was thinking in terms of a few weeks, at most a few months, of hostilities. Then our side would thrash the enemy and peace would return. So simple, as I imagined then — so impossible, as I know now.

War came to our island out of a clear moonlit sky in the shape of a flight of metallic bees emblazoned with blood-red discs whose bellies rained down sinister grey eggs on an unsuspecting population.

We were awakened from our sleep by the drone of low-flying planes overhead, followed by a series of explosions nearby which shook the old wooden dormitory. As soon as we heard those moonlit explosions, the same eager faces that had crammed the window space at the Katong Beach convent now lined the balcony outside the boarders' dormitory. Those who had cheered on the brash young Aussies now stared in terror and fascination at the unfamiliar planes with their strange red markings as they dived low over the chapel roof, released their deadly cargo, then rose again, seemingly just missing the tall spire. Then came the sound of gunfire — and finally, belatedly, the wailing air-raid siren.

Outside the perimeter fence, we glimpsed smoke and flames, heard screams and later the clanging of fire engines. At this point the duty nuns rushed us downstairs to the nearest staircase-shelter to await the All Clear.

To our anxious queries ('Has War begun?' 'Those planes we saw, were they enemy planes?') our guides nodded in an uncomprehending and dazed way and their fear and disquiet transmitted itself to us so that we returned to our beds subdued and troubled.

Sleep was out of the question. Some chose to talk until the Mass bell knowing that on this occasion there would be no punishment for disobeying the strict rule of silence during bedtime hours. I lay quietly in my bed thinking, 'This is IT, WAR!' Was I still in favour of it?' I called up in my mind a vivid snapshot of those gleaming Japanese Zeroes above the chapel roof of the convent and relived that memorable moment in history; equally distinctly I heard again the agonised screams that followed the thudding of the bombs and the acrid smell of smoke. Could War have two faces, one exhilarating, the other horrendous? I faced the new day feeling both excited and terrified.

We crowded round the small radio, nuns and boarders together, to hear the eight o'clock news. Listening to news bulletins was not part of the daily routine; we were all aware that the occasion was special, the matter serious.

The calm tones of the news announcer confirmed for us what we already knew. War had come to the Far East, Japanese planes had bombed Singapore in the early hours of the morning and an invasion force had landed on the east coast of the peninsula at Kota Bahru. The Japanese had taken the British completely by surprise, just as they had, without warning, devastated the American fleet at Pearl Harbor, a few hours earlier on the night of 7 December 1941.

The news bulletin ended with the assurance that Singapore was impregnable and the Allied forces would soon overcome the enemy.

This bland assurance of security was put into question a couple of days later when the battleships *Prince of Wales* and *Repulse* were sunk by Japanese aircraft off the east coast of Malaya. Reverend Mother St James, the Mother Superior of the Singapore convent, decided not to put her faith in the promises and propaganda of the British authorities. Instead, she resolved to send as many of her charges as possible away from the island city to Seremban, a small, quiet, semi-rural town about forty miles south of Kuala Lumpur, the Malayan capital. This was to be our rural refuge.

The Order of the Holy Infant Jesus, or Les Dames de St Maur as they were known in France, where the Order originated, operated a number of convents strung along the western coast of the peninsula, roughly following the main north-south rail and trunk line linking Singapore to Penang. Its major institutions were in Penang, Kuala Lumpur and Singapore. Some, like Seremban, were medium-sized, others quite small.

The larger institutions were little worlds in themselves, comprising living and sleeping quarters for nuns, boarding pupils (first- and second-class) and orphans, a baby house (for abandoned infants), chapel, infirmaries, playing-fields, storerooms and, of course, blocks of classrooms. All classifications had their own areas and seldom mingled, and the boarders and orphans were further subdivided into Big Boarders and Little Boarders, so that older and younger siblings met only at weekends. Even the nuns were divided into two groups. Those who taught in the classrooms were addressed as 'Madame St —'; those who performed domestic duties were known as 'Sister'. Most convents were situated on major roads in good city locations, isolated to a certain degree from unwanted worldly influences by high walls totally enclosing the premises. Some of these convent walls were topped off with broken glass — a clear message to intending escapees and would-be invaders alike!

St James, our Mother Superior, was one of the company who had survived World War I in France. This experience may have taught her that invading armies tend to pick strategic targets and concentrate their biggest efforts and firepower on them. Singapore appeared the obvious target for the fiercest fighting, the heaviest bombing and the highest casualties, and so she selected Seremban as an area of little or no strategic importance. The dear lady was right on both counts. When she announced her intention to send most of the boarders north before Christmas she must have met with gasps of incredulity from many of the assembled nuns. 'Sending them upcountry? Into the arms of the invading Japanese troops?' they might have said, had they ever dreamed of challenging anything this tiny human dynamo decided. St James' keen analytical brain and independent and courageous action says something about the quality of the missionaries that came to the Far East between the Wars.

The nuns who taught us, and in some cases inspired us, were no group of jilted maidens running away from the scene of their humiliation, as popular misconception would have it. They were, on the whole, good-looking and talented young women who would not have lacked for suitors but had chosen to follow a life dedicated to the service of God. Some, naturally, fell by the wayside, not worthy of the cause they espoused, but many more kept the divine flame alight to the end.

An obvious question: If I found so many admirable individuals in the convent ranks, why didn't I join the saintly throng? Three main reasons provide the answer: POVERTY, CHASTITY and OBEDIENCE, the vows taken by the novices on completion of their training.

POVERTY, as interpreted in the daily life of the Order, meant that nuns did without numerous creature comforts, their only possessions being essential personal items. The Order fed, clothed and housed them, but they owned nothing individually — not an attractive prospect to a young girl who had enjoyed an extremely comfortable life before becoming a convent boarder.

CHASTITY and the thought of renouncing forever the search for the partner of my dreams raised an even higher barrier. Today, when primary schoolchildren receive sex instruction, it is hard to comprehend how innocent we were then. Our boy/girl encounters consisted of smouldering looks exchanged across the aisles of a crowded church on Sundays. Would I have to give that up and keep my eyes cast down modestly forever and a day?

But most of all it was the rock of OBEDIENCE that stopped me in my tracks. Obeying without question one's religious superiors; submitting totally in mind and body to somebody who could conceivably be fallible — the idea did not bear thinking about.

A doubting Thomas from my early years, I was incapable of taking that great leap of faith which would have carried me over all obstacles, major and minor, that blocked my path to the religious life. There were times when the idea of 'taking the veil' seemed quite appealing, especially during one of the elaborate feast day celebrations inside the lovely chapel, when the voices of the choir soared in four-part harmony up to the vaulted roof, while rainbow-hued shafts of light coming through the stained-glass windows gave an unearthly glow to the interior space, highlighting the marble altar decorated with masses of fresh flowers, their heady perfume blending with the aromatic smoke from the incense burner.

On such an occasion, who would not have been tempted to join the band of nuns gliding up to the altar rails, an other-worldly look upon their faces, to receive the host out of a golden chalice at the hands of a figure resplendent in embroidered silks or satins? Was I responding to a true religious experience or to a hunger for beauty in an otherwise austere life?

For the chapel was an oasis of splendour in an otherwise spartan environment. All living areas — dining-rooms, dormitories, dressing-rooms, recreation halls, classrooms — lacked any soft decorative touches such as curtains, carpets, flowers or pretty lights. The chapel alone provided a feast for the senses to those starved of loveliness in daily life. So I was tempted, but not taken up into that rarefied atmosphere of union with Christ.

There was nothing rarefied about the atmosphere of the Singapore railway station about ten days after that first air-raid on the island. The southbound train had just disgorged hundreds of travellers, mostly European women and children, looking tired and bewildered, clutching bulging suitcases and untidy bundles. These were definitely not holiday-makers or visitors on a shopping spree; they were refugees seeking sanctuary in the Lion City (as Singapore is known). The air of uncertainty and unease was palpable. Our northbound group attracted a certain amount of attention and some curious looks. As we stood uneasily on the platform waiting for the signal to board the train, a young British army captain approached and with a note of surprise in his voice enquired, 'You young ladies heading north?'

Fifty pairs of eyes focussed on him; he was tall, good-looking, well-spoken. The nuns immediately lowered their gaze, but the boarders were happy to keep on looking. 'Yes, we're going to Seremban,' one of them told him.

'Seremban!' he exclaimed. 'A delightful spot. I was stationed there for a short time. So green and fresh — you'll be able to go for walks in the Lake Gardens.'

We girls exchanged glances. From what the Captain said, Seremban didn't seem such a bad place after all. Yet Singapore represented home, family and friends. One brave soul blurted out, 'We'd really prefer to stay in Singapore.'

'Oh, never fear, the war will be over in a few weeks and you'll be back on the island,' he replied, then with a friendly wave he disappeared into the crowd.

Somewhat reassured, we climbed aboard the train in a fairly cheerful frame of mind, telling ourselves we were taking a country holiday. We noticed that none of the accompanying nuns had scolded us for speaking to a strange man, especially one who was a soldier; in fact, one of our younger chaperones remarked, 'That was a very pleasant young man — let's hope he survives the war!'

Amen to that, we all thought as we spread ourselves out in the carriage which we had to ourselves, since all the population movement was southward. No one else seemed to be travelling north. There was a sense of barriers coming down: nuns, first-boarders, second-boarders and orphans shared the same carriage for the upcountry trip. As the train moved slowly out of the station, we waved openly to all and sundry on the platform, and a couple of the younger nuns even joined in the farewells.

Those of us among the boarders who had family and friends in Singapore had said our goodbyes during the disastrous week after the first air-raid; a week that had included the bombing and surrender of Penang as well as the sinking of the *Prince of Wales* and the *Repulse*.

Despite leaving two sets of first cousins behind, my sister Olga and I weren't as upset as we might have been about our departure from Singapore because we had expected to meet up with Dad again after a separation of approximately eighteen months. As the Senior Engineer with the Straits Steamship Company, he had operated from Singapore for several years, but in 1940 he had retired from his maritime position and taken up a shore job at Pacific Tin Mines, outside Kuala Lumpur.

As our train headed north the Japanese troops were steadily moving south. Ipoh was about to haul up the white flag. The Allied troops kept retreating 'according to plan' or had accomplished 'a strategic withdrawal' to prepare positions further south. There was considerable speculation about Kuala Lumpur, the Malayan capital, which seemed the logical choice for a major battle to stem the Japanese advance. If this happened, lost territory could be recovered and all refugees would be able to return to their homes. Along with everyone else, I hoped and prayed for a speedy Allied victory and a return to peace. My taste for war had ended very quickly. This ten-year-old warmonger had turned pacifist within the space of a week!

As we sat in the carriage, bearing us closer by the hour to the enemy lines, we were not terrified at the prospect of meeting the enemy face-to-face because we all firmly believed that at some magical moment quite soon, the war would turn in our favour and victory would be ours.

Like my classmates, I peered into the dense jungle on either side of the tracks hoping to spy tigers, elephants, snakes and other exotic wildlife in their natural surroundings. For most of us the Malay Peninsula was new and strange territory. We'd all been across the causeway to Johor Bahru, but anything further north was unexplored terrain. This was real jungle and we certainly hoped to glimpse a prowling tiger or two, but after a fruitless hour or so we turned our attention to our black-robed chaperones. Several of them had sisters or cousins at the Seremban convent whom they hadn't seen in a long time, so they were being given the opportunity of a brief reunion before returning to Singapore.

In the last row of seats, wide shoulders resting against the carriage wall, sat St Coleman, a large, solid, reassuring presence, radiating warmth and goodwill all around. Beside her, dainty and fragile, sat St Raphael, angelic of face and temperament, a great favourite with the Little Boarders.

Across the aisle from St Coleman sat St Ignatius, tall and gaunt, sallow of skin and sour of disposition, aptly nicknamed *makan chukar* ('vinegar-eater' in Malay). With her sat the pleasant and unflappable St Bernadine, the guardian angel of the Little Orphans, who called her *malaikat* or 'angel' in Malay. They believed she looked like the statue of the Archangel Michael that stood just inside the altar rails of the chapel, one foot firmly planted on a prostrate Satan, his benign countenance at odds with his warlike stance.

Closest to me sat St Gerard. Plump, chatty, amiable, she had been my form mistress the previous year and was indirectly responsible for my nickname. She had written on my Report Card: *Maisie would be an excellent student if she didn't spend half her time dreaming.* In all Dad's subsequent letters to me he called me 'Dreamy Daniel'.

Now St Gerard asked me, 'What news of your father? I believe you heard from him recently.' I deflected the question towards my sister Olga. It was in fact the question uppermost in both our minds.

'Do you think we'll see Dad soon?'

Olga pulled a crumpled letter out of her pocket. It had been read and re-read many times. The postmark was Petaling, a small village near the mining compound outside Kuala Lumpur. It had been written the day after Singapore's first bombing raid. Dad enquired after our safety and expressed the wish that we might meet soon. He spoke of train timetables becoming quite erratic since the start of hostilities and of every train being crammed with people fleeing south. He promised to try his utmost to stop at Seremban and collect us if he was forced to evacuate from Kuala Lumpur. He spoke also of his great distress concerning John, our brother, who'd been sent north to Penang when his boarding school at Katong, Singapore, had been taken over as a temporary military barrack.

'We'll see Daddy again, I know we will.' Olga lifted her chin confidently.

'But what about John?' I countered. 'Penang has fallen.'

Olga looked cross. Why did younger sisters have to torment their older siblings with difficult questions? 'I don't know — just make sure you pray hard!'

Obviously I wasn't going to get anything further out of her, so I sat still, trying to visualise Penang, the lovely island where we three had been born and where John, the eldest, was now trapped behind Japanese lines. As the train bore us onward to Seremban, I fell into a reverie made up of family stories I had so often heard repeated and my own memories …

2

EASTERN ENCHANTMENT

In his novel *Youth*, Joseph Conrad writes:

> *And this is how I see the East. I have seen its secret places and have looked into its very soul; but now I see it always from a small boat, a high outline of mountains, blue and afar in the morning; like faint mist at noon; a jagged wall of purple at sunset. I have the feel of the oar in my hand, the vision of a scorching blue sea in my eyes. And I see a bay, a wide bay, smooth as glass and polished like ice, shimmering in the dark. A red light burns far off upon the gloom of the land, and the night is soft and warm. We drag at the oars with aching arms, and suddenly a puff of wind comes out of the still night — the first sigh of the East on my face. That I can never forget. It was impalpable and enslaving, like a charm, like a whispered promise of mysterious delight.*

The island of Penang lies off the west coast of Malaya, approximately four hundred miles north of Singapore; a forested, flower-scented, hilly terrain, very different in appearance and atmosphere from low-lying, bustling, business-oriented Singapore.

As a young ship's officer, my maternal grandfather Peter Vaz had sailed from British Cochin in India and settled permanently in Penang in 1876. His Portuguese ancestors had emigrated to the west coast of India more than a century earlier. The family prospered and there were numerous offspring. Some sons carried on the seafaring tradition while others involved themselves in the business and community life of the region.

Four years after Peter Vaz dropped anchor in Penang, he obtained his Master's Certificate, the second to be issued in the colony of Penang and thereafter he captained many ships of the Straits Steamship Company, a British shipping line which serviced the eastern seaboard extensively. He married a local Eurasian girl.

Peter Vaz had been the tenth child in a family of twelve. He in turn had twelve children. Girls were very well represented: he had no less than seven daughters. Alice, my mother, was his tenth child. I recall my mother pointing to a row of faces in an old wedding photograph and getting me to recite the names after her: 'Belle, Edward, Therese, Martha, Joan, Alice (me), May, Peter, Frances … '

Captain John Prout, my paternal grandfather, was also a proud family man but compared with Captain Vaz, he only had a 'small' family of five; three girls and two boys. Stanley, my father, was the baby of the family and his older siblings were Lily, Ethel, Arthur and Maud.

Devon, England, was Captain Prout's home port, so his journeys to the Orient took him a lot further and longer than the trips made by Captain Vaz; therein may lie the explanation for his 'small' Victorian family. In his time he had raced clippers around the Cape of Good Hope in order to command the best price for his precious cargo of tea, but sail gave way to steam, and his younger son Stanley was to spend a great many years of his life aboard steamships as a marine engineer. His elder son, Arthur, less robust than Stanley, settled in Shanghai and worked in a bank. He died of tuberculosis in his early twenties.

At an early age, my father acquired a taste for life aboard ship, for foreign travel and exotic locations. On the occasions when he sailed with his father, he used to study for part of the trip and sit for his exams on his return. Dad usually performed well; a feat he attributed to his near-perfect memory. 'I'm not clever,' he used to say 'but I do have a good memory.' At some stage in his late twenties, he joined the Straits Steamship Company, called into Penang and shook hands with Captain Vaz, who was destined to become his father-in-law.

Consider the position of Captain Vaz. He had seven daughters to marry off at a time when young ladies did not get jobs and become self-supporting. Instead, they stayed in the family home acquiring the social graces and counting the days until a suitor would ask for their hand in marriage. Faced with a task that might have felled a lesser man, this father appeared to take on the challenge with considerable gusto. After all, part of the solution was already in place on the deck of his ship! All those bachelor officers and engineers could be invited to his home to meet his daughters. Marriage was definitely on the menu, but not of the shotgun variety.

At his home on Arratoon Road, he would offer the warmest of Eastern hospitality to his European crew. East met West in a succession of curry tiffins, musical soirees and beach picnics; and success crowned his efforts. In order to keep everything respectable and above-board, he made certain that all the gatherings were very strictly chaperoned; a seaman himself, he obviously believed that one should 'never trust a sailor.'

My mother and Aunty May, her closest sibling, were the star turns at the musical soirees, Mum being the singer and May the pianist. Both were able to provide numerous examples of Grandpa's infuriating narrow-mindedness. To him, sex before marriage was a cardinal sin, while the religion or nationality of his prospective sons-in-law was of less concern. He appeared to welcome several different races and cultures into his family: three Englishmen, a Russian, a Dutchman, and two Eurasians, while his grandchildren carried on the tradition of mixed-race marriages, adding more Englishmen, an Australian, a Welshman, a German, a Siamese, a Dane, an Indian and several others to further enrich the multi-racial brew. Long before the term was invented, we were a 'multi-cultural' family as well as a mini-United Nations.

Imagine a society before radios were commonplace, when only the more affluent possessed gramophones, and the piano was the main focus of entertainment for most families.

Mum and Aunty May performed on a nightly basis, not just at parties. On a still night in a quiet street, devoid of any noise from cars, motorbikes, radios and television sets, their music was heard from one end of the street to the other. People from that area I met years later told me how much they had enjoyed the free concerts and how they would request special items for the next programme if they happened to run into May or Alice outside. No doubt it wasn't solely the singing that entertained the neighbours, but the frequent comings and goings of the assorted seamen (or sacrificial lambs) that added a certain element of spice and speculation to the otherwise placid and uneventful tenor of suburban life in Penang.

In due course, Stanley Prout proposed to Alice Vaz, but she had to break off a prior engagement before she could accept the proposal of this English marine engineer. She had been taking singing lessons from Ivor

Jones, a Welshman in the Malayan Civil Service. Mr Jones had wanted to marry his student and even obtained the requisite permission from the 'powers that be' for the marriage to take place. It was then the policy of the British Raj, while not openly forbidding marriage between its officials and the local population, to discourage it. Mum's teacher/suitor had encouraged her to sing in public and she appeared at various concerts and recitals in George Town. According to family history, she sang at a concert held to welcome Edward, Prince of Wales, when he briefly visited Penang as part of his tour of the Far East. There was more than a hint of pride in Uncle Peter's voice as he recounted the incident, adding that his sister Alice was the only female singer in an otherwise male choir.

When Mum decided to return her first suitor's ring, she confided in Aunty May, 'Ivor's a good man and I'm very fond of him, but it's Stan I love,' then asked her sister to take the ring back for her. But her sister told her she had to do that job herself. After Mum became Mrs Stanley Yerward Prout, the musical evenings continued but she had a different singing teacher, of course!

Not surprisingly, my earliest memories of Penang feature a number of gatherings with people singing near a piano while others danced slowly and sedately around a leather ottoman that occupied the centre of a large downstairs parlour. A tall, thin youth with large brown eyes used to carry me in his arms as he danced and sang to me in those far-off days; this gentle dancer was my cousin Dennis Pientowski, only child of Aunty Belle, my mother's eldest sister.

By the time Dad got transferred to Singapore as Senior Engineer with the Straits Steamship Company, all the aunts had been married off with the exception of Aunty Therese, who was destined to remain single for the rest of her life.

Therese did not complete her education at the Penang convent and so was not considered as eligible as the other sisters. A silly incident that would be thought too trivial to mention in a modern classroom was considered sufficient grounds for her expulsion. Therese was seen undressing a doll at her desk in the class, the nun in charge spotted the no-knickers doll and the poor girl was considered unfit for the society of nice young children! For Therese there was no more schooling, and further down the track, no husband either. Such were the puritan attitudes of the time.

Belle and Martha had short-lived marriages. Belle's husband left her not long after my cousin Dennis was born; divorce was out of the question for a good Catholic, so Belle lived the life of a chaste widow while still officially married, bringing up Dennis on her own in the family home.

Martha's husband also departed from her, but not by choice. He was killed in a freak accident when a falling coconut bearing his name crashed into his skull as he sat under a shady palm.

Meanwhile, Singapore's importance had grown apace: its strategic location, entrepôt facilities and large naval base made it a Mecca for ambitious young men seeking promotions and prosperity. Like my father, Aunty May's husband, Uncle Willem, also headed south and occupied a similar position with the Dutch KPM line. About the time of Dad's transfer, his long-service leave became due and Mr and Mrs Prout spent six months in England minus their three children, Olga, John and Maisie — for we had all made our appearance in the world by this time. Dad's British shipping line did not provide passages for children, whereas Uncle Willem's company paid for children as well as an amah (house maid), so whenever his leave fell due, the whole family was able to travel to Holland first-class.

It was probably not Mum's first trip to England so the most important aspect of the visit was not the tourist attractions but the opportunity it gave her to discover whether the medical specialists in London's Harley Street could do anything to alleviate her asthma problem.

As a young woman, she had enjoyed robust health; shortness of breath and bouts of coughing and wheezing were foreign to her. All that changed the day she caught a ferry to Butterworth to visit a cousin who lived there. She'd just turned thirty, life was good for this happily married mother of three and she was dressed to the nines. A tropical downpour caught her unprepared and she got drenched to the skin. Her cousin offered her a change of clothes, but Mum was adamant she wouldn't wear anything that didn't fit her properly (her cousin being somewhat shorter and a great deal wider). So she sat around all day in her wet but fashionable outfit until it was time to catch the ferry back to Penang.

On her return she felt ill and feverish and started coughing and wheezing off and on for several days. A doctor diagnosed asthma; it may or may not have been the direct outcome of that fateful ferry ride to Butterworth. Aunty May was quite certain there was a direct link. 'Poor Alice,' she once remarked, years later. 'She paid a high price for her vanity.'

So Mum did the rounds of specialists in England but no cure was forthcoming, though she subsequently obtained some relief from injections during bad attacks of her illness. She might have fared no worse and saved Dad a pile of money had she followed the advice of the Malay medicine man she consulted before the trip to England. His prescription was easy to obtain and dirt cheap, literally. Five large cockroaches fried and eaten with bread or rice.

'I'd rather die first!' my mother exclaimed.

3

FAMILY LIFE

While our parents were in England, ten-year-old John was placed at a Christian Brothers' boarding school, eight-year-old Olga was looked after by Aunty May, and I was placed with another family of cousins, less closely related and less kind. I was five years old at this time. Aunt Marcia did not appear to like me at all; I don't know why she agreed to take me unless it was the prospect of material gain for her effort. I was acutely aware of the change from a loving, nurturing atmosphere to a cold, uncaring, slightly hostile environment.

Marcia and Maurice Vasey* had five children. The youngest were twin girls, Prudence and Priscilla. The eldest, Marion, was in her mid-teens and there were two sons, George and Andrew, in between.

The twins were my daily companions; we were about the same age, and on the whole we got along fairly well — but whenever there was a squabble, their mother regarded me as the culprit and I felt the brunt of her annoyance and disapproval. The earliest Christmas I remember was the one spent with the Vaseys. A few days before 25th December, the bigger children decorated the seldom-used parlour with streamers and balloons while Aunt Marcia put up the Christmas tree in the centre of the room. We little ones were told several times that Father Christmas would bring presents if we were good, so there was much excitement on Christmas Eve, as we were tucked in tightly under the mosquito net in the one large bed we shared.

I was awakened the next morning by happy cries of 'He's been here! Father Christmas has visited us!' as the twins pointed to a number of gaily wrapped parcels under the large bed. These were dragged out in a hurry and paper lay torn and scattered all over the floor to reveal a number of gifts — two of everything, one for Prudence, one for Priscilla — dolls, teddy bears, china tea-sets. I looked in vain for a third

* The names of my host family have been altered but the events are exactly as described.

matching gift that could possibly be mine, some tangible sign that I hadn't been totally overlooked. Further searching disclosed a shoe-box tied with some tinsel string.

'Could that be my gift?'

'Open it up,' said Prudence.

'Hey! That's my old doll!' Priscilla exclaimed possessively.

Their mother walked in at this point. 'Let Maisie have that doll, Priscilla, we've got to give her something for Christmas. You both have lots of new things today, so you can spare that.'

I cradled the doll in my arms, grateful not to have been completely ignored. Obviously Prudence and Priscilla had been very good indeed while I'd been quite naughty.

There was one bright moment late in the evening that Christmas Day. Marion, who had always treated me kindly, took me on her knee and read me a story, then whispered as she set me down: 'Your Mummy and Daddy are coming back soon, and they'll bring you lots of lovely presents.'

Soon, what did that mean? One more sleep? Two? Three or more?

Going to bed at night had become an ordeal. Now, when I was told to be good, I was aware Aunt Marcia meant 'Don't wet the bed'. That was hard to avoid when the net got tucked in so tightly that getting out from underneath it in a hurry was a tricky business. Even if I extricated myself in time from the bed, an accident was likely to happen while I frantically tried to untie the drawstrings of my pyjamas, elastic and zips not being part of daily life in those days. Often I'd return to bed wet and miserable and lie awake afraid of what the morrow would bring. A big scolding for sure, maybe a spell in the yard with the sheet wrapped around me. Prudence and Priscilla, who never needed to get up during the night, would be playing near me in the shade of the coconut palms — oh, how I envied them their flawless bedtime routine.

One Saturday (it must have been a Saturday as the boys were at home in the morning), my aunt decided to shock me out of my bed-wetting habit. The punishment was carefully planned and willingly carried out by George and Andrew. The whole family knew that I was terrified of the beetles and cockroaches that flew and crawled or leapt through the windows and up and down the walls of their old wooden home — 'all those coconut trees', somebody said by way of explanation. None of the Vaseys seemed to mind the horrid creatures and regarded my fear with amused contempt.

So that Saturday morning after breakfast, George and Andrew took me by the hand and told me they had something very interesting to show me. Normally they ignored me completely, so when they sought me out I was both curious and apprehensive. They led me upstairs to the wide wooden verandah and from their pockets produced three or four matchboxes, slid back the lids and tipped the live, seething, leaping contents all over my head, shoulders and arms. Then they stood back laughing while I screamed and sobbed, 'Mummy, Mummy, I want my Mummy, I'll tell Mummy about you!'

I cannot recall the incident being repeated, though it's unlikely the bed-wetting would have stopped forthwith. A more likely cause of their forbearance would have been the imminent return of my parents and the fear that I might succeed in getting them into trouble.

And Mum and Dad did return one wonderful day when a taxi pulled up in the driveway and they climbed out and stood amid a mountain of boxes, bundles and suitcases with arms outstretched to scoop me up. My nightmare ordeal had ended.

I was not quite finished with my cousins but the atmosphere at the Vasey home had altered completely. Mum and Dad stayed with them for a few days while they went house-hunting. I was no longer the little nuisance that could be ignored or punished at will but a delightful little girl to be petted and indulged, the treasured daughter of Lord and Lady Bountiful. For my parents had indeed scattered their bounty lavishly. Marion received a lovely wrist-watch and so did Andrew, while George got a bicycle and the twins got cooking sets and a doll's house. Marcia and Maurice received a handsome financial reward for their trouble. I wonder if Marcia felt any shame over her meanness and cruelty to a five-year-old. Luckily, I was never again at her mercy.

My ordeal had ended but my mother's continued. Frequent and heavy bouts of asthma dogged her days and the doctor's visits became an inescapable part of her routine. The word 'sickness' belonged to Mum, while the phrase 'sickly and delicate' applied to me, because I suffered bouts of high fever and lethargy which left me unable to join in the rowdy, energetic games enjoyed by my robust older siblings. 'Noisy, cheeky and quarrelsome' were the words thrown at them.

Olga's special word was 'tomboy'. It summed up her appearance and behaviour perfectly. Whenever aunt or uncle, cousin or friend asked my parents 'How's the tomboy today?' everyone knew they were talking about Olga, whose solid frame was topped by a head of tight dark curls, an unflinching gaze and impudent grin. John was two years older and proportionately taller and stronger, yet Olga constantly challenged him in every way — running, jumping, tree-climbing, even punching and kicking. Her motto was 'Anything you can do, I can do better'. I seldom had the energy or inclination to join them in their war games, but I'd watch with great interest from the sidelines as the battles raged loud and long until Mum would make a dramatic appearance wielding a long, thin bamboo cane. With a few well-aimed whacks of her rattan, peace and quiet would be restored.

A well-meaning neighbour once offered us a pair of puppies from her litter but Mum rather ungraciously refused the gift, saying, 'Every day I have to referee cat-and-dog fights between my children — why would I risk battles of the four-legged variety?' So we never acquired any household pets, though I daresay Olga and John would have claimed there already was a household pet in residence — ME!

I shadowed my mother around the house, seeking extra cuddles and security, and when she was absent (usually in hospital), I'd stay very close to the amah. As a result I was scornfully dubbed 'Mum's pet' or 'amah's pet' by my more independent siblings.

There was, however, a serious and sensible side to my tomboy sister. When she wasn't sparring with John, she was conducting her own private school. Any visiting child was liable to be coaxed or coerced into her classroom, where she'd hold forth in front of a small blackboard, chalk at the ready, while passing out slates and slate pencils to her temporary and sometimes unwilling students. From a very early age, all Olga ever wanted was to be a schoolteacher. Dad sometimes took us to the movies and we collected photos of film stars, male and female; but the Hollywood dream was not Olga's dream — nor was the mystic religious world of the cloister. Her goals were set much closer to home and everyday life. Her guiding stars were not the celluloid heroines of film but the flesh-and-blood Queens of the Classroom who gave orders to their captive subjects each weekday. Every order was instantly obeyed — 'Sit! Stand! Come! Go! Speak! Be silent!'

Female schoolteachers were powerful figures and what's more, they were fashionable as well. Unlike the nuns, they wore make-up and high heels and displayed a different outfit everyday. Some of these classroom queens even possessed their personal coaches; snappy little Austin or Morris motor cars.

This was the world Olga regarded as her chosen arena. When no outsiders were available, class numbers would be reduced to two — John and myself. He would pretend to follow the lesson quietly for a few minutes, then ask questions or make comments destined to start an argument or provoke a fight. 'Does Mum know you've borrowed her lipstick and high heels?' he'd inquire. He was seldom disappointed when he looked for a battle.

Unlike John, I could sit still and listen for long periods, so I was often rewarded by 'teacher Olga' with stories from her Fairy Tale collection, or legends of the Saints which she'd heard in her Catechism class. These were often accompanied by pictures of the said Saints, complete with golden haloes. Other holy pictures depicted beautiful angels with powerful wings. Angels were supposed to protect people, especially innocent children, from harm, and it was these Guardian Angels I most admired and wanted to encounter. 'Can I meet one NOW?'

'No, only when you die and go to Heaven — if you're good!'

'What if I'm naughty?'

'Oh, then you'll go to Hell and burn forever with the Devils.' Olga dealt with the great mysteries of Life and Death just as she had memorised them from her catechism. She spoke with the authority of someone whose world view was fixed and unambiguous, even matter-of-fact.

I had no trouble accepting her moral certainties that the good would be rewarded, the bad punished; my problem lay in a different direction, in separating fact from fable, what was real from what was imagined — in essence, I struggled with the Nature of Reality.

My universe was filled with family and friends (real); creatures from fairy tales (not real), movie stars (real people acting out unreal stories), angels and saints (real? Olga said they were!), bogey men, especially the local version of a ghost, the *Pontianak* (real and unreal), my toys — especially my dolls (real, maybe?). Red Riding Hood and the Big Bad Wolf were not likely to come knocking at our door, I knew that much. Nor were Snow White and the Seven Dwarfs, though they would have been most welcome. There was a craze for collecting Snow White memorabilia connected with the recent Walt Disney film, and my sixth birthday cake had been decorated with a Snow White candle set, but only six dwarfs were allowed to circle their Princess on the icing; the seventh had to sit in the box while I blew out my candles.

Not long afterwards Olga celebrated her ninth birthday and received a large doll with a beautiful porcelain face, long-lashed eyes that opened and shut and a rosebud mouth that pronounced 'Mama' whenever you pressed a certain spot in her chest. I coveted that doll as soon as I saw it. Of course I had dolls of my own that I loved, including two that always slept beside my pillow at night — I was convinced they chatted together and even went for walks in the garden while I was asleep. But Olga's doll was extra special. It had the face of an angel: it had to be alive! I begged for it on several occasions but she kept on saying 'No'. Olga did not cherish her dolls the way I did; I suspect she regarded them as mere inert decorations, and once the pleasure of acquisition wore off she tended to put them aside for something more practical, more user-friendly, like a toy sewing machine that actually stitched, or a box camera that took snapshots.

Meantime I kept up my pursuit of the angel-doll, and one day Olga actually said 'Yes'.

The scene remains vividly etched in my memory. A warm afternoon, Olga and John playing hopscotch on the concrete driveway leading to the garage, Olga winning, the precious doll flung carelessly onto the lawn nearby. Every time Olga returned to the hopscotch starting-point, I'd implore, 'Please give me the doll!'

'No,' she'd reply, 'I will not,' and then she'd hop and jump away to the other end of the chalk marks on the driveway. I persisted with my pleas and finally, after about the tenth attempt — or was it the twentieth — she roared back, 'All right, take the silly doll and go!'

For a long moment I couldn't believe my ears. Had she really and truly said that? I needed confirmation. 'Come and get it NOW!' she exploded. Still unbelieving, I walked slowly to the other end of the driveway, but my hesitation had cost me the doll. Before I could reach the spot and scoop up the prize, Olga picked up the doll and smashed its head against the pavement. 'It's dead now,' she stated coldly, while I sobbed bitterly. Between my sobs I asked 'Will it go to Heaven?'

'NO,' she shouted back, 'It's gone to HELL!'

At that final blow, I howled in pain and sorrow and it took Mum several minutes to calm me down and reassure me that Dolly had really gone to heaven. Finally she cheered me up with the promise of an equally beautiful doll for my next birthday.

Today, in her seventies, Olga has mellowed; she is the most generous of sisters, the most loyal of friends — but she still hates ditherers!

We were to move house a couple of times the next year on the doctor's advice, first to Fort Road and then to Brooke Road, in search of fresh sea-breezes and parks. We moved away from a townhouse-type apartment on busy Killiney Road into the leafy, seaside suburb of Katong, with large colonial bungalows adjacent to the Park. Here, Mum's condition did improve to the extent that she went out and about a lot more and whenever Aunty May dropped in, their musical sessions were resumed. Most days I was taken to play in the park by my Chinese amah. Olga and John were now attending school, so they only joined me occasionally. Oleanders grew there in profusion; their heady, cloying scent is a smell I always associate with those happy, carefree days in Katong Park.

On the corner of Fort Road, in an imposing house across from the park lived Mrs Jardine, a tall, handsome woman who wore lots of unusual, expensive jewellery. I recall in particular a diamond encircled jade ring and a waist-length amber necklace. She was a member of the family of merchant bankers operating in the Far East. While Mum and Mrs Jardine had tea and cucumber sandwiches in her parlour, I was usually provided with a plate of Jacob's biscuits and some rose syrup and sent out into the garden with the warning 'Don't tease the monkey'. Not much chance of a timid six-year-old provoking a wild and vicious chimpanzee that only waited one second for his mistress' back to be turned before taking a flying leap at me from the branch where he'd been sitting, in an attempt to relieve me of my precious biscuits. In a just world, the caution would have been directed at the monkey, not the child!

True, a chain did impede the monkey's movements somewhat but it was a long chain and I wasn't fleet of foot, so it remained an unequal contest. I certainly did not enjoy my encounters with this screeching, grimacing, razor-toothed resident of the Jardine garden.

In fact the animal enjoyed greater mobility than the poor Down's Syndrome boy who had lived three doors down from us in Killiney Road. He was kept closely chained to their wrought-iron gate every day because his parents believed him to be mad and dangerous, as did everybody in the neighbourhood.

Our house on Brooke Road was another colonial bungalow set in a large garden. The main building was connected to the servants' quarters by a long covered walkway, and the front porch descended to the driveway by means of a wide, curved concrete staircase. We were still in Katong, much closer to the beach but further from the park. With the beach practically at our doorstep, at one end of a narrow gravelled lane, we were able to go swimming whenever we wanted, and sometimes Dad or John would show me how to float and how to tread water. My swimming skills did not progress much beyond that stage.

The local cinema, the Roxy, was also within easy walking distance, and to us children, it now proved a far greater attraction than Katong Park.

The Prout family patronised the local cinema so regularly that a special five-seat balcony was always set aside for us, so that even if we arrived late and the theatre was full, 'our' seats were always available. Dad joked that the theatre management should not be charging him full price because he had only one good eye and so could see only half as much as everyone else! At a succession of Saturday matinees, we children saw Laurel and Hardy, Abbott and Costello, Donald Duck and Mickey Mouse movies. Sometimes our parents came too for the romantic, grown-up films starring Fred Astaire and Ginger Rogers, Dorothy Lamour and Ray Milland, Errol Flynn and Olivia de Havilland. Mum's favourite stars were the wonderful singing duo Jeanette MacDonald and

Nelson Eddy. She collected their songs and played them on her wind-up HMV (His Master's Voice) gramophone, that bore the trademark picture of a dog beside a gramophone just like ours.

Sundays were 'curry tiffin' days in Malaya, when all the big hotels and clubs competed to provide the most mouth-watering selection of curries and side-dishes to tempt well-heeled and very selective customers. If we missed out on curry tiffin on board Dad's ship, we usually had a curry dinner at home, followed by the traditional sago pudding. Now and again, we'd have our curry meal at the Tanglin Club with the Pijpes (pronounced 'Pipers'), who lived nearby, or we'd call in on the Van Vliets, who ran a very successful boarding-house in the Tanglin area. Flora and Dick Van Vliet had an excellent Chinese chef and Dad was certain not to be deprived of his favourite cuisine during his shore leave.

The proximity to the sea must have had a beneficial effect on my health as well as Mum's because I was now able to join Olga and John in most of their activities. I began to join in their escapades too, like sneaking off to the beach without permission, and as a result I discovered that I was no longer exempt from the sting of the cane.

Early in January 1938, after attending kindergarten classes on an irregular basis, I started Primary School. This meant that I joined Olga and John every day for the car ride into the city. Olga and I were dropped off at the Holy Infant Jesus Convent, while John's destination was St Joseph's nearby.

Mabel Wickwar was my first teacher. Legend has it she selected her pupils in a highly unusual manner. Her method had nothing to do with kindergarten records or enrolment forms but everything to do with — ear-size! Kitty Fogh, the 1B class teacher, claimed that Mabel Wickwar used to move around the new Primary One pupils waiting in the hall, checking out their ears.

'Small ears,' she'd say, 'my class, 1A. Medium ears, Miss Fogh, 1B. Big ears, Miss Chin, 1C.' Thus she'd organise the whole group of newcomers without any bureaucratic form-filling and tedious paperwork.

Miss Wickwar was the senior teacher, and once she'd taken her pick, all three staff would go off to their separate rooms to record students' names in their registers, the new 'ear-tested' pupils following in an orderly crocodile. While I must have passed muster 'ear-wise' with Miss

Wickwar (since there I was, sitting beneath her dais) in other ways I was probably a disappointment to her; I remember virtually nothing of the year spent in her class, apart from the fact that she was somewhat irritable and had a very hoarse voice from chain-smoking. I must have dreamed my way through most of the day, coming to life only for the lunch hour when Olga and I would meet up with Mary and Cora Pijpe, then 'tuning out' again until it was time to go home.

We saw a lot of Mary and Cora outside school as well. They often arrived with their parents for a Friday night sing-song at our house, with their brother Willie in tow. The children would contribute a musical item before being allowed to run off and play while the adults then sang on or talked among themselves without us eavesdropping. I cannot recall Cora or Willie or John doing solo items, but I know that Olga excelled in comic sketches or skits of popular songs such as "Daisy Bell" *(Daisy, Daisy, give me your answer do …*). Mary Pijpe was fast becoming an accomplished pianist and her renditions of "Poet and Peasant Overture" or "Liebestraum" were always highly acclaimed. My party pieces at the time were the songs "Sin to Tell a Lie" and "Some Day My Prince Will Come".

In those distant days, anywhere in the neighbourhood was safe territory, even at night. So after we left the grown-ups, off we'd go, equipped with torches, to traverse one end of the lane to the other playing hide-and-seek. Sometimes the sound of music would follow us wherever we went and eventually guide us back to base. Cora was usually my partner, Olga and Mary were inseparable, and the two boys stuck together even though John was a lot older than Willie. One still night, I remember being terrified by the sound of an eerie voice singing '*Oo-ooo-oooh*'.

'Is that a ghost?' I whispered to Cora, trembling.

'Silly girl, it's your mother singing,' she replied, amused, and as I waited still feeling nervous, the rest of the "Indian Love Call" followed and I realised that the high-pitched voice did indeed belong to a living person, not a spirit.

While I was prepared to concede that no ghost lay in wait for me that night, my mother was sure they existed and in the latter part of that same year, this conviction began to assume major proportions. However, the early months of 1938 were full of happy and memorable events.

Towards the end of January I turned seven and an evening party was held in my honour. Small tables were set up in the front garden and all the trees and shrubs glowed with paper lanterns. Our Hokkien cook produced a number of special dishes, and a couple of itinerant hawkers were on hand to provide on-the-spot local favourites like satay (small pieces of barbecued meat on wooden skewers), mee goreng (a fried and spicy noodle dish) and assorted local cakes.

The parlour couch was piled high with gifts, and the loveliest present of all was the large baby doll from my parents. Mum had kept her word! She seemed in her element that night, full of fun and good cheer. Standing beside the piano in her favourite black satin evening dress, she sang several numbers in full-throated celebration of life. She wore that dress for Dad's birthday in April and again in May for her thirty-sixth birthday, when there was much laughter and song and a little wine. (Dad's favourite drink was the local Tiger beer, while Mum occasionally had a glass of Wincarnis port).

It could have been that night, or not long afterwards that Mum had a very bad asthma attack and had to spend a few days in hospital. Then she took up her normal routine again, visiting friends and relatives, buying groceries and going for fittings to the dressmaker and shoemaker — few people in those days bought clothes off-the-peg, or selected shoes off-the-shelf. The island was full of talented craftsmen of all kinds who could copy and manufacture any item from a mere photograph.

Not all the outings were pleasurable occasions. Mum made duty visits to certain charitable institutions, her main charity being The Little Sisters of the Poor. Sometimes I was taken along to rooms full of sick and elderly poor people while Mum distributed little parcels of soap, talcum powder and other small items, and the syce (chauffeur) carried a basket of tinned provisions to the kitchen. These face-to-face encounters with the needy and neglected took a heavy emotional toll on my soft-hearted mother. After one such visit, she cried all the way home in the car and Aunty May advised her not to go there again but to send her donations in the car with the syce. 'It upsets you too much, Alice,' she said. I think the advice was heeded because I can't recall a subsequent visit.

A task Mum really enjoyed was her Saturday morning stint of flower arranging. The long dining-table would be covered with an oilcloth and all the clean, empty vases stood there ready to be filled from a huge pile of yellow cosmos and asparagus fern, delivered fresh every Saturday morning by a Chinese boy on a bicycle. Sometimes there was a small sheath of red roses as well, which meant there'd be a dinner party that night, when the three-tiered silver vase would stand proudly in the centre of the table showing off its cascading pyramid of scarlet blooms.

The dhobi-man (laundry-collector) would appear with his cart by the time the flowers had been arranged in their respective vases. He would present Mum with a pile of fresh linen, starched and ironed, and she would tick off the date in his book while amah counted out sheets and tablecloths and towels, the current week's tally, which was tied up together in a large sheet and placed in the cart for him to take away. The freshly laundered items were then checked for holes, tears, missing buttons and so forth, and mended. Like most convent girls, Mum was a good mender; many an odd sock was preserved even though worthless, because of the beauty of her darning.

Usually we children were up early on Saturdays in order to spend time at the beach, or just to play around the house. We'd be on our best behaviour because we didn't want to be barred from the Saturday matinee. But one Saturday in four, by common consent, we dawdled; we feigned sickness, tiredness, anything to avoid getting to the breakfast table where we knew that three identical glasses of orange juice laced with castor oil awaited us. The routine never varied. Our eyes would implore as our lips mouthed, 'Do we have to?' Mum, firm and unyielding, would first coax then command us to drink the contents down and not waste time if we wanted to go to the pictures in the afternoon. She always won and somehow or other we swallowed the vile mixture.

Despite the air of normality after Mum's latest hospital stay, there was an undercurrent of unease due to the increasing frequency of her asthma attacks and the need to send for the doctor almost on a weekly basis. As if this weren't enough, a second, more insidious problem was surfacing: the matter of Dad's *liaisons*, which were undermining Mum's emotional stability. The first ailment was, to a degree, treatable, but it goes without saying that a cure for the second was far more elusive.

The asthma bouts usually reached their peak late at night or early in the morning and Mum's first reaction would be to give herself an injection, as she'd been taught and see if her breathing settled down to normal. If she continued to struggle for breath, Olga and John were despatched to ring the doctor from the nearest phone box. (Dad, of course, was away on his ship). Nobody in the street or neighbourhood had a phone in those days; with hindsight, it seems amazing that a family with a car and chauffeur, two amahs and a cook didn't own something as basic as a telephone. It may be that until the 1940s, the phone cables covered only the central business district and in the outlying suburbs, phone links were restricted to doctors, hospitals and senior government officials.

Getting to a phone, even at night, was not too difficult while the syce was living on the premises, but after a rowdy and bruising fight with his wife, he moved back to his kampung (village) about a kilometre away. Olga and John had to walk there to get him to drive them to a phone box to alert Dr Herron, who sometimes turned up with a jacket thrown over his pyjamas.

I was considered too young to be involved in these late-night excursions, but the commotion usually woke me up and I'd watch Olga and John take off into the night, Olga purposefully brandishing a stout stick, while John walked alongside carrying a large torch. It never occurred to me to ask Olga if she was scared of making these midnight dashes. In my estimation, ten-year-old Olga was afraid of nobody and as for John, boys were supposed to be brave, weren't they?

Aunty May visited more often now and occasionally stayed overnight when Dad was away at sea. When they thought I was asleep, I'd occasionally overhear snatches of conversation in which several names were mentioned. One name in particular was repeated on numerous occasions: 'Bobs'. Mum would begin to see evil spirits lurking everywhere while her sister tried, not very successfully, to calm her down. In her troubled state, Mum confused 'Bobs' with the Pontianak, the ghostly Malayan she-devil and irresistible temptress, the downfall of countless erstwhile faithful husbands. She became convinced that this evil creature had taken up residence in the cotton tree outside her bedroom window, so to humour her, Dad had the tree chopped down. The drama should have ended there but it didn't. The she-devil had many disguises and the next source of contamination was supposedly our drinking water. All tap water was suspect and undrinkable unless boiled beforehand, and we children were encouraged to drink only the bottled drinks in the ice chest. Naturally, we weren't averse to helping ourselves liberally to the lemonade, orangeade or Coca-Cola, then newly available on the market.

One day when Aunty May was on her own, I asked, 'Who's Bobs?'

'Oh … you heard us, did you? Well, she was once a good friend of your Mother's, but she's not her friend any more.' I had to be satisfied with that. I knew my mother was behaving strangely and that something was wrong, seriously wrong, besides her usual ailment. At times, I'd go up to her and say 'Mummy, you're very sad today.' She'd nod her head a few times and hug me tight, murmuring, 'My little girl, my lovely little girl.'

In an attempt to cheer our mother up, Aunty Frances, the baby of the Vaz family, came visiting. She brought young Thomas with her, leaving her other three children behind in Penang. Mum brightened up considerably and there were several happy get-togethers when the sisters and their families managed to set aside unpleasant problems and enjoy each other's company. But the improvement was only temporary. The medical men my mother now saw were no more successful in dispelling her fits of depression and hysteria than the London doctors had been in attempting to cure her asthma.

'They tell me I'm just imagining things!' she'd complain to Aunty May, 'but I'm not; I can actually see these things.' Aunty May would shake her head sadly; often there were tears in her eyes. On one of these occasions, Mum stalked off into her bedroom and returned a few minutes later holding her black satin evening dress up against her body. 'When I'm dead, will you bury me in this?' She put the request in a calm and matter-of-fact way.

'Alice, don't talk like that,' Aunty May protested. 'You're going to get better.'

'I'm not getting better, it won't be long now. Promise me!'

'All right,' her sister answered unwillingly, 'but I don't believe you're going to die soon — and you shouldn't talk like that in front of the children.'

4

'AFTER THE FIRST DEATH THERE IS NO OTHER'

But Mum did talk 'like that' and mentioned the 'D' word fairly often. She wasn't about to avoid it lest it cause discomfort and dismay. She'd always been an outspoken, direct sort of person. Hints and evasions were foreign to her nature.

She had come close to death on numerous occasions and must have known that if the next onslaught of asthma didn't kill her, then the one after that definitely would. So she went on saying 'When I'm dead' or 'when I'm gone'. She wanted us to take her seriously. More poetically, she might have said, 'I'm dying, not raving!' Deep down, we didn't doubt her words. We just didn't want to believe them.

The year's end was fast approaching and thankfully Mum was still around. We'd begun to talk of Christmas celebrations and drop broad hints about the gifts we'd like Santa to bring. Then, on a night in early November the ambulance paid its last call and Mum was carried down the porch steps on a stretcher. Before the ambulance doors were closed, she raised her arms and waved to us in farewell as we stood watching in silence. The vehicle then sped off towards the hospital. It was a Thursday night, and we went to school as usual the next day, telling ourselves that Mum would be out by the weekend.

That evening, a very agitated Aunty May came to tell us that Mum was very ill; she had developed pneumonia and had sent for Dad. May herself was heading straight back to the hospital to spend the night with Mum. The news was most unsettling, but being young and optimistic we managed to sleep until we were awakened early in the morning by the sound of a car pulling up in the driveway — not our familiar Hillman — and we rushed out to see a taxi dropping Dad off. One glance at his face and we knew that he was going to tell us what we most dreaded, yet expected to hear. 'Your mother — your mother — has gone to heaven.' Tears were pouring down his face. I'd never seen him cry before. In no time, the servants had joined us and there we all stood on the porch; father, children, servants, dazed, uncomprehending, sobbing openly, united in our sorrow over the loss of the pivot around which our lives had turned.

Minutes later, the Pijpes' car pulled up and a grief-stricken Aunty May rushed to embrace us as she assured us that Mum wouldn't suffer any more, that we weren't to worry, Mum would keep an eye on us from heaven. She fetched Mum's favourite black frock and said that she would dress her in it and that we would all have the chance to say our goodbyes later. She hardly spoke to Dad as she went off to carry out Mum's request. Lost in a timeless moment of grief and bewilderment, Olga's remark brought us back to ordinary life and weekend routines.

'It's castor-oil Saturday,' she whispered. 'Let's not remind amah.'

Needless to say, John and I were unlikely to do anything of the kind, and all three of us congratulated ourselves on our lucky escape. On the one hand, we felt genuine distress at the death of a beloved parent, but that didn't prevent us from appreciating this release from the customary dose of the hated castor oil! If Mum had been watching us from her heavenly vantage point, she might have said, 'Look at them! I've only been dead a couple of hours and already they are ignoring my wishes.'

Some time that day Dad took us to view Mum's body laid out in her coffin. We walked into the reception area and hesitated. 'Don't be afraid. She looks very peaceful,' he told us, trying to sound reassuring. 'Come and say goodbye to your mother.'

Slowly we approached the glossy wooden box and gazed down at the lifeless shape which had once given us life and love. Softly and sadly, I whispered in Dad's ear, 'Mum's not wearing her party dress!' Instead, she was covered from neck to ankle in a loose, white hospital nightie. I couldn't help feeling cheated on her behalf as well as mine. I had expected her to look the way she had on the night of my seventh birthday party, resplendent in her satin gown. And here she was in a shapeless white shift. I wasn't alone in my disappointment. Olga, always more direct, fired the question at Dad. 'What happened to Mum's black dress?'

'You'll have to ask Aunty May that question,' countered Dad, looking relieved that the lady herself had just arrived with her family to view the body.

'The dress didn't fit her, it got stuck halfway,' Aunty May replied, looking uncomfortable as she faced three pairs of accusing eyes. 'But you could have cut the back with scissors,' persisted Olga, to which Aunty May murmured something we couldn't catch and looked miserable. (Possibly a black satin gown was not considered appropriate as a Christian woman's shroud). 'Come and kiss your mother,' she said. We each in turn planted a kiss or two on those cold, cold cheeks and forehead. Would those eyelids suddenly flutter and open? I asked myself. Mum appeared to be sleeping, but maybe, just maybe, she'd wake up. After all, Snow White and Sleeping Beauty had woken up after they were kissed. I stared at her face for a long moment, but there was no movement.

'Kiss her rosary. It's the last thing she touched,' said my Aunt and obediently we planted several kisses on the large wooden beads wound around the stiff fingers, then stood back while some discussion took place concerning how much longer the coffin should remain open. I didn't want the lid to go on, I just didn't.

We spent the rest of the day with our cousins while Dad finalised the funeral arrangements. Aunty May described Mum's final moments. 'Your father arrived on the first plane from Penang about an hour before your mother died. They were together for some time and then your mother called me aside. I felt she didn't want your father to hear what she was about to say, so I asked him to fetch something from the hospital shop. He refused at first, saying the errand could wait, he had to stay beside Alice, but I insisted, and so he went to avoid making a scene. As soon as he'd gone your mother made me promise that I'd take care of the three of you after she'd gone. 'May, look after my children — promise me that,' she said.

'"Of course I will, Alice, I promise," I told her.

'"Bobs won't want them, you see," she said.

'We said a few Hail Marys together and her voice became very faint, she seemed to be choking. "I'm going, May … I'm going," she said, "… where's Stan?"

'Your father returned only minutes later but she'd gone — to Heaven,' Aunty added, trying to reassure us and possibly herself. 'Your father took one look at your mother, then he called me names and started to cry. "Why did you send me away? I should have been with Alice when she died!"

'But Alice wanted to talk to me privately — she really did, children.' Aunty nodded her head to emphasise the point. 'It was your mother's wish, but your father believes I did something wrong.' She looked at each of us in turn and we stared back at her in silence. The issue was too complex for us, we could not pass judgement.

I recall nothing of the funeral service, but I remember a long drive to Bidadari cemetery and I have a mental snapshot of the sealed coffin smothered in white frangipani wreaths, borne shoulder-high between rows of graves towards a freshly dug hole where it came to rest.

My next snapshot shows me sitting in the car with the amah and syce, well away from the burial scene so that I am spared (wisely, I think) the sight of the coffin being lowered into the ground and the sound of stones thudding on the closed lid. As I write this, a line from Dylan Thomas comes into my head: 'After the first death there is no other.'

Only the fragrance of the occasion stays with me, the all-pervasive, sickly-sweet scent of hundreds of frangipani blossoms from the wreaths and from row upon row of frangipani trees lining the graveyard.

In Singapore, the dead pushed up neither poppies nor daisies, but frangipani.

Olga and John put me to bed that night and I'm certain they'd never done that before. Both were so kind, gentle and attentive to my needs that I've a strong suspicion I feigned illness to prolong their unaccustomed care of me.

All three of us missed Mum very much; we were aware that something fundamental had gone from our lives, but the full impact of her loss would only seep through to us gradually, further down the track. Initially, the daily routine did not alter a great deal. We were driven to and from school during the week and on Saturdays we'd drive to the wharf to fetch Dad. On Sunday evening or Monday morning, Dad would sail away again, giving Olga sufficient money for the week's groceries. In slow, measured tones he would ask us to be good children, to obey amah and to avoid doing anything silly. To amah he'd say, 'If they're naughty, tell me and I won't give them any pocket money.' Naturally we'd promise to be model children and off we'd go and begin another week, like the previous one, full of mischievous escapades. Dear, sweet, loyal amah never complained about us so we were generously supplied with spending money.

The dhobi-man came as usual on Saturday mornings to hand over the clean linen and take the week's soiled bundle away in his van, only now it was Olga who presided over the laundry delivery, ticking and signing the book with a flourish. Sadly, the florist no longer delivered his armfuls of living colour to brighten and sweeten our home, but we three fully supported another departure from routine — the castor oil Saturdays came to an end.

There were changes to the weekly menus. We'd persuade amah to provide our favourite items on a regular basis instead of just occasionally. Chicken, for instance, began to appear much more frequently — at that time it was more expensive than beef, pork or mutton, so we were used to having it only as a treat. But now — 'Chicken tonight,' Olga would tell amah before we drove off to school. 'Chicken, please,' I'd pipe in and amah would snap back, 'Chicken, chicken, chicken — you think your father is *orang kaya!*' (a local millionaire). But mostly she'd carry out our wishes because she wanted to please us in any way she could. She must also have suspected her days with us were numbered.

Some weeks after the funeral, a bright and brassy young woman was introduced to us by Dad as a long-time friend of Mum's. 'I'm Barbara Neil,' she said, 'but you can call me Aunty Bobs.' I looked into her large green eyes and stared at her coppery-red hair and the penny dropped. So this was the woman who was likely to become our stepmother! She seemed friendly and pleasant enough. She attempted to gain our confidence by telling us about her three children, who were about the same age as us and most anxious to meet us and become our friends, she said. She also made overtures to the servants regarding their staying on and working for her when she moved into Brooke Road. They, loyal souls, turned down her offers, explaining to an embarrassed Dad, and to us later, that they 'didn't trust this new *mem* and would leave if she ever came to stay in Brooke Road and take over the running of the household.'

Aunty May was livid when she found out about Bobs' visits. The strained relationship between her and Dad had been patched up following the funeral, when the possibility of the Prout children being adopted and raised by the Pijpes was discussed. Dad had surprised them by making a spirited declaration of his affection for us and his firm intention to dedicate his life to raising his children himself (with the help of the family servants, naturally). He sounded so convincing that he won their grudging respect and Aunty May was prepared to forgive and forget. And now, with the advent of Bobs, came this apparent about-face! Aunty May didn't swear but I'd never seen her so angry. From then on, she took to visiting us only when she knew Dad would be away. Understandably, she was less than complimentary whenever the conversation turned to Bobs or Dad. However, there were times when she had to deal with him directly. One such occasion was the forthcoming Children's Christmas Party held every year at Government House. When the formal invitation arrived there was some discussion about whether it was appropriate for us to go because of Mum's recent death.

Dad was all in favour of our going; my Aunt was no killjoy either, but she wanted us to be suitably dressed for the occasion according to an elaborate colour-code that probably had its origins in our maternal Portuguese-Catholic background. It certainly didn't come from Dad's side of the family, so he was content to allow Aunty May full reign in the choice of our going-out attire for the period of mourning.

Some latitude was acceptable in the case of young children, so while Aunty May wore unrelieved black for the first three months, we children wore black-and-white polka-dots, or floral-patterned fabric with white collars and cuffs. For those who observed the code strictly, plain black gave way to grey or navy blue and the last phase of mourning allowed the use of pastel shades to complete the twelve months.

We three were in the black-and-white stage when Aunty rummaged through our wardrobes to find something more festive for the event. She discovered the pale blue and pale pink organdie and lace confections that Mum had brought back for us from England, nearly three years previously. Waists were adjusted, hems let down and the outfits were pronounced perfectly suitable party dresses, so we curtsied to Lady Thomas and shook hands with Sir Shenton (the Governor of the Straits Settlements) in our pastel finery and enjoyed our last party at Government House. The following year there were no big decisions about appropriate attire for the Christmas Party; by that time not only were we out of mourning, we were also out of circulation.

Meanwhile, we managed to chalk up a few more escapades that counted against us when the temptation to put us into boarding school loomed large on Dad's horizon.

John was solely to blame for the driving accident. From his usual seat beside the driver, he was sometimes allowed to steer the car once we got off the main road and onto the lane leading to the house. One Friday afternoon we were returning from school when he coaxed and cajoled the syce into changing seats with him, so that he could show off in front of his sisters. He tried to park the car in the usual spot, but instead of stopping at the staircase he crashed into it, demolishing the three bottom steps. Fortunately there were no broken bones among the riders in the chariot, but the Hillman bonnet sported massive dents and scratches. Tough car that it was, it was still driveable and it carried a very contrite and nervous John to the wharf next morning to explain to Dad what had happened. We never did find out exactly what John said to Dad or what Dad said in reply, but that weekend we missed out on our treat at the Polar Café, an ice-cream parlour on North Bridge Road where Dad used to take us on a regular basis.

Acting as a threesome, our most serious crime was the almost daily practice of pulling back the sunroof of the Hillman and sitting side by side on the roof, dangling our legs in the well of the car behind the driver's head. From that vantage point we'd drive through the city, waving to cyclists, pedestrians and other motorists who'd be too startled to wave back. What a wonderful feeling we shared, the wind in our faces, sitting on top of the world!

Naturally, the syce would beg us to come down, but we'd take no notice and repeat the performance next day. One afternoon, we were aloft again, giving the royal wave to all and sundry when we realised the car following us contained two convent nuns, who got their driver to pull up alongside as they shouted, 'Get down, children, get down!'

Quick as a flash we were in our seats below, feeling chastened and fearful of the consequences. Retribution was not long in coming. We were summoned the next morning to Reverend Mother's office and severely scolded for acting so foolishly and dangerously. We were informed that Mr Prout would be advised to put us in the boarding school because of our wild and reckless behaviour.

Time had run out for the Three Musketeers.

5

BEHIND THE CONVENT WALLS

Perhaps Dad had been waiting for something to force his hand. He hated making tough decisions. Our reckless behaviour gave him the excuse to shift the onerous responsibility of raising three motherless children onto the capable shoulders of Reverend Mother St James. He could always claim that he'd tried to tackle the job himself (for a few months) but that our irresponsible actions had given him no choice.

Once our fate was decided, events moved very swiftly. The servants were paid off and departed tearfully; amah embraced us and promised to visit us at the convent, where Olga and I would now change our status from day girls to boarders. John was taken out of St Joseph's, which was a day school, and placed at St Patrick's in Katong, which had a boarding department.

Dad and Bobs moved into a new flat at Tiong Bahru, one of the first skyscraper apartment buildings that would subsequently become a feature of the Singapore landscape. Bobs declared she didn't want to live in a large bungalow waited on by a team of servants, adding that in any case, Dad could no longer afford such a lifestyle; Mum had left a mountain of medical bills in her wake which could only be paid off by thrifty housekeeping. We began to hear all sorts of critical comments about Mum's extravagant ways — her monthly accounts with the dressmaker, shoemaker, florist, silk merchant and so forth. Naturally it was our stepmother who fired all the bullets while Dad merely sat quietly, nodding his head. 'We're poor, now, very poor indeed,' he remarked sadly.

We got the message loud and clear; they would pay our boarding fees but there would be no expensive extras and birthdays and Christmases would be low-budget events. We just had to make the best of our changed circumstances. Dad and Bobs were going to set the example by embarking on a frugal and economical lifestyle, unlike the previous wasteful regime of our 'spendthrift' mother.

There is a convent school in Victoria Street
Where they eat rotten eggs ten times a week.
Oh how the children yell when they hear the dinner bell,
Oh how the curry smells — ten miles away!

The transition from a free-and-easy existence to a rigid, institutional life was not easy.

I remember first being shown my bed in the Small Boarders' dormitory. The iron-frame beds with plain white sheets faced each other across bare polished floors, reminding me of the hospital wards I had visited. If anything, the latter were more cheerful places because of the softening touch of brightly coloured curtains and fresh flowers. In this austere sleeping area for young children, not a single toy was visible. Clutching my doll tightly, I ventured to ask, 'May I take dolly to bed with me at night?'

'No, dear, dolly stays in the toy cupboard until Saturday.' St Daniel attempted to soften the blow. 'You may take your rosary to bed with you and offer up your prayers and your tears for your mother.' It wasn't the response I'd hoped for but I recognised in the tone of voice an underlying kindness. At the age of eight, I was aware that even good people did not enter the heavenly portals at the moment of death — only saints went straight to heaven. Ordinary Christians got to heaven eventually, after spending some time at a waiting station called Purgatory. As dead people couldn't pray for themselves, their families and friends had to intercede on their behalf.

I was to become very familiar with this standard response to every personal difficulty. Whatever the pain or provocation, one was exhorted to offer up prayers for the sick, dying, dead, the starving children in Africa, South America, the soldiers in the trenches and so forth and so on.

A little bit of self-denial was doubtless good for the soul but occasionally it was carried to extremes, when genuine individual needs were brushed aside for the so-called 'general good'.

Virtues promoted at the convent were those that underpinned a religious community: piety, self-discipline, modesty, self-denial and scholarship. We boarders and orphans virtually lived the lives of young novices waiting to take their vows.

The rule of silence was rigidly imposed and not lightly waived. We took our meals in silence every day; only weekend lunches and dinners were exempted from the ban on speech. Study periods were times for absolute quiet and of course no chatter was permitted during the frequent chapel and church visits. Talking in the dormitory was a punishable offence. On those nights when sleep was slow in coming, you counted sheep, said your rosary, or escaped into a dream world where rules, barriers and boundaries disappeared.

Cocooned in my mosquito-net, if I sat up in bed, I could see the friendly red beacon of the Capitol Theatre, glowing in the dark, through the open window — a telling symbol of my pleasant, vanished past. From the verandah behind my bed, the ghostly white spire of the convent chapel stood for the present, imperfect regime. Floating away on my magic carpet I often revisited my happy past or escaped into a fabulous future.

But the daily routines of the present were not always easily set aside. One had, for instance, to be fully alert when taking a bath. This was another activity conducted entirely in silence and modesty was another essential of the bath ritual. The bathroom consisted of a large, concreted, enclosed space dominated by a low rectangular water-tank, into which the bathers, twenty to forty at a time, dipped small metal buckets and poured the contents over their chemise-covered bodies. Water was strictly rationed: when the water supply was quite plentiful, three buckets before soaping, six buckets to follow; otherwise, two buckets before and four to follow.

The trick was to dress and undress under the chemise without exposing a single inch of flesh between the shoulder and the knee. Hindus bathing in the Ganges perform remarkable sleight-of-hand tricks with wet and dry saris; Balinese women accomplish graceful, dexterous movements behind their flimsy batik sarongs — but these bathers are practised performers, worlds apart from awkward and amateurish convent girls. As a result, mistakes did occur and naked bodies were sometimes inadvertently exposed to the shocked gaze of the bathroom audience. When this happened, eyes were immediately averted and no comments were made. Only the brave dared to laugh, for this was a serious world and the human body was not an object of levity.

During my first few months as a boarder, if anyone had told me that I would come to regard my convent days with some degree of nostalgia, I would have laughed out loud.

En masse, the nuns were rather daunting, but gradually I came to know them individually. For every nun who was severe and chilly, there were two who were friendly, warm-hearted and even fun-loving. They were not 'touchy-feely' people — it wasn't part of the culture, yet they did not avoid physical contact altogether. Kisses tended to be regulated by the calendar; Easter and Christmas, and of course St Patrick's Day were occasions when kisses were part of the exchange of greetings. St Patrick's Day was a special feast day because most of the nuns were Irish.

There were some nuns who could convey a great deal of affection without needing to hug and kiss. St Raphael was a prime example. She brushed hair, tied ribbons and patted cheeks so lovingly in the daily dressing-for-school routine that there was always a queue of adoring young boarders awaiting her ministrations, whereas St Daniel, less gentle and patient, seldom had any customers.

St Raphael became my mother-substitute; her warm brown eyes and friendly smile brought comfort to the bleakest surroundings; and when her Saturday morning stint with the Little Boarders was over, St Madeleine of the Big Boarders would take me under her wing and make a place for me among her charges. Her trainee teachers and Senior Cambridge students would good-humouredly make way for me every Saturday afternoon at the big table in the recreation square while they talked freely about current events, religion, politics, fashion and local gossip. St Madeleine would direct and widen the debate and correct any inaccuracies. A lot of the talk went over my head but it was very flattering to be regularly included in an adult gathering.

Less surrogate-mother than teacher and mentor, St Madeleine encouraged me to use my brain, not in so many words of course, and I was happy to comply. Having dreamed my way through most of my early schooling, I decided to start taking my classwork seriously and my grades improved markedly. The dolls that had been brought out for their Saturday airing would sit behind me neglected. No doll-play could be as riveting as the conversation all round me. Gradually I was weaned from my dolls and took to reading in a big way. Books were permitted on toy-ban days. Like the weekly discussions, they opened up amazing new horizons.

While the observer in me was given free rein, I was also pushed into participating in a whole range of school events — plays, sports, dance displays — and I started to make friends with a number of children in my own age group, forging a number of lasting friendships. Olga didn't have to learn how to make friends; the art of friendship came naturally to her and within a few days of becoming a boarder, she had acquired a close-knit circle of bosom companions. For anybody attempting to interact with other people, the cosmopolitan community of the Convent, while French in its inspiration, offered an abundant smorgasbord of racial and cultural mixtures, a microcosm of Singapore society. Within the religious community, the Irish dominated in numbers, but there was a good representation of Italians, Spaniards, a sprinkling of Poles and Belgians, Chinese and Indians, and one English and one Eurasian nun.

Not long after I became a boarder, there was great excitement over the news that we would be welcoming St Anna, a Vietnamese princess no less, who had been educated in Paris and would spend some time with us. Petite and vivacious, St Anna was an instant hit with her young charges because she livened up the uneventful afternoons with the introduction of French folk-dances and songs. English folk-dancing was already part of the school curriculum, but we were always happy to learn new dances of any kind. It goes without saying that the Irish nuns had taught us a number of jigs and reels; we certainly weren't deprived of the pleasant sensation of moving in time to music. However, the kind of dancing we boarders most enjoyed was ballroom dancing. Yes, ballroom dancing! On special feast days, the wind-up gramophone with the universal totem of the listening dog was trotted out and the Big Boarders would 'trip the light fantastic' to the music of Victor Sylvester. A number of the older girls were really fine dancers and shone not only at the waltz, foxtrot and quickstep but the rhumba and tango as well (the last supposedly banned by the Vatican). The younger girls watched carefully and tried to copy their steps and sometimes received personal tuition from the 'experts'.

But long before I'd mastered all the fancy footwork, we found ourselves moving to the frantic drumbeats of war rather than the measured cadences of Victor Sylvester's band. A week after that first air attack on Singapore, the decision was made to evacuate the boarders and orphans to Seremban, in the Malayan state of Negri Sembilan, some two hundred miles north.

6

SEREMBAN STOPOVER

I came out of my daydream as the train slackened speed and hissed its way into Seremban station where a row of smiling 'penguin' figures pressed forward to embrace their sisters, cousins and close friends, welcoming them to this rural retreat.

We boarders felt a bit left out because there were no familiar faces on the platform to greet us on our arrival. As we looked around awaiting instructions, a tall imperious 'penguin' strode towards us and introduced herself as Sister Finbarr, the sister of our St Coleman. 'No doubt you girls will be delighted to stretch your legs and walk to the convent,' she surmised. 'It's not very far.' We exchanged glances. *Walk*? No bus? Something in her manner discouraged any discussion, so we squared our shoulders and set out behind the trishaws that were conveying the nuns to the school. A couple of our chaperones walked ahead of our straggly crocodile as it slowly made its way down Birch Road. Truckloads of troops passed us, waving and whistling, calling out in surprise, 'Wotcha doing up here? Meet you in Singapore!' A marching column of infantry bringing up the rear sang a Gracie Fields number, 'Wish me luck as you wave me goodbye —'

Soon we were walking alongside the convent fence, a fairly low corrugated-iron structure backed by a line of wide-leaved Travellers palms, Alexandra palms and Oil palms with their fringe of red-gold berries hanging below their round spearheads. At first sight, the Seremban convent appeared as a lush green oasis, self-assured and at ease in its occupation of a large segment of the main road. At our approach the wrought-iron gates swung wide open to allow the inflow of evacuees into the circular driveway. Baggage of all shapes and sizes littered the porch and every incoming pair of feet added a bundle or two to the pile. In the middle of all this activity stood a small intense figure, in build a replica of Mother St James, directing the traffic, and like St James, not needing to raise her voice to be obeyed instantly.

'Gather around me, children,' Reverend Mother St Pauline invited us. 'Madame St Finbarr will be taking you to the refectory for afternoon tea and then she'll show you where you can sleep. Welcome to Seremban!'

The tea was hot and sweet, the bread fresh with a good crisp crust, the locally grown bananas were honey-flavoured, so we didn't mind too much that for the first time in our lives we were eating off tin plates. More little jolts lay ahead of us, as if we needed to be reminded that we were no longer in Singapore (dear old Singapore!) and there was a war on.

The dormitory was totally lacking in the one item of furniture usually associated with such places — beds. Instead, piles of fibre mattresses were stacked against the walls, and one by one we were assigned a mattress and a pillow (no sheets or pillow-slips) and shown how to place the mattresses side by side, touching the walls and leaving a clear space down the middle of the room for access. Hard times were indeed upon us but we were not about to complain. For a bunch of refugees, our morale was quite high. We were young and healthy, Christmas was around the corner and if the war wasn't over by then it would surely end early in the New Year!

The choir mistress came looking for recruits the next morning and was delighted with the enthusiastic response from all the evacuees. 'May I join too? I know all the Christmas hymns, including the French and Latin ones,' I pleaded. Small boarders didn't usually sing in the choir, but St Matthew was happy to be persuaded. Her tall, angular frame bent over towards me and her brown eyes twinkled behind thick lenses. 'How can I refuse anyone who is so keen? Of course you may!'

And so a lot of time that might have been taken up with worrying about our desperate situation was instead channelled into rehearsing the lovely traditional melodies of the Christmas season. We could do nothing directly to help the war effort, but we were encouraged to think that if we prayed earnestly enough, sang beautifully enough and made sacrifices of sufficient magnitude, somehow the impending disaster could be averted. This 'miracle mentality' was not just a pious hope, cherished by religious communities, it was the official government policy pursued in the misguided belief that telling the ordinary citizens and the fighting men the unpalatable truth about the war situation would be bad for their morale. Which meant, of course, that nobody was prepared for the coming debacle.

One afternoon before Christmas the boarders were taken for a walk. All the Singapore nuns came along, and for us evacuees, it was our first glimpse of the world outside the convent walls. We headed for the Lake Gardens first and after a pleasant stroll we had to admit that the English captain we'd met on the platform at the Singapore railway station was right when he called Seremban a 'green and pretty place'. We returned along the main street, walking slowly past several open-fronted provision stores which were doing a brisk trade, the busiest of all being Lee Kee's, diagonally across the road from the school. Our crocodile was poised to re-enter the convent gates when several more troop-laden trucks heading south slowed down to exchange pleasantries with us. Cheeky and chirpy as usual, they called out: 'Don't worry, girls, we'll lick the Japs in no time — be seeing you!' From the nuns' ranks came the surprising response, 'God bless you, boys, and keep you safe!' Obviously the lads were no longer regarded as threats but as defenders and patriots.

We now included our defending troops at every prayer session. Irreverently, I liked the short and pithy supplication, 'Oh God of Battles, steel/steal our soldiers' hearts!'

The Midnight Mass that Christmas was a joyous occasion. All doubts and anxieties were stifled while we raised our hearts and voices in glorious song, praying that the Divine Child would bring peace to all mankind.

Then we returned to the dormitory to catch up on our sleep. It was customary for Santa Claus to call during our absence and leave presents on every bed. We'd been warned not to expect anything this year because of the 'W' word, and were pleasantly surprised to find a small parcel on every mattress; toilet articles mainly — soap, toothpaste, combs, and holy pictures from all the nuns left behind in Singapore. Gifts and greetings from family members sometimes arrived on Christmas Eve and were delivered together with the present from Reverend Mother, after Midnight Mass. Olga and I had told ourselves from the time we arrived at Seremban that we'd be hearing from Dad very soon. Every morning we woke up thinking 'This could be the day'. Then, as one day faded into the next, we convinced ourselves that the big moment would come with Christmas, when we'd be handed an envelope with the familiar handwriting. But for the Prout girls, there was no letter, no card, no word at all from their father. It would be understating the case to say that we were bitterly disappointed. The nuns had sent their greetings, but apparently not Dad. Was it the postman's fault? It's true that the postal system was no longer reliable. A host of unanswerable questions sprang to mind, but were not voiced. No point in asking Olga whether she believed Dad had already left Kuala Lumpur. Nobody could have told us. Perhaps — perhaps, he wasn't writing because he was coming in person and would appear at the convent gate any day now, definitely before New Year. In much the same way as everybody was waiting for the turn of the tide in the Allies' favour, Olga and I waited for our personal miracle.

There was no question of Dad ringing us; the only phone in the school had to be reserved for convent business and emergencies. Besides, all interstate calls had to go through the exchange and delays of hours, even days' duration, were becoming common. In his book *Sinister Twilight*, Noel Barber describes several events surrounding the fall of Singapore and says that business people were able to follow the battle lines southward by the announcements of banks closing their doors 'until further notice'. In a similar way, Mother St Pauline had a fair idea how far south the Japanese had penetrated because one by one the phone links with the convents north of Seremban were cut off. Their nuns had remained in residence but they could not be contacted. Special prayers were offered up for them on Christmas Day. We hoped that the convents would provide true sanctuary as they had in ancient times, in faraway places.

For those of us who were still free, this was a day to eat, drink and be merry, because a big question-mark hung over the morrow.

Every meal that day was extra special: bread and jam for breakfast, a thimbleful of sherry in each glass for lunch (for this was a French convent, where wine was usually served on major feast days), and after dinner, *la pièce de resistance*, a large, luscious trifle, fruit-filled and brandy-flavoured, courtesy of St Coleman. What a feast to remember!

There had been singing at the midnight service and there was dancing after lunch. The Seremban boarders brought their precious gramophone to the recreation hall with a small pile of records and generously allowed the refugees to select the songs and dances, even wind up the machine. They had not been so forthcoming with their sewing machine and had to be firmly persuaded to share that prized possession with the new arrivals.

The record selection comprised mainly sacred songs, Irish ballads, singers like John McCormack and Gracie Fields and several jigs and reels for dancing. No Victor Sylvester, but nobody complained. We were happy to be dancing at all. It was an occasion when there was peace and goodwill to spare among all the thirty-odd boarders, regardless of our convent of origin.

At Seremban, the inevitable tensions in our enlarged family were diffused when we sang together as a choir or participated in netball or volleyball games or other team sports. The attitude of the host nuns was crucial in promoting harmony and good relations and most of the Seremban nuns were anxious to achieve this. However, St Finbarr appeared to have a personal grudge against the Singapore girls which she demonstrated in various ways. When drawing up the duty rosters she would single us out for the most unpleasant tasks, making comments like, 'That's a job for the Singapore girls — or should I say "ladies"?' The full force of her venom was reserved for the five First Boarders, Mary and Annie Dragon, Monique Dupire and the Prout sisters. She regarded us as having led a useless, pampered existence and was determined to bring us down to earth with a crash-course in sweeping, dusting, washing and cleaning, especially bathroom and toilet cleaning. No doubt it was a sensible idea to teach us domestic skills, but we suspected that her motive was humiliation, not education.

We should have been a soft target, easily squashed, but St Finbarr came up against two seasoned rebels: Olga and Monique, a French girl whose parents were in Saigon. Olga refused point-blank to carry out any chore she considered excessive or unnecessary, while Monique would not only refuse but would also fire off a few salvos in French at St Finbarr, who would then trot the two insubordinates to Reverend Mother's office. A heated exchange would take place and the two miscreants would have to forfeit a meal or recreation time. Punished they might be, but they were not cowed. After a few such battles, St

Finbarr reduced the level of provocation and a sort of armed truce existed until we returned to Singapore.

Approximately two weeks later, the time had come for the nuns from Singapore to return to our convent there. Tears flowed freely on both sides as our nuns took their leave of their family members and the boarders. By now, a deep sense of foreboding had replaced earlier optimism, and we all sensed that we were in for a grim time.

The rapidity of the Japanese advance had begun to sink in; Olga and I had ceased to expect the small, lithe figure of Dad to stride through the convent gates and ask for his daughters, as he had on so many occasions when paying his weekly visit to the Singapore convent.

Holding St Vincent's hand, St Raphael whispered, 'Take good care of my little treasures.'

'I will, my dear,' her sister promised in as firm a voice as she could muster. Then St Raphael hugged us all silently and departed along with the other nuns who were returning after their sojourn in Seremban.

A phone call from Singapore informed St Pauline of their safe arrival and also mentioned the growing problem of the refugees from upcountry. These unfortunates, mostly women and children, had been rushed south at a moment's notice. In many cases they had lost contact with their husbands, had no money and nowhere to go. They had taken to roaming the streets looking for food and shelter. Raffles College and certain schools helped billet them and a few convents had opened their doors to them. St James had taken in as many as she thought she could feed, housing them initially in the empty boarders' dormitories. But the almost daily bombing from the beginning of January forced everybody to abandon the upper floors and seek whatever shelter was possible in the ground-floor classrooms and passages.

This telephone conversation may have prompted St Pauline to get her Seremban charges to make a similar change from upstairs to downstairs in search of the greater perceived safety of ground-level classrooms.

One upstairs dormitory had been large enough to accommodate all the boarders but we couldn't all fit into a single classroom with our mattresses, so two rooms were required, with the older girls in one space, the younger ones in the other. This meant that several pairs of siblings were separated (including Olga and me) and considerable unease was generated. 'This will only be for a night or two, until we know what happens in Kuala Lumpur,' we were told. The morning before our move downstairs, a Radio Malaya broadcast had stated that the Allied troops were preparing to engage the enemy on the outskirts of Kuala Lumpur. We didn't need to be reminded that Kuala Lumpur was only some forty miles to our north and that if our side retreated once again, the road to Seremban would be clear and unprotected; an easy ride for the enemy.

Getting to sleep that night was not easy. There were several things on my mind. I missed Olga's reassuring presence. Had I asked, 'What if the Allies are defeated?' she would have said firmly, perhaps with a hint of irritation, 'Stop worrying, you can't do anything, just pray.'

Somehow I must have dropped off, because when the bombs came screaming down and shook the building, it took me a few seconds to get my bearings. In the dim pre-dawn light I noticed several crouching and trembling figures like mine, then near the door I picked out the tall, gaunt figure of St Ignatius, who'd been delegated to stay behind when her companions returned to Singapore. She now produced her rosary and asked us to do likewise. The familiar roll of the 'Hail Marys' did have a calming effect, until the next screech and thud signalled another bomb and little cries of 'I want my sister' were heard — was that me, or somebody else? Sternly, St Ignatius addressed her frightened charges. 'Stay here quietly, children. Your sisters will be all right. Now let us say the Act of Contrition.'

That prayer! Was she hinting we were facing Eternity?

'Oh my God,' she began, 'I am heartily sorry that I have sinned against thee.'

A full chorus joined in fervently; after all, none of us was certain we'd see another day.

Suddenly everything was silent, the planes had gone and the early morning sun was a welcome sight. We were alive — and hungry. We looked forward to the fresh, crisp white bread that was always there for our daily breakfast. Today, however, hard, stale, yellowing crusts sat in the middle of each tin plate. As we stared in shock at the substitution, we were told there would be no more fresh bread from the bakery because the baker had fled at first light. He was just one of many who had been terrified by the bombing and decided on the spur of the moment to drop everything and escape — but where? Mostly southward, where the Allied troops had gone and were now engaged in sporadic battles with the enemy. Surprisingly, we had not witnessed the movement of Allied troops past our door after the fall of Kuala Lumpur. Possibly they had moved to their 'prepared positions further south' under cover of darkness. The Japanese bombing raid may have been aimed at them, rather than at the non-strategic town of Seremban.

Very likely, a major battle would be waged in Johor and the tide would turn in our favour. Despite all the evidence to the contrary, the myth of British superiority lived on. Meanwhile, those townspeople who had not fled southward after the retreating British Army dispersed into the surrounding jungle or hid out on rubber estates, waiting out the Japanese arrival in Seremban.

7

THE ENEMY ARRIVES

Once the road was clear of the human flood, an eerie silence followed. The normal sounds of town life had ceased.

We became acutely aware of our isolation. The Christian Brothers, like us, were staying put but they were not visible or easily contactable. On the grapevine we'd heard that the so-called Suicide Squad usually preceded the regular Japanese army. This was made up of the dregs of the military machine and was sent on ahead to capture a town or village. Once that was accomplished, its members were at liberty to pillage, rape or murder for three days as a reward for their efforts.

Despite our desperate situation, I cannot recall any signs of panic among the two hundred or so souls waiting behind the flimsy fence for the arrival of the all-conquering foe. Mother St Pauline had spoken to us briefly after the bombing. Calmly and concisely, she had told us the unpalatable truth. 'All our defenders have gone or are leaving. We are now solely in God's hands — pray very hard, my children.' I expect that we took our cue from her, telling ourselves, 'All will be well. We'll come through it!'

So we carried on with our various tasks, filling in the hours somehow with prayers, sewing, cleaning and gardening. As we worked in the fields on this particular day we asked ourselves, 'What sort of people are these Japanese?' We would soon be meeting them face-to-face. We speculated on their appearance, hoping they would not prove as ugly as their caricatures in the newspapers or as ferocious and cruel as rumour had depicted them.

When it came time to put the gardening tools away, I was one of a small party carrying the rakes and cangkuls (hoes) to a storeroom near the perimeter fence. For hours it had been strangely quiet outside, but as we approached the fence, a rising volume of sound caught our attention. Curiosity overcame caution as we crept up the stairs to take a peek at the source of the commotion. Crouching behind the wooden verandah rails, we spied the dreaded foe.

Were they the vanguard of the bloodthirsty desperadoes that made up the Suicide Squad?

At first glance, this swarthy, sweating army on push-bikes pedalling its way down Birch Road, wearing peaked canvas caps with back flaps, water bottles and food cans strapped to their waists, inspired unease rather than terror. Then, one noticed the rifles strapped to their shoulders and the cold glint of steel of the fixed bayonets and knew that any opposition they encountered along the route would be met with a swift and bloody response.

A group of riders on their left flank brushed past the convent fence and glanced sideways and up in our direction. Loud, excited chatter followed. Horror of horrors! Had they spotted us? We crawled downstairs, hearts pounding, fully expecting them to smash open the gates and come looking for us. But the minutes ticked by and there was no invasion. The street was empty once more so we started breathing freely again and vowed not to speak of our escapade with the others. Very subdued, we filed into the refectory for dinner.

Over boiled sweet potatoes and spinach, St Finbarr spoke of the possibility of Japanese soldiers dropping in to search the convent on one pretext or another. We were to go to bed in our day clothes, not to wash our faces or brush our hair, to lie still on our mattresses and to do nothing to call attention to ourselves. 'As if we would!' protested Monique indignantly and several heads nodded in agreement. St Finbarr glared at her and continued, 'Never ever look directly at them — you wouldn't like them to take you away!'

She got no argument on that score.

That night we prayed intensely and at length for our safety and that of all our loved ones. With all that prolonged Heaven-storming going on, it may have seemed rather cheeky of me to have included a quick personal plea for the speedy return of our fugitive baker to provide us with our all-sustaining daily bread!

Around two in the morning, the bicycle warriors of the evening before leapt over the fence or clambered up the gate and in no time they were swarming all over the place in small bands, rushing up staircases, smashing locked doors, checking all manholes in the ceilings to capture the English women that some terrified townspeople had told them were hiding in the convent. They had met with some resistance at first. A wall of black-robed nuns waiting in the porch attempted to bar their way, but they were thrust aside impatiently by unkempt, tough-talking ruffians demanding ever more stridently, 'Egirish-u-man, you show!' The NCO in charge singled out one nun (St Dennis) and placed the barrel of his pistol against her temple, barking, 'You Egirish *ka*?'

'No, Irish,' she replied in as calm a voice as she could muster, her heart fluttering wildly while she prayed frantically that he wouldn't pull the trigger.

'Egirish, Egirish!' he insisted.

'Irish, Irish,' she responded, wondering whether her inquisitor understood the difference between the two words. After what seemed a lifetime, he replaced the pistol in its holster to join his men in their search for those elusive English women they were convinced lurked somewhere in our midst.

Our night-duty nuns merely had time to call out, 'Girls, they're here — eyes closed!' before feet pounded outside the doorway and the soldiers crowded in, stumbling past mattresses at one end, working their way to the other end, food cans and water bottles rattling at their waists, torches sweeping the dormitory area, checking out every face on the floor. Before they even entered, a stench of raw or rotting fish and sweaty rubber shoes engulfed the sleeping area; we smelt them before we heard them. Lying very still, I chanced a lightning glance through half-closed lids, and spied a soldier shining his torch at a face two mattresses away from mine. 'He's coming,' I thought and no sooner had I pressed my lids together than a warm disc of light played on my face for — seconds? Minutes? Then just as suddenly, the probing, scary warmth was gone and the welcome cooler darkness returned. 'I'm safe now,' I told myself.

Orders were shouted in guttural, staccato tones and immediately the invaders rushed out and off across the quadrangle towards the orphans' dormitory. Their departure was the signal for all the prostrate figures feigning sleep to sit up and compare notes. 'They might be back any moment, better be still,' we were warned.

A clock in the adjoining passageway kept us informed of the passing moments, yet time seemed to be standing still. An hour had passed since we'd seen the invaders rush up the staircase of the orphans' dormitory and nothing appeared to be happening. We couldn't hear a thing. What were they doing?

We lay still, imagining all manner of things, and of course, we prayed. Rosaries rotated like worry beads through sweaty fingers. The clock struck four — still no movement on the other side. Then the girls nearest the door peered across the yard and whispered in surprise, 'They're sitting in the verandah outside the dormitory, cooking and eating!'

Five o'clock came and then a stampede back in our direction — were they re-visiting us? Oh hell! The clamour built up to a crescendo as we braced ourselves for an awful encounter and then — the noise went past us and out onto the street and silence, blessed silence, returned. For several minutes, no one spoke and then there was a general resurrection of prostrate figures asking, 'Have the Japs gone?'

'Yes, girls, they've left. We must thank God for His deliverance and ask for His continued protection.'

'Did they take anybody away?' At that point a nun from the orphans' side popped her head in the door to say nobody had been harassed or removed and we all joined in a thanksgiving prayer immediately.

Over breakfast, we heard all the details of that memorable night. When the intruders reached the orphans' dormitory, they were met by three nuns and — surprise, surprise — a man! A Mr Singham, a Catholic layman who had very bravely offered to camp on the premises until the situation was calm again. His dark skin did not protect him from the unwelcome attentions of the same thug that had earlier intimidated St Dennis. 'Japan ZIS!' shouted the NCO, giving the thumbs up sign; 'British ZIS,' giving the thumbs down sign, to which Mr Singham, with a gun to his head, readily agreed. But our Indian protector could not agree to the next proposal put forward by the Japanese soldier. The gun was lowered and the belligerent manner replaced by a more reasonable approach. 'These girrs' — a khaki-clad arm indicated the eighty or more orphans lying on mats on the floor — 'people outside tell, no one want, Japanese Army take, orright? We give food.'

As one voice, Mr Singham and the nuns replied loudly, emphatically, 'No, no, no! You cannot take God's children, convent holy place, girls pray all day.' Kneeling down in the middle of the room they produced crucifixes and rosaries and started a circle of prayer.

The NCO and his men looked nonplussed. Had they really imagined the convent would willingly hand over its orphans to a bunch of soldiers, any soldiers, merely to save itself the trouble of feeding them?

Looking back on this scenario today, it still amazes me that this bunch of cut-throats didn't just grab as many girls as they wished and take off. Why were they so patient? So restrained? Who could have stopped them had they lived up to their reputation for getting their own way in the most vicious and violent manner?

Instead, they opted to play a waiting game. It looked as if they wanted to remove the orphan girls by stealth rather than by force, and to that end they hung around waiting for the nuns to fall asleep at their posts. And while they waited, they decided to have a meal. Ration tins were removed from their waists, portable kerosene stoves were set up on the verandah and a bizarre breakfast session began.

When the meal was over, the nuns were still awake, and still praying! At this point the enemy decided to withdraw and vacate the field.

They had raided the convent to ferret out fugitive English women and had planned on carrying off several of the orphans to act as 'comfort women'. On both counts they had been thwarted and left empty-handed. Yet they took no reprisals. Was somebody up there actually listening to our prayers?

As soon as the Japanese had left, Mr Singham was dispatched to fetch Brother Joseph, the Principal of St Paul's, and after early Mass, St Pauline, Brother Joseph and the parish priest set out across the Padang to the KGV (King George V) School, where the Japanese Military Governor had taken up residence. St Pauline put her case for protection from marauding troops. The Governor spoke little English but his aide-de-camp was fairly fluent, so Reverend Mother was able to put her argument and be understood. She knew nothing of Japanese culture or history and yet she used the best argument, perhaps the only one, capable of swaying the Japanese authorities in her favour. In her slow, precise way, she stated that it would be SHAMEFUL if it were known that the Japanese Army had defiled a convent, a sacred place, full of nuns and innocent children.

She won her case.

She returned to the convent armed with a scroll she'd been instructed to hang from a pillar supporting the main gate. The Governor had assured her there would be no further problems caused by unruly troops, and he was right.

The scroll read: ENTRY FORBIDDEN UNLESS AUTHORISED BY THE GOVERNOR. SOLDIERS FOUND DISOBEYING THIS ORDER WILL BE BEHEADED.

A few days after the Suicide Squad invasion, the Governor and his aide came on a goodwill visit.

The whole convent population assembled in the quadrangle, filled with curiosity about the new man in charge. From his crisp white shirt collar to his shiny leather boots he looked very different from the scruffy ruffians that had provided us with our first glimpse of the Japanese Army.

Through his aide, the Governor announced we were now under the protection of the Imperial Japanese Army and expressed his wish for us to feel safe and happy! He predicted that the rest of Malaya and Singapore would soon be in Japanese hands; when that happened school would re-open and we would all be lucky enough to learn Japanese — Nippon-go. Smiling broadly, he produced a banknote from his wallet and handed it to Reverend Mother with a flourish, declaring, 'Japanese people children very much like — buy cakes!'

After he'd left we gathered round St Pauline to get a closer look at her prize, the first example of Japanese currency we'd seen. Face-up, it read:

The Japanese Government promises to pay the bearer on demand FIFTY DOLLARS.

In recent times, I received what might be considered a partial explanation for the sympathetic hearing and immediate assistance accorded to St Pauline when she pleaded for the protection of the convent after the invasion by Japanese troops.

There is no doubt that her use of the word 'shameful' aided her cause, but there may have been other factors in the equation. Such as the long-standing and distinguished role of the Infant Jesus convents in Japan. This connection had its roots in the early 1870s.

The Infant Jesus nuns were the first missionary nuns to go to Japan and their first students were Japanese ladies from the Imperial court. Their welcome at the Imperial Palace assured them of a ready acceptance elsewhere. Several schools and boarding houses were established in various parts of the country. All Infant Jesus convents in Japan bore the prestigious name of *Futaba* (two leaves).

This royal connection is confirmed in *Mother Mathilde's Call to Japan*, where it is written:

> *Haruko (Spring Princess), the Imperial Spouse of Mutsu Hito, the Emperor of the Restoration, had founded, not far from the Imperial Palace, a magnificent establishment where young girls of the nobility were receiving an excellent education ... Daily, because of the distance, some sisters were transported from Tsukiji to the property in order to give required courses.*
>
> *The proximity of the Empress' palace made it possible for her protégés, when their Japanese classes finished, to go willingly to the sisters in order to supplement their instruction and receive some European education for which they were eager.**

Conceivably, the Governor would have heard of the Futaba schools and have been prepared to help an institution with Imperial links. However, it is highly unlikely that the unruly mob that overran the

* Published by the St Maur International School in Japan in 2003, *Mother Mathilde's Call to Japan* is a translation from a French document found by Sister Carmel in the Mother House in Paris a few years before.

convent on that memorable night had any inkling of these connections and therefore been inhibited by them. Their forbearance on that occasion remains a mystery to me.

It was now considered safe enough for us to move upstairs again to the boarders' dormitory on a more or less permanent basis, so beds were found for everybody and we placed our mattresses and pillows on the wire frames, and were issued with pillow-slips, but still no sheets.

However, we soon came to realise why the sheets previously available for the Seremban boarders were no longer on offer. They had been set aside as an essential resource — the raw material for convent underwear, seeing that we could no longer purchase these items outside. The sewing mistress began to cut out panties and petticoats for those in need. Our first attempts were somewhat rough and ready, but with practice and persistence, our 'underwear factory' began to turn out very durable, wearable items, compensating in fine finish for what they lacked in style.

Venturing outside the convent walls to attend church services was another sign of returning normality, albeit Occupation-style. The traffic didn't flow the way it used to because every major intersection now sprouted a sentry-box with a grim-faced sentry in attendance exacting the homage of a low bow from all who went past, whether on foot, bicycle, trishaw or truck. The civilian population soon learned to bend at the waist Japanese-style … or else! Virtually nobody drove a car at this time, except Japanese military personnel and the sentry always waved them past.

Another sign of the times, on our first visit to church after the occupation, was the demolished shop-house across the road from its main entrance. A popular photographer had plied his trade there until a bomb destroyed his home and business in one hit. Most of the debris had been cleared away but for weeks afterwards, people were still discovering unclaimed photographs on footpaths, roadways and in drains. The railway station had also scored a hit or two during the bombing raid. Both sites were close to the convent — no wonder we had felt the impact in our downstairs classroom!

Various regulations and restrictions came into force entailing the loss of several freedoms we had hitherto taken for granted. We were permitted to move outside the convent but forbidden to visit other towns or leave the state without the authority of the Japanese government. Most of the European nuns now discovered they were Enemy Aliens and were obliged to wear armbands proclaiming their new status every time they set foot outside the gates. They were also warned that they could be interned at any moment, and to that end were obliged to keep a small suitcase with the bare essentials packed and ready just in case.

Just after the Japanese Occupation of Seremban, two new boarders, Nellie and Pauline Plachel, joined our ranks. They had both been educated at the Seremban convent, so they weren't new girls in that sense. They had gone home for the holidays to a French-owned rubber estate some miles outside Seremban, and now that the Japanese forces were in control, their mother thought she and her two daughters, who were both in their early twenties, would be safer at the convent than at a remote plantation several hours drive from the town.

The need for medical assistance was possibly a high priority as well. I cannot say whether Pauline, the younger sister, had been diagnosed with tuberculosis before she joined the boarders in January, or whether it was a condition that only became apparent then. Being seriously ill during a war is to be doubly disadvantaged. Most hospitals weren't admitting patients and those that did lacked the necessary drugs to treat their sick. Pauline had struck us all as being extremely thin and pallid, but then several of us, healthy enough types, were not looking particularly robust after a few weeks on a diet of tapioca, sweet potato and boiled greens. However, it soon became clear that she was dangerously ill. Like Nellie, she had at first joined in the daily routine without expecting any special consideration, until it became apparent that she barely had the strength to drag herself out of bed. She was assigned a small cubicle off the dormitory in an attempt to isolate her; visits were not encouraged lest we should contract her disease. But some of us paid fleeting calls, staying just long enough to murmur a few 'Hail Marys', positioning ourselves at the foot of the bed, hopefully out of harm's way. Nellie and her mother nursed Pauline devotedly, but she faded fast, every bout of coughing and spitting taking her closer to her final farewell.

Pauline's condition and the war situation seemed to run a parallel course in disaster. Then, in the fourth week of January, suddenly, at long last, came hopeful news from the battlefront.

'The Aussies are giving the Japs a hiding on a rubber estate on the east coast near Mersing.' Mr Singham grinned broadly as he passed on the good news to St Finbarr. The Asian grapevine was alive and well. 'Listen to those lorries outside. The Japs are racing reinforcements to Johore.' For three days the Japanese were pinned down and their advance delayed until help reached them. Then they resumed their drive south.

No reinforcements reached the Aussies, nor did they have the benefit of air cover, so retreat was inevitable. Together with the other Allied forces fighting on the west coast they withdrew across the causeway on 31st January, blowing it up behind them. Last across were a valiant band of Scots, the remnants of a regiment that had lost most of its men but not its fighting spirit. To the swirl of bagpipes they marched over to the doomed island.

During that brief 'good news' interval, Pauline seemed to pick up and improve, but even before the bad news came clamouring back she had coughed for the last time and died, peacefully and prayerfully.

No elaborate funeral service was held, for obvious reasons. An armful of fragrant white lilies from the convent garden celebrated Pauline's youthful beauty and innocence. It bore the inscription: *Blessed are the pure of heart, for they shall see God.*

8

SURRENDER

During the two weeks in which Singapore moved from siege to surrender, most people upcountry had no idea of the actual situation on the island. Our usual news sources had dried up. Perhaps the brave souls who'd kept us informed had heard about the horrific punishment meted out to people who owned radios or listened to outside broadcasts.

It would appear that we weren't the only ignorant ones; even Singaporeans were kept in the dark by a ruthless censorship. Troops as well as civilians were confused and insecure. Courage and the will to fight were not lacking but no charismatic figure emerged to direct the efforts of the population in a concentrated effort to hold back the invaders. While the island trembled on the brink of chaos, insane and interminable wrangling continued among the decision-makers. The civilian government, the military authorities and Whitehall seemed unable to agree on uniform goals and the strategies for implementing them.

The Japanese officers who came to the Seremban convent on brief inspection tours were happy to boast of their military victories and confidently predicted the imminent surrender of Singapore. Secretly we knew they were right — only a first-class miracle could have saved the island once the causeway linking Singapore and Johore had been severed. The causeway had carried the Island's main water supply, so there was an acute water shortage. Nor was there any air cover, and the army food and petrol reserves had almost run out. This is why the so-called 'Invincible Fortress' proved indefensible. In the end, all was lost. The Union Jack sank — Singapore's sunset. The Rising Sun rose — Syonan-to's sunrise.

The dreaded announcement of Singapore's fall came from a loudspeaker truck moving slowly up and down Seremban's Birch Road with the news being relayed in English, Chinese, Malay and Tamil. The announcement began and ended with a song called '*Ichi-ban*' written specially for the occasion. (The only words I recall describe the Japanese flag floating proudly for the first time in the dawn breeze of Singapore.)

The news was then repeated and confirmed by a Japanese official who produced a pamphlet depicting General Yamashita taking the surrender from General Percival. The Lion City was henceforth to be called Syonan-to ('Light of the South'), and Malaya, Sumatra and Borneo and all British and Dutch territories in the region would become part of the South East Asia Co-Prosperity Sphere.

In this 'brave new world', all contact with the outside world was prohibited. That meant no letters, broadcasts or phone calls were supposed to penetrate the bamboo curtain. Any acts of defiance, any criticism of the Japanese authorities brought immediate retribution. Unquestioning obedience was the only way to ensure survival. Furthermore, no unauthorised movement away from home base was allowed.

Word of a punishment centre located down a side street of Seremban filtered in and the name 'Kempeitai' was mentioned with fear and trembling. The Kempeitai were the 'thought' police or secret police, the Japanese equivalent of the Gestapo. At their headquarters, acts of unbelievable cruelty were carried out against their victims. People going through the town avoided the Kempeitai building if they possibly could, because they didn't want to hear the hair-raising screams that emanated from it.

The boarders were warned to watch their words carefully. 'Speak freely to God, but mind what you say to anybody else,' we were told, 'walls have ears.' Terms like 'informer', 'betrayal', 'torture' became part of our vocabulary.

In this atmosphere of anxiety and suspicion the nuns designated as Enemy Aliens received their marching orders. Off they went with their packed ports, inwardly uneasy, outwardly calm and untroubled. No doubt the most anxious member of the Order was Mother St Pauline, who was French, even though she herself did not have to join the group heading for the police station. The French, Italian and Spanish nuns could stay put (France had surrendered to Nazi Germany in 1940).

Eire was neutral, but that still put the Irish nuns offside, though of course to be English or American was far worse. The Irish sisters made up the largest component of the religious community and the convent would have been in dire straits without them.

Towards evening the Enemy Aliens returned, very happy to be released from captivity. Apparently they'd spent the day sitting around at the police station doing nothing in particular. Nobody could tell them how long they were likely to stay there and whether they were destined for the POW camp in Singapore. Then before dark, a staff car pulled up, an officer got out and told them they could go back to the convent. No explanations, no apologies. Needless to say, the detainees didn't wait around and completed the journey back in record time, hardly stopping in their rush through the gates till they reached the chapel where they could be heard joyously chanting the *Magnificat*, the song of celebration:

My soul doth magnify the Lord,
and my spirit hath rejoiced in
God my Saviour,...
For He that is mighty hath magnified me,
and holy is His Name ...

That mood of exultation quickly turned to one of shock and grief when a few days later, we got our first detailed news from Singapore.

The convent had scored two direct hits in a bombing raid during the final stages of the siege. The presence of stationary military trucks right round the convent site was no doubt a contributing factor. One dormitory and several classrooms had been reduced to a heap of rubble, but worse still, two refugee women had been killed and a number of them wounded. That was not all. St Pauline resumed the recitation of bad tidings.

'We have also lost one of our nuns. It was not a bomb that killed her, she died a week after the surrender.' She paused. 'God does not always take the old and feeble, sometimes He takes the young.'

My heart started racing. Surely not ...

'St Raphael is now with God,' St Pauline continued.

A great gasp went up from all who were present. Through tears, I vaguely remember seeing St Vincent some distance off, her shoulders shaking with sobs, while I continued my monologue with the Lord: 'Why did You have to take my gentle guardian angel? You took Mum not so long ago … So why, why, did you have to take HER?'

Several girls went up to St Vincent to press her hand and offer a message of sympathy. I believe she saw and heard nothing beyond a blur of faces and a patter of incoherent sounds. The blow had come too suddenly. St Raphael had appeared to be in good health and spirits at the time of her departure from Seremban. However, soon after her return to Singapore, she entered the quarantine block of the Middleton hospital as a suspected carrier of diphtheria. On her return to the convent, she was suffering from acute malnutrition, a speedy recovery was unlikely on a besieged island on the eve of surrender. Two days after the Fall, a very frail St Raphael was sitting beside St Madeleine in the chapel, waiting for Bishop Devals to begin early Mass. Suddenly two Japanese soldiers rushed into the chapel, yelling '*Kunci! Kunci!*' ('Keys!'). They had climbed over the main gate and were demanding the convent car. When the keys were handed to them, they jumped into the car and drove off. The bishop and his flock, including St Rapael, had run down the chapel steps to see what was happening. In her weakened state, St Raphael was unable to cope with the sudden exertion and the shock — she collapsed, was taken to hospital and died there a week later.

No formal funeral service was possible at the time, and only three people were present at her burial: St James, St Anselme and the officiating priest. St Vincent herself had not had the chance for a proper farewell.

As one, nuns and boarders headed for the chapel where the prayer of lamentation, the *De Profundis*, was slowly and solemnly recited:

Out of the depths have I cried unto Thee, O Lord,
Lord, hear my voice …

'St Raphael spoke of you often, Maisie. She was very fond of her Little Boarders.' These precious words from St Vincent validated my grief for St Raphael and deepened my growing bond with the speaker.

In their time of sorrow, both St Vincent and Nellie were able to draw on a fund of affection and sympathy from nuns and boarders alike, and those of us who had already suffered bereavement had something extra to offer the newly desolate.

Now that the war was over, refugees of the whirlwind Japanese campaign began to make their way back to reclaim abandoned homes and properties in an attempt to re-establish their lives and businesses in whatever way possible. High on the list of priorities was the need to acquire a ration card from the authorities; without one, buying basic food items would have been beyond the reach of most families. Some of the refugees had amazing tales to tell of the last days of the fighting. There were incidents of shining courage and despicable treachery, of sudden death and miraculous escapes.

Perhaps the most memorable of the survival stories we heard concerned a band of Eurasian families who had fled south to stay with relatives on an isolated rubber estate in Johore. During the time they were there, friendly links had been established with the local Allied forces. Many of their young men were members of the Eurasian Volunteer Reserve, so when the Allies withdrew across the causeway, mainly women, children and older men were left behind on the estate.

The few young men who had stayed behind to be with their families after the British withdrawal decided to contact the Japanese authorities in order to obtain ration cards for all the people on the estate. Alas, their good intentions invited disaster both for themselves and the other members of their party. They themselves were never seen again; presumably they were executed. And now the Japanese were aware of the existence of several Eurasian families on that secluded Ulu Tiram estate, families that had supported the British cause, whose sons had fought alongside the Allied troops.

A Japanese killing squad descended on Ulu Tiram and a number of group executions were organised and carried out. The last batch of victims had already dug their shallow graves and were kneeling beside them, hands tied behind their backs, awaiting the word that would blast them into eternity. The soldiers stood in line, quiet and alert, rifles loaded and poised, eyes focused on the commander, ears straining for that word which would end the ominous silence, the simple deadly word '*Ute!*' ('Fire!')

A sound broke the silence, a different sound, not the one the soldiers had been expecting. It came from the prisoners' side, the plaintive cry of a young child, growing louder as they listened, begging, pleading — 'Don't kill my Mummy and Daddy!'

The officer-in-charge froze. His eyes sought out the source of the commotion. He spied a child of about six. Her large brown eyes returned his stare with such eloquent entreaty that the inexplicable happened. Facing his men again, he barked out '*Yame!*' ('Cease-fire!') and the bemused shooting party dropped their rifles while the overjoyed prisoners laughed and cried for joy and embraced their young saviour. What was it about Florrie George that had touched the heart of their executioner?

The officer attempted a brief explanation. 'This child, same my child,' he said, pointing to Florrie before scooping her up in his arms, whisking her off in his car and disappearing down the gravelled track of the estate, heading for the town.

Several hours later, the distraught parents observed car headlights through the straight rows of rubber trees. Rushing to the front of the bungalow, they were just in time to see Florrie alighting, cherubic face beaming, arms crammed with toys from her benefactor. A brief wave and he was gone, away from the estate and out of their lives.

Standing amongst the excited group welcoming Florrie back was nineteen-year-old Fanny Browne, to whom this unexpected gift of life was a poisoned chalice. Her fiancé, Basil, was one of those intrepid young men who had gone down that estate road never to return.

Some time after this incident, both Florrie and Fanny returned to Seremban, their home town, and joined us in the boarding department. Little Florrie did not have much to say about their terrible ordeal, but Fanny was more forthcoming; it was from her that we learned the details of what had happened that day.

9

RETURN TO SYONAN-TO

Towards the end of March 1942, the Singapore girls received the long awaited summons to pack up and go home. In Japan, the school year begins in April and there was a serious attempt to bring the newly conquered territories into line with the Japanese model. In every school Japanese was to be a compulsory subject, as the Governor at Seremban had promised.

We were excited about going back and also apprehensive about what we might discover. For three months we'd had no news of family or friends. Very soon we'd know whether our loved ones were alive or dead, imprisoned or free, or perhaps 'missing'. We were also anxious to see how much remained of our battered and blitzed city and our bomb-damaged convent.

There was some regret at parting with friends we'd made during a short but very tumultuous period in our young lives. I had regarded all the nuns except one with affection and was sorry to have to say goodbye to special friends among the boarders. Nellie Plachel and Olga had hit it off from their first meeting and this bond had grown stronger after Pauline's death. As we packed our few possessions to leave, Nellie presented Olga with a stylish off-the-shoulder evening gown in burgundy silk velvet. The opportunities for displaying such a garment in a convent environment were not promising; it was not a practical gift. But what young woman could have refused such a lovely creation at a time when new clothing was scarce and likely to become scarcer? Olga was delighted with her present and packed it away carefully in her suitcase, but not before I'd run my hands up and down the smooth, caressing fabric several times and indulged in a fantasy or two in which I featured as a famous film star parading before an admiring crowd.

Before departing from Seremban we obtained a document from the relevant Japanese authority stating that our group of nuns and boarders was permitted to leave Negri Sembilan, our host state, for Singapore — or Syonan-to, as we were now supposed to call it.

Highly excited, we retraced our steps to the railway station after the evening meal. Our departure was to be far more humble and less comfortable than our arrival. Instead of a proper railway-carriage to ourselves we were assigned a cattle-wagon, a large metal container with small slats near the roof instead of windows and a sliding metal door for access or exit. The normal carriages on the train were reserved for Japanese troops.

The wagon contained no seats of any kind. In the light of a single torch, we glimpsed some lumpy hessian bags in one corner, which the luckier ones managed to sit on or lean against while the rest of us sat on our suitcases. During the day the heat would have been unbearable; even at night, our dark, metal box bore many resemblances to the infamous Black Hole of Calcutta.

While the train was in motion, the wide sliding door was left slightly ajar, but whenever the train stopped, it was opened to its full width and we filled our lungs with fresh air and descended in groups to use the station lavatories. In between the frequent stops along the route we managed to snatch a little sleep.

Towards morning, we arrived at Johor Bahru station in Southern Johor, not far from the causeway, and our spirits rose as we knew that our destination was close at hand.

The door slid back to reveal a score or more Japanese soldiers standing just a few feet away on the platform. They were idling away the time, smoking, talking, looking around. They saw us immediately and came forward as one so that we were virtually face-to-face. On our part there was fear and disquiet. The soldiers, on the other hand, thrust forward eagerly, with expressions of anticipation.

We didn't understand their rapid-fire chatter or the catcalls, but their body-language told us loud and clear that they were delighted to see us and wondered if we were available. They grinned, laughed and waved their arms forwards and backwards towards themselves several times in a series of come hither gestures, while a few of them started to whirl and gyrate around clumsily, calling out what sounded like 'Jiggy jiggy, uman, dansu, singu.'

At this point, St Ignatius, our trusty watchdog, pushed herself forward to the edge of the van and thrust the permission-to-leave document in the face of the most senior-looking soldier, who read it aloud and then called off his young hopefuls. They backed away casting a few doleful glances in our direction and muttering curses at spoilsport St Ignatius.

Just before the train moved off again, two Indians jumped aboard and pushed through our ranks to the far side of the van. They weren't looking for young women. Their quarry was far more mundane. They seized on the lumpy hessian sacks located in one corner, heaved them up across their shoulders and jumped off as swiftly and nimbly as they'd come, leaving a trail of salted fish behind them. We looked at one another grinning widely. So that's where the funny smell had come from! During the wakeful and uncomfortable night we'd falsely accused one another of being the source of the odour.

There were no further incidents along the way and soon we were moving slowly across the patched-up causeway and were at last on home territory again. At the Singapore station, we boarded a bus for the convent with eyes searching the road on either side. We witnessed something of the legacy of the recent conflict. We cried out in dismay at the horrendous battle scars.

Several buildings had been reduced to rubble. In some places the road was barely passable. The bus driver had to pick his way around and between large craters, shattered bridges and wastelands which were once parks and level roads.

Our eager chatter ceased. We had no words to describe the devastation we saw and the human misery it represented. Only the corpses were missing; mercifully the dead had been buried. Several thousands had lost their lives in this short, brutal conflict. How could I ever have imagined that war was exciting, even glamorous?

As we pulled up at the large, wrought-iron main gate of the convent we wondered nervously what further unpleasant shocks might be in store for us. The Victoria Street façade appeared to be intact. As we alighted, a joyful cry went up from the whole congregation waiting in the driveway, 'They're here!' We were enveloped in a forest of arms that reached out to hug us, while a chorus of voices repeated over and over again, 'Welcome back, welcome home, dear girls.'

The usual emotional restraints were absent as our nuns openly celebrated our return to their fold. Three figures stood a little apart from the rest: St James, tiny, intense; St Gerard at her side, plump, homely; and St Anselme behind the pair, towering over them. *Kachang panjang* (long beans) was her apt nickname. All three came forward to kiss and hug us with a spontaneity and warmth previously lacking.

St James took Olga and myself aside. 'I saw your father a couple of times during the siege,' she told us. 'He left Kuala Lumpur on the last train out of the town. It did not stop at Seremban. In any case, he assumed you would already have returned south to wait for him in Singapore — he had hoped to evacuate you to Australia.' She paused then. 'He questioned my decision to send you upcountry and couldn't comprehend how I could leave you and the other boarders in Seremban to the mercy of the Japanese.' She shook her head. 'I did not abandon you, *mes enfants*, I thought you would be worse off here if the island was heavily bombed.'

This frank disclosure of a difference of opinion between Dad and St James was a novel experience for us. We were usually given the decisions but seldom the reasons for them. St James had taken a huge gamble with the lives of her charges and now that we had survived the ordeal, she appeared to be presenting both sides of the argument as honestly as she could.

'I last saw your father two or three days before the surrender,' she went on. 'He'd been digging a trench outside the convent and came in to say goodbye. He was caked in mud and dust and looked extremely tired. I sat him down to some tea and biscuits — he was very grateful because he couldn't remember when he'd last eaten. We both knew then that Singapore was doomed and he said he'd make his way to the beach and escape if he got the chance. He was still very upset at your absence, and I made him a promise. He told me that his wife, your Aunt Bobs and her three children had managed to escape on one of the last ships to sail out of Singapore, bound for Perth, Australia. He hoped to join them.'

At this point, two thin, bony arms encircled us and a slight tremor came into St James' firm, clear voice as she said, 'I promised your father that I would take care of you both until the war was over. And so I shall, my dear Olga and Maisie.'

Our hearts were heavy and tears came to our eyes at the realisation that it would be a long time before we saw Dad again, if ever. We had lost a father, either temporarily or permanently, but our august and formerly aloof Mother Superior was offering herself as our guardian and protector. We raised our heads to look directly at this amazing woman and saw that she was dabbing at her eyes with a handkerchief. We knew she shared our sorrow. She was human too! For me, that moment marked the end of my fear of her and the beginning of a deep, abiding affection and respect.

St James ended on a note of optimism. 'Your father is a fine seaman; he knows the waters around Singapore as well as other people know its streets. It is quite likely he has made a successful escape — so, my dear children, continue to hope and pray!'

A few moments later, we walked to the chapel to offer our thanks for a safe return to Singapore and as we took our seats in the front pews we observed two long dark shadows on the altar, from the pair of boarded-up stained-glass windows in the sacristy. One of the eight bombs to fall within the convent compound had created a huge crater in a playing-field barely four yards from the chapel and the windows on that side had been blown out by the blast. In other parts of the convent there was more serious damage. Whole buildings had been razed and planks and loose bricks blocked the gaps in the perimeter wall until such time as workmen could be found to repair it and restore a semblance of protection and security.

10

NIPPON-GO

School re-opened in Syonan-to in April, as planned by the authorities, but most of the girls who'd been my classmates from Primary One up to Standard III were missing. The only familiar faces belonged to the other boarders who had weathered the recent upheaval with me. The convent clientele as a whole had undergone a dramatic change. Many of the students now attending our school were previously enrolled at government English schools or other missionary schools.

The biggest change to the curriculum was the deletion of all English language classes and their substitution with Japanese language classes. The Japanese envisioned replacing English and Dutch as the official languages of this region with Nippon-go. To this end, all Singapore teachers had to attend crash-courses in the new tongue. As there was no pool of native Japanese language teachers on hand, the first classes were taught by Army officers who had a smattering of English. Later, qualified civilian teachers were sent from Japan to continue our introduction to the Japanese educational system.

Singapore's Holy Infant Jesus Convent, so centrally located, was one of the major teaching centres for compulsory staff courses held by the Japanese. The instructor would stride into the room in full military uniform, mount the teacher's dais, unbuckle his sword, drop it on the desk, then scoop up a fistful of chalk and cover the blackboard with an assortment of characters. Pointing to his handiwork, he'd command, 'You learn today!' For those who had grown up with a 26-letter alphabet and basically a single script, allowing for cursive and printed forms, the task ahead was formidable. It was a case of 'look, listen and imitate'.

Japanese bears no resemblance whatsoever to English in its spoken or written forms and the acquisition of two new scripts was mandatory. It was permissible for pupils to use *Romaji* (Japanese words spelt phonetically in English letters (DOG = INU), but teaching staff were obliged to know and use both the printed and cursive forms of the language, as well as a few hundred *Kanji* (Chinese ideograms).

For instance, for the word 'dog' there are the four following forms:

inu = Romaji (Roman)
イヌ = Katakana (printed form)
いぬ = Hiragana (cursive form)
犬 = Kanji

The military instructors' English seldom allowed for detailed explanations. There were no grammar books available and the material had to be ingested very rapidly by the teachers before passing it on to their pupils at a more leisurely pace.

Surprisingly or not (given the 'No Nippon-go, no jobs' policy of the new masters) most teachers acquired the basics of the language within a few weeks. Some struggled, a few seemed to take it all in their stride as an intellectual challenge.

St Madeleine belonged to the second category and I found her enthusiasm for this exotic language infectious. Initially, I held back a bit, regarding any serious attempt to learn the enemy's tongue as a betrayal of my British heritage. Then I got the crazy notion that fluency in Japanese could make me a valuable asset in the Allied cause, as a spy.

For whatever reasons, I applied myself earnestly to my Nippon-go studies and soon advanced beyond the basic stage of memorising and writing the fifty or so sounds or syllables which are its building blocks.

Writing short compositions or essays in Japanese scripts became an enjoyable exercise; the pictorial quality of the characters appealed to me and before long, I was covering pages and pages of my exercise books with my writings. St Madeleine praised my efforts highly and invited me to her classroom during their language period in order to write up my little essays on her blackboard for the edification (entertainment, more like!) of her older students. I was received with great warmth and friendliness by the 'big girls' who seemed hugely amused, in a nice way, by this precocious little eleven-year-old. Naturally, I lapped up the attention. I was surely on my way to becoming a credible spy — step aside, Mata Hari!

Ministry of Education officials made regular inspections. An ingenious survival routine was worked out for those teachers who had problems acquiring basic language competency, and this was used successfully for the duration of the Occupation.

The top drawer of the teacher's desk was furnished with one large sheet of foolscap paper on which were written classroom drills and essential phrases in Romaji with their English equivalents. As soon as the word 'visitors' was flashed around the school corridors, the teacher would pull open her drawer and glance at her survival kit. No sooner did a Japanese face hover into view than the command '*Tachi nasai*' (stand up) would ring out and forty children would spring to their feet, bow deeply, then resume their seats at the second command, '*Suwari nasai*'.

From a repertoire of well-prepared lessons, the teacher would call out one topic, such as *Teisha-ba-de* (At the Railway Station) or *Yaoya-de* (At the Greengrocer). The pre-selected actors would come forward furnished with diagrams, pictures or stage props and enthusiastically play out the charade for the benefit of the visitors, who never failed to be impressed and go away murmuring '*Joozu desu ne*' — 'Aren't they clever!'

Lionel de Souza, the Eurasian Inspector of Schools, whose task it was to accompany each group of observers/intruders, must have heard the same material over and over again, but he feigned great interest every time and never let on that he'd heard it all before and guessed at our cunning strategy.

There were a couple of teachers who were beyond the help even of the survival kit. These included Mabel Wickwar, my former Primary teacher. Mabel would have wholeheartedly endorsed the words of one of the first Jesuit missionaries to visit Japan. He claimed that Japanese was a language invented by the devil in order to make it virtually impossible for Christian missionaries to convert the native population. There was no question that Mabel found Nippon-go fiendishly difficult, but she was forced to learn it in order to keep her job. So St Madeleine arranged for me to give her some lessons. The poor lady must have been desperate to accept me as a tutor. She would have found it less galling to accept the help of one of her 'good' ex-students instead of dreamy, inattentive Maisie Prout of all people!

Mabel Wickwar now lived in the convent annexe, a two-storey wooden building on the perimeter fence of Stamford Road. Her former abode, the Oranje Hotel, across the street from the annexe, had been taken over by Japanese officers. Many of the annexe residents, such as Kitty Fogh, were teachers. Others, like Mrs Freeman, who had two daughters in the boarding department, did secretarial work.

I cannot recall our opening remarks when I first presented myself to chez Mabel, but she received me cordially enough and explained that she was unable to remember the Hiragana and Katakana characters that went with the syllabary. Actually it wasn't just the script, she wasn't even making the sounds correctly. Like a few of the other teachers, she tended to anglicise the vowel sounds, making dipthongs where pure vowels were required. On the whole, the pupils had better accents than their teachers because young people are not self-conscious about attempting different sounds and speech patterns and are happy to experiment.

Laboriously, I'd call through the *Go-juu-on* (fifty sounds). Mabel would repeat these after me and write down the characters one by one until she had a nodding acquaintance with them. Any problem characters would be singled out and written up large on pieces of cardboard which we attached to the edge of Mabel's dressing-table mirror so that she'd see them daily. The impossible-to-learn characters scored pride-of-place, smack in the middle of the mirror: every time she went to peer at her face, these 'monsters' had to be pushed aside deliberately. This meant she was obliged to handle them a few times a day — and hopefully remember them.

In time, Mabel's mirror became character-free, but I don't think she ever advanced beyond the most basic stage of Nippon-go proficiency. Her heart just wasn't in it. Dear Mabel, I hadn't liked her at all when I was her pupil, but as her tutor, I became very fond of her. Perhaps I understood her better. For my pains, I received small packets of biscuits or cakes and occasionally syrupy desserts that I had to eat on the spot. No money ever changed hands. I was perfectly satisfied with the little gifts of food because by then, hunger had become a daily irritant in the pattern of life during the Occupation.

11

KIMURA-SAN

The scarcity of food must have been a twenty-four-hour nightmare for St James, the person responsible for feeding the entire convent population.

She broached the problem of dwindling food supplies to the first official Japanese visitors to the convent, singling out the babies in the orphanage for special consideration. The senior officer dismissed her concern with the confident claim that in a month or two, Japanese forces would have added Australia to their new empire and then there would be food a-plenty for everybody and gallons of milk for the babies!

In the light of what had just happened to the former British and Dutch colonies, the officer's words were no idle boast. On the grapevine, we heard that the Japanese Navy was assembling its fleet for a big push 'Down Under'; ships and naval personnel formerly stationed off Penang now took up their positions in Singapore.

So it came about that a young Japanese naval officer presented himself at the visitors' gate of the convent, enquiring for the Prout sisters. He explained that he had a message from their brother in Penang. It transpired that sixteen-year-old John and our cousin Albert, the eldest son of Aunty Frances, had managed to get some casual work on the wharves. With her husband Uncle Bertie in a POW camp, they were now the breadwinners. In the course of their work, they had met several Japanese seamen, some of whom had a smattering of English. The boys picked up many Japanese expressions and soon they were able to communicate in a mixture of both languages. One young Japanese officer became a special friend and was invited to the house to meet the family and sample a Malayan curry, one of Aunty Frances' specials. He enjoyed himself immensely and became a regular visitor, always bringing greatly appreciated food parcels. It was evident that he missed his own family and was happy to attach himself to the Coules family in their place.

When the order came to transfer to Singapore, he was sad to have to leave Penang and the Couleses were sorry to see him go. They asked him to take a letter to us at the Victoria Street convent and he readily agreed.

When he turned up as promised, the gate-duty sister despatched a young orphan to summon the Prout sisters to the parlour. 'A Japanese man wants to see you!' our fleet-footed messenger could barely contain her curiosity, and Olga and I were just as anxious to know the reason for this surprise visit. Was it good news, bad news? We ran across the playing-fields and down corridors towards the parlour just inside the visitors' gate. Pausing for breath, we pushed open the swing doors and came face-to-face with a slim young man in naval uniform who rose to his feet on our arrival, bowed slightly, and said, 'Your brother John, he ask me — visit you. Here is letter.' And he handed Olga a sheet of paper torn from an exercise book, covered in John's neat and distinctive handwriting.

Looking over Olga's shoulder I read: *We are all well. Aunty Frances sends her love. Kimura-san has been a good friend to us and when we heard he was leaving for Singapore we asked him to visit you to give you our news …*

St Madeleine sat in on our meeting in her capacity as interpreter and chaperone. We were happy she was there; at that time, my Japanese was very limited, while Olga had no Nippon-go at all. She had elected not to learn the language of the enemy.

Kimura-san produced a small black-and-white photograph of his 'adopted' family. With the long pointed nail of the little finger of his left hand, he indicated John and Albert, Aunty Frances, Lizzie and Thomas.

'All have good health, all *genki!*' He smiled as he offered the photo to us. Then he explained how he had met John and how much he had enjoyed spending time with the Coules family. Did we have a letter for them? He offered to post a letter for us if we had it ready when he called again a week later.

At this point, St Madeleine said we had a big favour to ask. She wondered if Kimura-san could possibly enquire at all the POW camps in Singapore for Mr Prout. He had been on the island until the surrender but since then we'd had no news of him. Kimura-san said he'd be happy to help. He wrote down Dad's name and details in his pocket-book, gave a smart salute and strode off through the gate. Watching him go, I thought, 'I don't hate him, even though he's supposed to be my enemy.'

I had learnt much earlier that there were nuns *and* nuns — now I was learning that there were Japanese *and* Japanese. Obviously, the enemy came in different shapes and sizes and some behaved more like friend than foe.

Our obliging young man was back a week later as promised, and we had a letter for him to post to Penang, as well as a small gift to thank him for his trouble. This was St Madeleine's idea — 'Perhaps one of your watercolours,' she suggested to me. She looked through my painting-book. An arrangement of bright floral shapes against a dark background caught her eye. 'That one, quite striking, I'm sure he'll like it,' she said — and he did. He said he'd hang it up on his cabin wall alongside his family photos.

His search for Dad had proved fruitless but we'd half-expected that: Olga and I felt sure that if he'd been in Singapore, he would have contacted us somehow. But it had been worth a try.

There was no third visit. Maybe this Good Samaritan went to the bottom of the Coral Sea or perished in the Battle of Midway, when the hitherto invincible Japanese military machine suffered two crushing naval defeats that turned the tide for the Allies in the Southeast Asia war zone and staved off the invasion of Australia.

St Madeleine's linguistic skills were soon in demand once again. The Changi internees had obtained permission from the Japanese authorities to run a school in the prison camp. Teachers were not lacking. Highly qualified instructors in almost any discipline were held captive there, willing to share their expertise with any prisoner prepared to listen and learn during what promised to be a long period of enforced inactivity.

It is likely the Japanese approved of the scheme because they believed that schoolroom work would render their prisoners quiet, orderly and less rebellious. For whatever reason, a number of educational institutions were contacted and the convent agreed to donate some desks and chairs towards the project.

When a group of Australian POWs came to collect the furniture, our nuns made them very welcome — not openly, of course! That's where St Madeleine had to play her part. She was delegated to give the two Japanese guards a guided tour of the school while the Australians were working, thus enabling nuns and boarders to approach the prisoners, exchange a few words and even offer them some food.

It was only a year since we boarders had covertly watched the 'wild colonial boys' from an upstairs window at Katong, while the nuns kept watch below, effectively blocking any conversation. Amazingly, instead of keeping us apart, those same nuns were throwing us together, albeit very briefly.

The convent kitchens had little food to spare, but some biscuits and bananas were passed on to the grateful men, who were very hungry — but still cheerful, cheeky and boisterous.

It seemed no time at all when the guards' voices were heard outside the classrooms. In one fluid movement, the Australians, acting in unison, transferred all food remnants into their upturned hats, which were then crammed onto sweaty heads while they saluted their returning gaolers. The latter appeared not to notice how high those slouch hats sat on the heads of their grinning captives.

As the lorry pulled out of the grounds, heading for Changi, strains of a merry song could be heard, something about a track winding back on 'the road to Gundagai'.

12

FOOD AND PROPAGANDA

Olga and I were to receive a number of visitors that year but no more young men came calling.

Dad, of course, wasn't around, nor was Aunty May. The Pijpe family had sailed to Batavia (Jakarta) not long after our departure to Seremban. After the Dutch colony of Batavia was occupied by the Japanese, the family lived under a system of house-arrest for the duration of the war.

Our mother's sister, Aunty Joan Bruce, was still in Singapore with her family and she took to visiting us fairly regularly at weekends, often bringing a large homemade cake for her nieces. Nobody made a better sujee (Semolina), chocolate or fruit cake than Aunty Joan. We sometimes indulged in a 'pre-taste' before handing over the spoils to be carved into wafer-thin slices for everyone. But there were occasions when hunger or greed dictated a different course: we would hide our treasure in a desk or wardrobe to enjoy a furtive feast with a few select friends like Mary and Annie Dragon or Mary and Doris Liew.

The Liews were great treat-providers, frequently including the whole boarding department in their generosity. They carried on the tradition established by wealthy Chinese boarders in pre-war years of sharing their abundance with everyone when they celebrated their birthdays and special festivals. Convent rules prevented them from going to a grand restaurant to mark the occasion; instead, the chosen restaurant brought the meals to the school and a good time was had by all. Chinese New Year, which occurred not long after the start of the school year, always got us off to a flying start in the feasting stakes — we could count on several days of mouth-watering food.

Our main benefactors were two multi-millionaires, Mr Pun and Mr Eu. Pun Koon San was a mining magnate from Kuala Lumpur, Eu Tong Sen, a Hong Kong business tycoon whose true or fictitious rags-to-riches story was the stuff of convent legend. There were four Pun girls and at least five Eu daughters; together they made up about a third of the First Boarders. Surprisingly, this millionaire class displayed no airs and graces and neither dressed nor behaved differently from their less affluent schoolmates. No wonder they rated so highly in the popularity stakes and enjoyed enduring friendships.

Another Chinese connection that stood the test of time was the link with our old Chinese amah. She had made a point of dropping in every two or three months, just staying long enough to observe with her own eyes that we looked fairly well and seemed reasonably happy. She would say things like, '*Maisie banyak kurus! Olga, jaga Maisie baik, lah!*' (Maisie is very thin, take good care of her, Olga!) From a carefully knotted handkerchief she would produce two mandarins and two small slabs of Nestlé chocolate for 'her children'. The gift offering never varied and although we accepted all contributions to our diet gratefully, we always felt uncomfortable in accepting hers because we suspected she had given far more than she could afford. Her visits ceased after the bombing raids on Chinatown. Very likely she was an anonymous casualty of the war.

Contrary to what one would have expected, we got out and about a great deal more during the Occupation than we did in peacetime. Previously, sporting events and concerts were intra-school affairs held within the confines of the convent compound, but the Japanese changed all that by ordering us to participate in massive sporting carnivals at venues such as the Jalan Besar Stadium. These events lasted all day and involved thousands of children. Under a green banner, Victoria Street School (as we were now known) and other former English schools had to compete against Chinese, Indian and Malay schools, which carried yellow, blue and red banners respectively. In the sporting sky, the green banner frequently flew high.

Large-scale musical events were held at the Town Hall and all the major schools were told to prepare a few items for the occasion. The Ministry of Education supplied every school with a list of Japanese folk-songs and our choir mistress, Miss Isobel McIntyre, taught them to us in preparation for the concert. St Madeleine had overall control of the convent programme, a task she had carried out very successfully for years. Previously, she had produced Shakespearean plays; now she presented a number of short plays in Japanese based on popular folktales, as well as graceful Eastern dances choreographed by a very talented Filipino student, Rosie Domingo.

These concerts were usually held at night, so it was a special treat for the boarders involved in the event to be allowed out for the occasion.

As the youngest member of the concert-party, it was considered advisable for me to have a minder, a certain Yvette Da Silva, who was an older member of the choir and a day girl. She turned out to be a very kind and generous sister-substitute who always provided a tasty snack for me at interval. Her family must have stocked up on cream crackers and tinned cheese before the surrender — she appeared to have an endless supply of these items.

The musical fare was not exclusively Japanese in origin. European music was acceptable provided it was not from English or American sources. So we heard the work of German, Russian, Italian or Czech composers and works from other Axis-occupied countries. Hungarian music featured quite largely because the classical music section was coordinated by a Hungarian couple, the Karenzas.

The finale was always provided by a Japanese military band playing martial numbers. One in particular, "*Teki Bei Ei Gekimetsu*" ("Annihilate the American and British Enemies") sticks in my mind. These young soldiers who had sat quietly, impassively even, at the back of the hall listening to children's songs and lilting Viennese waltzes underwent a total transformation on-stage. In their performance, they acted out the belligerent sentiments of the title. Never before or since have I witnessed drums being pounded with such ferocity and abandon. The display was both electrifying and terrifying. I think everybody secretly sighed with relief when the pounding stopped and the frenzied tempo gave way to the slow, sedate measures of their national anthem, the *Kimi gayo*.

Smaller events, such as mini-concerts, took the school choir to factories and hospitals, and on one occasion to the radio station set up in the Cathay building where we broadcast our repertoire to Tokyo.

The Cathay cinema screened free films for the benefit of schoolchildren. Some depicted city or rural life in Japan while others showed scenes and events in the newly acquired territories of Southeast

Asia. I recall watching an amusing short item about the celebration of a local festival in the former Dutch colony of Java (Indonesia). Young Indonesian boys were gleefully wielding water-hoses and spraying everybody within reach, including truckloads of khaki-clad Japanese troops who appeared not to mind at all when they got a drenching at the hands of the water-sprites. I remember thinking at the time, 'Were the soldiers only laughing for the benefit of the camera? Did they seek out and punish the hose-culprits afterwards?'

The loosening up of school routine was accompanied by some relaxation of boarding-school rules, even taking the sting out of Sunday 'Notes' or 'Judgement Hour', which had always been the most dreaded event on the weekly timetable presided over by Reverend Mother. During the 'Notes' ritual, every boarder's behaviour for the past week was judged and either praised or condemned. Marks were awarded for punctuality, orderliness and conduct. The first two categories usually found me wanting but normally I scored well in the last and most important one. However, there was the day when I obtained '0' for conduct. I'd been overheard criticising one of the nuns for being too hard on us girls. This was a major crime and I had to forfeit dessert for a week.

Either deliberately or otherwise, St James now softened the hitherto stern approach to the supervision of her flock. The 'Notes' session turned into a fairly relaxed discussion period, when important current issues were aired and spiritual values uncovered in a topsy-turvy world.

One Sunday she arrived very late for our session. This was a highly unusual occurrence: 'Punctuality is the politeness of Kings,' she used to say, and we had to repeat it in French. She proceeded to tell us the reason for her tardy appearance. 'A very distressed woman came to seek my advice about ration cards. The authorities had refused to provide cards for her two sons.

'"Why?" I asked.

'"How about your daughters?"

'"Oh, Lily and Mary have received theirs," she told me, "but they refused ration cards for Roosevelt and Churchill!"'

With a twinkle in her eye St James continued, 'Can you imagine the Japanese feeding Roosevelt and Churchill? I advised the woman to change her sons' names and the sooner the better — so, there's a moral in this tale for you, *mes enfants*. When you marry and have children, make sure you give your offspring suitable, *sensible* names!'

Further changes were afoot in 1943, changes that were to alter radically the direction of several lives in the institution. St James was transferred to a smaller, less demanding post upcountry, none other than our erstwhile rural retreat, the convent at Seremban.

For two decades she had been at the helm of a sprawling, challenging, multi-faceted community which had weathered many storms. No period of her long reign could have been as gruelling as her final year in Singapore that took in the three months of brutal fighting which ended in the surrender of the island. The ordeal had taken its toll on her health and so the next big trial facing the convent was to be undertaken by her younger, more robust successor, Reverend Mother St Charles, whose task was to relocate virtually all the nuns, orphans and boarders to a remote jungle village called Bahau, some distance from Seremban. Only a few nuns would remain in Singapore and they would keep the school open with the help of the lay teachers.

The escalating food shortages and the perception that their boarders and orphans might be at risk from predatory Japanese soldiers were major factors in what must have been an agonising decision for Bishop Devals and the Reverend Mother. In August 1943, many of the Bishop's Eurasian and Chinese parishioners joined the convent's advance party sent to this jungle clearing of Bahau or Fuji village, in an attempt to set up a self-sufficient, food-producing community far removed from the stress and strife of the island city. No boarders were sent there till the following year.

On the whole, we who comprised the lower ranks of the convent hierarchy remained blissfully unaware that the ground was shifting under our feet. We carried on with our routines as if their current status were permanent. The school day started for everybody as usual, with *Rajio Taiso* (Radio Exercises) performed in the large playing field where the annual Sports Days was held. Then we went to our classrooms for a daily dose of Japanese and maths. Hygiene and geography were also part of the syllabus as well as sewing, drawing, cooking, singing and commercial classes. English as a subject was banned, yet most subjects were taught in English.

In the case of the commercial class, the students learnt no Japanese at all, apart from the formal greetings in case any visitors stuck their heads in the door. Shorthand, book-keeping and typing were taught in English, which suited Olga down to the ground, for she was determined to maintain her distance from Nippon-go. Monique, her former rebellious companion in the ranks, would undoubtedly have joined Olga in boycotting Japanese classes, but she was no longer around. With a group of French compatriots, she had departed the island on an epic overland journey, bound for her family in Saigon.

Olga did extremely well in her commercial studies; at the end of the year she was offered a tutoring job of a few hours a week. A Mr Erikson from the Danish Consulate was seeking shorthand lessons. He was taken aback when he learned that his prospective tutor was only fifteen.

'Can a mere child conduct a proper lesson?' he wondered.

'Try her out anyway and if you're not happy, we'll find you another teacher,' he was told.

So Olga got the opportunity to teach her first real lesson. It must have gone well because she was asked to continue. The tuition fees she earned went towards our boarding costs, with a few dollars left over to cover small essential items.

The handsome young Dane also provided something more precious even than cash — news of the progress of the war, for he was one of those intrepid souls who listened clandestinely to the BBC bulletins on his hidden radio.

On the whole, 1943 proved a good year for Olga. Besides giving shorthand classes, she was receiving free cooking lessons from Miss Khaw, an American-Chinese cooking expert who had taken up residence in the convent annexe. She had brought her tools of trade with her and was permitted to fit out an empty classroom with her modern kitchen equipment. St Coleman, our cooking teacher, could only marvel at all the new-fangled gadgets and appliances that Miss Khaw presided over, pride of place being given to the electric Mixmaster.

The new kitchen boasted more than gadgets — the shelves were stocked with provisions that had long ago disappeared from food stores and home pantries. Whenever Miss Khaw had a baking session she would invite two or three Big Boarders to help her turn out batches of cookies, breads and cakes. She shared the results of the afternoon's work with her helpers and they in turn passed on a portion of their spoils to their little sisters.

Like me, Bobby Freeman was one of those who benefited from an older sister's association with Miss Khaw. Bobby and I were possibly the only two boarders in the concert party. She was in the dance team and I was in the choir and drama group, so we saw a lot of each other. One day she asked me, 'Did you know that our fathers were great friends?' I shook my head. She went on, 'Well, on Mum's dressing-table in the annexe there's a portrait of a young man in naval uniform. When I asked Mum who he was, she said, 'That's Stan Prout, Olga and Maisie's dad. Ask them if they would like it.' And that is how that particular portrait came into our possession.

We valued the photo highly, yet feared to display it because an English father in uniform was a serious liability, one that could earn the possessor a quick entry to an internment camp. It was in fact mystifying to both the Prouts and the Freemans that we were still at large while the Bransons, fellow boarders and classmates, whose English connection was more remote, had been carted off to the POW camp. In a haphazard system, you never knew when your turn would come.

Through Bobby, I got to know Rosie Domingo, her classmate. Rosie, then in her late teens, used to complain about the shortage of clothes, particularly evening dresses, and had difficulty finding suitable outfits for her weekend performances. At the words 'evening dress', I pricked up my ears and told Olga she might have a buyer for her burgundy velvet gown. 'I'm not selling', she snapped. Then she came around. 'Well, okay, what do you think it's worth?' I plucked a figure out of the air. One hundred dollars sounded like a nice round figure. Olga agreed.

Rosie liked the dress but she offered sixty dollars only. Beggars can't be choosers. We accepted the sixty. Though less than we'd hoped for, the sum we now held in our hands was more than we'd possessed for ages.

The boarding-house mistress looked after any large amounts of cash belonging to the girls, so I took the money to St Madeleine, telling her about the sale we'd just made.

'You sold a dress to Rosie? How enterprising! But I think you'll have to inform Reverend Mother. She may not approve of buying and selling between day scholars and boarders.' That put a damper of things, just when I thought I'd been so smart!

St Charles spoke to me very sternly about my unauthorised trading, reducing me to tears. Then she said, not unkindly, 'Stop crying now,' and planted a kiss on my forehead, dismissing me with the warning not to sell any more goods to the day girls. She took the money away, saying she would look after it. Olga was very upset at the turn of events. She believed St Charles could have taken a softer approach.

It is likely that Reverend Mother was pre-occupied with the impending Bahau exodus and that was why she dealt more harshly than necessary with an entrepreneurial twelve-year-old.

Early in 1944, Olga and I were both summoned to see St Charles. This time she told us to pack our bags — we would be leaving by train for Seremban very shortly. St James had sent for us. We were to take one suitcase each; only essential items allowed. We had been given barely two days' notice, but that was in line with the convent's practice of uprooting people without much prior warning. It fitted in with the overall Christian philosophy of the need to be ready at all times to depart at a moment's notice for another earthly location — or even a heavenly one.

Our earlier sojourn in Seremban had not been especially happy, but St James was now in charge of the convent there and we looked forward to a reunion with St Vincent, St Matthew and the other nuns we knew, so we were not reluctant to go. We were fairly comfortable in Singapore, with lots of friends, outings and other diversions, but the die was cast. Our goodbyes had to be quick and smart. Unknown to us, several of those we now farewelled would be despatched not many weeks later to scratch a living out of the hard, unyielding soil at the vermin-plagued, malaria-infested jungle clearing of Bahau. While making our farewells, we called briefly at the annexe. Miss Khaw was very sorry to see us go.

For Olga she had a special gift, a navy-blue serge overcoat which she urged her to wear on the train. A highly impractical garment for Singapore, you would have thought, but it fitted Olga perfectly and she looked very grown-up in it. Mabel Wickwar was leaning against the verandah railing, puffing away at a cigarette as usual. 'I'd smoke papaya leaves, if I had to,' she told us with a smile, displaying small, even, nicotine-stained teeth.

Of Kitty Fogh there was no sign. She'd gone shopping as usual. Kitty was everybody's friend, always cheerful and ready with a joke or juicy tidbit of gossip. When she returned from the city, she'd often dawdle past the boarders' recreation hall and stop for a chat. We hoped we might see her later to say our goodbyes.

But the Kitty who came past on our last afternoon was somebody we'd never encountered before. Ashen-faced and trembling, she gasped, 'I've just seen a man's head on a pole!'

'Where?' we whispered.

'North Bridge Road,' she answered, collapsing onto a bench. 'Awful, awful — worst of all, he was grinning! There was a gold tooth shining in his black face.'

Later that evening we heard the background to the incident. Four men had been caught breaking into a rice store. They were beheaded on the spot and their severed heads were displayed on poles in four prominent parts of the city, as a grim warning — and a savage reminder of the dark side of life under the banner of the Rising Sun.

13

SAFE-HAVEN SEREMBAN

This unaccompanied journey was rather daunting because we had never before taken any trip, even a short one, without an escort. Now we were expected to travel on our own overnight, in dangerous times.

St Eugenie, our temporary minder between convent and railway station, was entrusted with our exit permits and the rail tickets and told to explain to any official querying our departure that both our parents were dead and we were going to join an aunt in Seremban.

'Let St Eugenie do all the talking,' St Charles advised us. 'You two just listen quietly and be ready to move quickly on to the train. You should be all right if you do nothing to attract attention.' From where Reverend Mother stood, it all seemed quite easy. She placed a sum of money in Olga's hand. 'That's the change from your sixty dollars after I paid for the tickets. Safe journey and God bless you.'

In the pedicab en route to the station Olga counted out the sum total of our worldly wealth. Approximately twenty dollars. 'Humph,' she snorted, 'you got roasted for selling the dress but the money certainly came in handy for buying the tickets. If there'd been no sale, what then?' It was my turn to snort 'Humph!'

The northbound train sat waiting to carry off its noisy cargo of people to various points along the peninsula. The crowd engulfed us in a solid wave stretching back yards before the arched entrance to the departure hall. Right under the arch stood a single, khaki-clad figure checking permits and directing traffic.

Our threesome, we felt, could easily disappear into this vast throng and escape notice. We shuffled our way to the top of the queue. Ahead of us, on either side, people were being waved forward after a cursory glance at the required form. But no sooner did the man in charge clap eyes on us than we sensed danger. St Eugenie held the permits out for his inspection. He thrust them aside. 'Why are you leaving Syonan-to?' he demanded. The through traffic came to a halt. We had an audience of hundreds.

St Eugenie, following instructions, responded, 'They want to attend school in Seremban.'

'I didn't ask YOU, I asked THEM!' the soldier spat out the words and the nun shrank a few paces back. Turning to Olga and myself, gimlet eyes boring into ours, he repeated, 'Why are you leaving Syonan-to? Plenty of schools here.'

Quite terrified now, we replied timidly, hesitantly, 'Because we have an aunt in Seremban — our father and mother are dead — we are going to live with our aunty.'

His thin hard mouth made an explosive sound, his eyes said, 'YOU'RE LYING!' The hate in his face was palpable. He scrutinised the permits, then barked out an order. Two burly Sikh guards appeared at his elbow. Pointing to us he shouted, 'Search their bags properly.' Why had he singled us out? Was it Olga's European overcoat? My brown hair, amidst a sea of black heads?

Our suitcases were upended onto a low table, the locks burst open, the contents spilled out on to the floor. We heard the sound of breaking glass — Dad's portrait! A sob escaped from Olga's tightly closed mouth, and I joined in. One of the guards whispered gruffly, '*Jangan nangis lah!*' ('Don't cry!'), '*Itu orang*' ('that man') — he stole a backward glance at our inquisitor — '*Kempeitai*.' He meant to reassure but the word 'Kempeitai' was enough to send a chill down anyone's spine. No wonder everybody obeyed his orders with alacrity. Hurriedly, we scooped up our clothes, shoes and other belongings, throwing them back into the cases higgledy-piggledy. St Eugenie furtively retrieved the photo, dropping it on top of one pile. It landed face-up: a white face above Royal Navy uniform, the face of a British enemy. Both guards saw it and exchanged a look — what would they do now? Show him the portrait? He looked in our direction; two turbaned heads shook from side to side and two pairs of open palms signalled 'nothing to declare'. The suitcase lids were rammed down, the whistle blew. The station clock signalled five minutes to departure time.

How would we get through the sea of bodies on to the platform? One Sikh guardian angel picked up the cases, the other forced a passage for us, urging, '*Lekas, lekas, lah!*' ('Hurry, hurry!')

'*Banyak terimah kaseh lah!*' ('Many, many thanks!') we said tearfully over and over again. We sat on our luggage in a crowded carriage, pleased beyond measure that we had succeeded in getting on the train. St Eugenie had followed hard on our heels. She'd been unable to do anything useful for us earlier on but now she walked up and down the crowded carriage seeking a single empty seat. Two magically became available side by side, and we sank onto the hard timber bench gratefully. Who knows? Perhaps there was an undercurrent of sympathy for the two young girls the Kempeitai officer had grilled. In the few minutes left, St Eugenie had persuaded an elderly Chinese lady to keep an eye on us overnight. Squeezing our hands in farewell, she said, 'God bless you, my children, say your rosaries now,' and then she was gone.

Barely two minutes remained. Was *he* around? Dared we talk, smile? 'Don't look now,' whispered Olga, 'he's just outside the window'. Would he pull us off the train? We stared straight ahead, aware of an ominous presence, aware of *him* watching us. No words, just a silent prayer — 'Oh God, *take him away*!' The whistle blew, the train lurched forward, the platform slid past. When we glanced back, he was heading for the departure hall.

Olga pressed my hand. 'Sweet Jesus, Holy Mary, have we really escaped?'

It grew very dark in the carriage. There was no electricity in third-class. Several people had come prepared with candles, a few had torches.

Our temporary guardian lent us a candle when we needed to use the toilet; a single cubicle with a hole in the floor. It was filthy and smelly, but preferable to leaving the train during one of its stops. The Chinese lady also provided us with some biscuits and mandarins. She didn't have an abundance of food herself, yet she willingly shared her meagre supplies with us. Who was it who said, 'Never underestimate the kindness of strangers'?

Olga and I sat huddled together through the night. Her overcoat made her appear a lot older than her sixteen years, while I probably looked much younger than thirteen in my plain school tunic. We spoke little though we were awake most of the night — the hard bench was not conducive to slumber, but we were better off than other passengers who had to stand up or crouch between seats.

There was nothing to see because even when the moon shone through the windows, a forest of heads blocked the light. However, on one occasion when I turned around to peer into the darkness, a stray moonbeam picked out the distinctive cloth cap of a Japanese soldier sitting behind on my left. A lone soldier amongst the local population — very unusual. He spotted me and smiled, then pointed to Olga's hunched figure. 'Papa? *Otoosan*?'

'*Iie*,' (no) I answered, '*Ane desu'* (elder sister).

'*Aa soo*.' He sounded friendly. Leaning towards me he placed a small something in a paper bag beside my knee. '*Purezento*' (present) he said and moved away. I held it where it could catch the light — a small banana, slightly squashy but still edible.

Olga had overheard the little chat and when she saw the fruit she was immediately suspicious. 'Don't eat it,' she hissed, 'it could be poisoned!'

I felt certain she was wrong, but Olga is a very forceful person, and she'd planted the seed of doubt. While I silently debated the pros and cons — to eat or not to eat, the train suddenly came to a screeching halt and a posse of Japanese troops stormed on board, working their way from one end to the other. They pushed and shoved their way through every carriage, leaping over reclining forms when necessary, bayonets at the ready. Their torches checked the face of every passenger. Had *he* sent them for us? We shivered with fear in the hot, steamy night. Passively, resignedly, we awaited the ordeal by torchlight. The fateful minute came and went without consequence. Thankfully, fortunately, they must have been chasing other prey.

The posse left. The train moved on again. I chanced a backward glance at my recent patron but his seat was empty. I looked again — no sign of him. Maybe he was the hapless prey, perhaps an army deserter! I offered the banana to a small, thin child nearby who downed it without a second's hesitation and suffered no ill effect. I glanced at Olga, 'See ...?'

Towards dawn, I urgently needed to use the toilet but the queue outside the lavatory door was never-ending. Olga advised, 'Just pee in your pants, but first pull up your dress at the back so that you won't have a wet stain when you stand up.'

Did she take her own advice? I never asked!

Around five in the morning we arrived at Seremban station. We thanked our Chinese friend for her help and scanned the platform for a glimpse of a nun's habit, but there was not a single black robe in sight. What now? Olga did not appear unduly concerned. 'We'll take a pedicab,' she said, and in no time we were bowling down the main street. The cool morning air was refreshing, the padang across from the school was lush with recent rain and the jacarandas just inside the convent fence were in full bloom. Our spirits soared. The pedicab stopped just outside the main gate. It was locked. No movement of any kind was detectable on the inside. Even the duty-sister's bench was empty. We were too early.

'We'll climb over,' Olga said, fully in control and she lost no time in showing me how. The ornamental grille design provided several footholds, and she was over in a flash, catching the suitcases as the pedicab driver, grinning from ear to ear, lobbed them over to her.

I followed slowly, carefully. I was no tomboy! I managed to get over and down without mishap. We were both very pleased with our efforts. 'We'll sit and wait here till sister comes to let the priest in for the early Mass,' Olga decided. We didn't have long to wait. Footsteps came pattering down the stone-flagged passage, a face came into view. '*Mais, mon dieu* — who are you? How did you get in?'

'We climbed the gate, Sister,' Olga replied, very matter-of-fact.

'You climbed the gate? You climbed — *mais, mon dieu* — you two wait here! I'll fetch Reverend Mother.' And she flew back along the passage.

Minutes later we heard a familiar voice, amused, reassuring. 'It's all right Sister, it's only Olga and Maisie Prout. I was expecting them tomorrow, but here they are now, God be praised! *Deo gratias*!' And she held out her thin arms in welcome.

So much warmth in her voice, so much happiness in her face. We shed a few joyful tears together, Olga and I, because we had reached a safe haven.

From the day of our dramatic return, the Seremban convent became our new home.

The Singapore trinity of St James, St Anselme and St Gerard had replaced the local duo of St Pauline and St Finbarr and with the change of government had come a warmer, friendlier atmosphere. St Finbarr was still around, less powerful than previously but by no means a spent force.

My daily routine was speedily organised. Quite simple really. I came out of Standard V in Singapore and went into Standard V in Seremban. By happy chance, my teacher was St Vincent! The Easter holiday break was only a couple of weeks away and the first term tests were imminent.

St James wanted me to attempt all the exams even though the text books were different and some of the work unfamiliar. At first I baulked at the idea, but on second thoughts decided to knuckle down and do my best as a small gesture of gratitude to my guardian and benefactor. I not only passed the exams overall, but did better than expected — third in the class. I shall always remember the happy smile on Reverend Mother's face when she presented me with a reward for my efforts. Over the years, I would receive other prizes and awards, but none, I think, meant as much to me as the carpet-bag in which I proudly carried my school books.

St James did more than provide me with a schoolbag. She used to invite me to her office for little treats of biscuits or cakes or bananas, all items she saved from her own breakfast in order to 'put some flesh on my bones.' With the aplomb of a conjurer she would whisk a teacloth off a glass jar to reveal its precious contents and I'd be instructed to eat it all there and then. I never needed a second invitation.

Olga was not included in these little treats. St James didn't attempt to fatten Olga up. She implied that Olga was sturdy enough. Any problems connected with my sister had far more to do with attitude than health. The main problem was her persistent refusal to attend school and learn

Japanese. Another Superior might have ordered Olga to 'just sit in a classroom and behave!' but not St James. Secretly, I believe she admired Olga's defiant spirit, just as in her own heart she would have supported General de Gaulle and the Free French.

St James found Olga a small out-of-the-way room, not likely to attract visitors of any kind, especially the Japanese. This private space was actually the chapel sacristy and the sacristan was the only regular visitor. Unlike Singapore, Seremban did not boast any embassy or consular officials with spare cash for tuition, but there were some local people, parents of convent students, looking for typing lessons. They were steered in Olga's direction, but she did miss the company of her peers.

It was St Bernard's cooking class that enticed her out of her secret room. Olga certainly knew her way around a kitchen and her occasional forays amongst the school population worked well at first. Then one day, Mr Kawashima, the Japanese Headmaster, stuck his head around the door. All the busy, budding cooks ceased activity immediately and bowed in greeting. All but one. No need to say who that was. She carried on creaming the margarine as if her life depended on it and pretended she hadn't seen the visitor, but she was forced to take notice when he roared at her, 'You! Come here!'

Olga downed tools then. Knees shaking, she walked to the spot indicated. Now she was scared, really scared! Kawashima-San turned to an ashen-faced St Bernard. 'This girl must go to Drill Master every day and learn to bow! Abruptly, he turned on his heel and left. It was St Bernard's job to take Olga to task for showing a lack of respect for the Headmaster. 'You got off very lightly this time,' she scolded. 'He could have slapped you across the face, or made you stand in the sun for hours on end, he could have punished the whole class if he'd chosen to. Don't you realise you put the whole class at risk with your stubbornness?'

Somewhat chastened, Olga apologised for the trouble she'd caused and promised to present herself the next morning for bowing lessons. Mr Jaganathan, the Indian Drill Master, put her through her paces the next day. It didn't take long, only a matter of ten minutes or so — bowing is not a complicated manoeuvre, merely a matter of lowering one's head and upper trunk while facing the person who is being greeted or acknowledged. (More sanitary than shaking hands or kissing!)

It wasn't as if bowing was a totally foreign gesture in the course of our everyday lives, either. All boarders and orphans bowed to Reverend Mother after daily Mass as we passed her elevated chair (her throne) just inside the chapel door. No, it was the symbolic gesture of submission to the enemy that irked Olga.

'You're not being asked to prostrate yourself, merely to incline your head,' reasoned St James.

But Olga was adamant. 'I know how to bow, I just don't want to do it!'

'Then, my dear, you will have to give up your cooking classes altogether and never show your face downstairs during school hours,' was Reverend Mother's firm decision. For Olga, it was back to solitary for the rest of the Occupation.

One person sympathised wholeheartedly with Olga's stance; our pretend aunt, St Norbert. It was her job to act as official chaperone to the convent day-girls and guide them past the sentry-boxes. At first, parents had hesitated about sending their daughters to school in these troubled times, so St Norbert was given the task of collecting the pupils from their homes in the morning and returning them in the afternoon. By nature she was a very independent and forthright individual, not given to hiding her opinions or feelings. And, like Olga, she displayed a very cavalier attitude towards the obligatory bowing. I overheard her sounding off to St Vincent on that very topic: 'A person of my senior years' (she would have been in her late fifties) 'should not have to kowtow to a young whipper-snapper in a sentry-box.'

I caught the warning note in St Vincent's reply, 'Be careful, St Norbert, be very careful!'

For several months, St Norbert went on her merry way completing the return journey without incident, despite ignoring the sentry. The pupils always bowed as required, but our rebel nun would walk past the sentry-box with head held high in defiance of the rules. One day, her luck ran out. As she strode past the box in the morning, a loud bellow stopped her in her tracks and a pair of muscular arms propelled her towards the sentry-box where she was made to stand without moving. A different, less tolerant sentry had replaced the previous one. St Norbert was left to reflect on her foolhardy behaviour while standing to attention in her heavy black robes, with the tropical sun beating down mercilessly on her head and sweat pouring down her body. Yet her greatest suffering came not from her discomfort or public humiliation, but from the knowledge that she had failed in her duty to her girls through her defiance of authority.

When she didn't show up at the usual time, a group of waiting mothers decided to go in search of her. As they headed for the convent, they passed the sentry-box and immediately all was revealed. A very distressed and crestfallen 'penguin' was doing sentry duty alongside the Japanese soldier. She was then released to rejoin her charges and she never again attempted to avoid that gesture of submission, without which she could not have survived in her allotted task of chaperone.

Later on, St Norbert was able to joke about the whole incident and give a blow-by-blow account, but she was not laughing that day!

The Prout family: Stanley, my father (left), with his sisters and brother — Lily, Ethel, Arthur and Maud.

Alice Olga Vaz, my mother, on the day of her engagement in 1921.

Mum and Dad at a New Year's Eve party, 1935.

My mother with the three of us, 1936.

Dad, in the uniform of the Royal Navy, in World War I. This was the photograph that nearly caused the Prout sisters serious trouble.

'Party girl' — a picture taken on my sixth birthday.

St Madeleine — teacher extraordinaire.

A picture of Olga and me within the cloisters, 1940.

Reverend Mother St James — not a person to be trifled with.

A guardian angel holy picture, given to me by St Raphael.

'Angel' St Raphael

An aerial view of the old CHIJ convent in Singapore.

In present-day CHIJMES (what used to be the CHIJ convent in Singapore), the old chapel is now a lavishly furnished wedding banquet hall.

'New-Look' nuns — our nuns in their postwar white coifs and scapulars.

Mary and Doris Liew, 1943.

Father Laurent, our 'New Age' (postwar) Priest.

A Japanese 50 cent note used during the war.

Prout family reunion, with John in the inset. Singapore, 1946.

A postwar reunion in the Singapore convent, 1946. From left: St Pauline, Olga, St Aidan and me.

Dublin Priest's Malayan Thrill

SWORD SOUVENIR OF VILLAGE CAPTURE

REV. MATHEW MALONE, a young Dublin priest and a former altar boy at the Sacred Heart Church, Donnybrook, who is now a chaplain with the British forces in the Far East, figured in the exciting unarmed capture of a town on the Malay Peninsula during the Japanese campaign and received the Japanese commander's sword as a souvenir.

Father Malone was landed with a medical unit on a strip of beach along the west coast of the Peninsula on "D" Day, September 9 last. Two days later they trekked towards the inland town of Seramban, which is about 20 miles from Port Dickson and 200 miles from Singapore.

NOT A SHOT FIRED

His unit was unarmed, and as they approached the town they wondered what their reception was going to be.

Not a shot was fired and the unit entered the town. The Japanese commander surrendered to them, and the Colonel of the British unit later presented the surrender sword to Father Malone.

On November last Father Malone delivered a sermon in the Catholic Cathedral, Batavia, at which Mass was offered for the British soldiers who fell in both Wars. His Lordship, the Bishop of Batavia, presided at the Mass, and the Cathedral Choir sang the Mass of Palestrina.

Father Malone, who is 29, is son of Mr. M. Malone, victualler, 25 Main St., Donnybrook, and of Mrs. Malone. He was educated at Synge St. Schools, and Mungret College, Limerick, subsequently going to Leeds University. He finished his course at All Hallows College, and was ordained there in 1942. He was a curate at the Church of the Holy Rosary, Leeds, until he became a Chaplain.

Rev. M. Malone.

An article about Father Malone (a conquering hero!) in a Dublin paper in 1946.

The Petersen sisters and Prout sisters with our soldier escort (I am standing on the right). Batu Ferenghi, Penang, 1950.

'New Floraville', the Van Vliet's boarding-house in Tanglin, January 1946: Aunty Flora in the floral dress, Uncle Dick in the rear, with several guests.

A boyish Welby Foley, Penang, 1946.

Welby in military uniform in 1948 — against the wildly unsuitable but quite characteristic photographer's backdrop!

The Foley boys in front of their home, Merah Estate, Kulim.

An isolated planter's bungalow, Jabi Estate, 1949.

Mary and Robbie Augustin — ready for action.

A daily line-up of the special constables who protected Jabi Estate.

An eventful tea party at the Jabi Estate in 1949 — I am seated with several members of the Foley family.

Geoffrey Beresford-Cooke, rubber planter.

'Farewell, Frank!'

Kelawei Road in Penang, Malaysia, the Vaz family house until 1952. The family did not own the house, but Uncle Peter managed the property for the owner.

Three trainee teachers — one went to England, two stayed at home! From left: Tessie, Louise and me.

John and Olga Prout

John as a weekend sailor on HMS Panglina *in the early 1950s.*

Twenty-one today!

Left to right: Olga, Mary, me, Cora and a ship's officer.

Mary and Cora Pijpe in Dutch costume.

A weekend on board Uncle Willem's vessel, Sanana. *Front row: Cora, Olga and me; centre: a friend, Aunt May and Uncle Willem; back row: crew.*

Lizzie (on the left) with her parents and three younger brothers.

Bob Duncan — in informal attire, complete with the racing pages, cigarette and tattoo.

Bob — scrubbed up and looking his best in dress uniform.

Lizzie with Billy and Harold.

Our wedding day, 8th November 1952. Left to right: Matty, my brother John, Ann Morris, Bob and Maisie Duncan, John Lucas, Olga and Eric Morris.

Two wedding photos, courtesy of Olga's Box Brownie.

14

THE UNASKED QUESTION

Occupying the desk beside me in St Vincent's class was a certain Tessie De Silva. Tessie and her younger sister Lyn had become boarders the year before when their mother died after a painful and protracted illness.

Because of the similarities in our situations, I could empathise with them straightaway. The loss of her mother weighed heavily on Tessie's mind, but my new friend was far too resilient, too full of fun and mischief to remain depressed and despondent indefinitely. Compared with her I must have seemed quite solemn and serious. Tessie possessed an insatiable curiosity about life; she wanted to know all about the people I met, the books I read, the experiences I had, and especially tidbits of gossip about the Big City.

It was flattering to have somebody in your own peer group constantly asking for information or advice and deferring to your opinion. I knew all about being a younger sister. Now I enjoyed the novel experience of acting like an older sister. It wasn't surprising that we were seldom apart. A certain amount of rivalry existed in the relationship but it never endangered the underlying bond of goodwill and affection.

As Olga was not in a classroom, her close connections tended to be with nuns and lay teachers. There were the 'old friends' from Seremban: St Vincent, St Matthew, Nellie Plachel, then St Anselme and St Gerard from Singapore and now she got to know and like several of the local teachers. There was petite and pretty Rose Charlie, plump and cheerful Eva Da Souza and brainy Ralda Lawrence, one of those Lawrences whose numerous family members were spread right through the school as pupils, teachers, secretaries and so forth. Even their brother, Alwyn, enjoyed special access to the convent in the guise of unofficial electrician, tracking down faulty wiring and fused bulbs in company with his form master and mentor Walter De Silva, father of Tessie and Lyn.

Most of Olga's new teacher friends remained two-dimensional characters to me until they became my instructors, briefly or otherwise, and then I got to know them in depth.

The Malayan Education Department had displayed a multi-cultural face from pre-war years. Chinese, Indian, Eurasian and European staff were well represented. During the Occupation, Japanese staff joined the service specifically to teach Nippon-go.

The Seremban convent boasted its own Japanese language specialist in the person of Miss Sugimoto, who took all the Japanese lessons in the higher grades. A Miss Kawaguchi joined her later to conduct the classes for the lower grades.

Miss Sugimoto was a person of great refinement and integrity, respected by teachers and pupils alike. Even St Anselme, who was wary of all Japanese, approved of her.

Miss Kawaguchi ('Miss Apple Cheeks' as she came to be known) was warm and friendly in manner and very well liked by her young pupils. She became popular with the whole school when she organised a picnic to Temiang Falls, a local rainforest area, when the boarders were allowed to join and freely partake of the largesse of the day-girls. Normally this was frowned upon. St Finbarr did not approve of boarders accepting food from day-girls, and punished any culprits she caught 'scrounging'.

In January 1945, Tessie and I found ourselves together in Standard VI. Our new teacher was Miss Jemiah. Malay high-school teachers, especially of the female variety, were not very numerous. Possibly that is why one wing of the convent had been taken over by the Education Ministry to house a Teacher-Training College for Malay women. They operated independently of our school and we had no contact with the occupants. We were not even allowed to walk around the building, but we managed to peek at them through the wooden window-shutters of the boarders' dormitory.

Miss Jemiah was intelligent, articulate and quietly confident. A lone Muslim in a traditional Catholic institution, she appeared to hold her own in an unfamiliar environment.

Tessie sometimes complained. 'Miss J gave you higher marks in arithmetic than me,' she would say.

'Maybe it's because I work a lot harder,' I'd respond.

'No, she likes you better — that's why!'

Once a week, Mr Kawashima would address the school assembly. Small brown eyes peering through bottle-top lenses, a calm monotonous voice holding forth about the duties and responsibilities of schoolchildren, the need to show respect to one's elders and superiors, the importance of study and so forth, he preached Confucian-type values, and, in so far as we could judge, appeared to adhere to his beliefs. He told us he'd been a schoolmaster before the call-up and spoke of missing his family in faraway Japan. At the end of every homily he would ask questions to see how much his captive audience had absorbed. Usually, only two hands were ever raised. One belonged to Lee Soo Sin, the school dux, who shone in every subject; the other belonged to Maisie Prout, daughter of an enemy alien. The rest of the school could normally cope with single, well-rehearsed question-answer type exercises, but found lengthy discourses beyond them.

The Headmaster did not give classroom lessons but did all the oral/aural testing for term exams himself. With my classmates, I went through the usual question-answer preparation — Name? Age? Address? Nationality? In answer to the last question I would reply 'Eurasian'. That word usually stumped the Japanese. They had no idea what sort of creature an Eurasian was. That word quite often got me off the hook when I was asked directly if I was English. My questioner would scratch his head, look blank, repeat, '*Eurasian*?' and go on to something else, such as 'How long have you studied Japanese?'

When my turn came to front up to Mr Kawashima, I raced through the first three answers and then, as usual, said 'Eurasian' in answer to the nationality question. Mr K looked puzzled; if I explained that it meant a mixture of Asian and European he might ask, 'Which of your parents is European?' While I was weighing up my course of action, he started the next question. '*Otoosan wa …*'

Here it comes, I thought. He's going to ask, 'Is my father English?'

Before I could jump in with 'He's dead', he had finished the query — 'Where is he?' Greatly relieved, I answered truthfully: 'I don't know, I think he's dead.'

'When did he die?'

'Recently, during the war.' Mr K listened, nodded a couple of times, then continued, '*Okaasan wa* — Your mother, is she alive?'

'No, she's dead too. She died a long time ago. That's why I live at the convent.'

A glimmer of sympathy in an otherwise impassive face? He began to chat rather than question. 'At school assemblies, you understand my speeches, don't you? Do you find Japanese easy?'

'No,' I answered, 'it's not easy, but it's good to study another language.'

'You may go now — continue to work hard.'

Phew — I was over that dreaded interview. St Anselme was waiting outside, anxious to know every word that was said during my time with the Headmaster. She would later relay it all to St James to reassure her that I had not let slip that dreaded phrase, 'English father'. No need to pack my port for Sime Road Camp yet!

Why hadn't Kawashima asked *that* question? Perhaps he had guessed my secret and didn't want definite confirmation, in case he might be forced to act on it. Obviously, he didn't regard me as a dangerous character requiring strict confinement. He may even have agreed with the State Governor, who was reported to have said, 'Prison, Convent — all same!'

If someone had asked any Malayan schoolchild of my era to name the chief products of the country, the answer would have come without any hesitation: 'rubber and tin'. These two commodities were the source of the region's wealth. If only they'd been edible, nobody in this hitherto prosperous colony need have gone hungry during the Occupation.

More resources, manpower and land had always been dedicated to these two lucrative enterprises than to food production; consequently when the war put a stop to the whole trading pattern of selling our goods and importing food, we were in serious trouble. Not only was the civilian population attempting to make do with its own limited supplies, there was the added imposition of two large armies, Allied and Japanese.

The authorities were constantly exhorting everyone to grow more food. Rural dwellers — the Malays in their kampungs, the Chinese in their market gardens — had traditionally grown their own rice and vegetables and kept chickens and other livestock. These country farmers had enough to sustain their own small communities but there was insufficient surplus to feed the urban population.

Townspeople had to utilise any vacant land around the place and turn into instant farmers or starve. Playing fields, parks, even footpaths went under the hoe. When our school ran out of usable land inside the convent walls, we were instructed to start on the footpaths outside the perimeter fence, and when that area was planted out we were ordered to start clearing and cultivating a site beyond the town limits. So urgent was the situation in 1945 that schoolchildren were informed they had to forfeit part of their Sunday holiday to till the soil.

The adoption of the Japanese-style timetable in 1942 meant that Saturdays were only half-holidays. Now that Sundays became half-days as well, our free weekends totally disappeared. No point in complaining about it; you just obeyed orders.

After the Sunday morning church service, the boarders would join up with the day girls outside the gates and walk to the work-site. The first time we sighted our new garden, we were filled with dismay. We'd hoped for some soft, yielding, easy-to-dig ground; instead we were faced with a burnt-out rubber plantation littered with heavy logs and large stumps which must somehow be removed before we could even swing a hoe. The task had to be accomplished without the benefit of mechanical aids — we had no bulldozers, no trucks, not even a humble wheelbarrow. Just muscle and will-power!

Teachers were officially exempt from Sunday duty though a few did turn up. The drill master was there to direct operations and Miss Sugimoto came to lend moral support. Fortunately for us, the boys from St Paul's had been assigned to the same work area, and while they rolled, shifted and shoved the logs to the perimeter of the clearing, we girls carried away the smaller branches and twigs in preparation for digging.

Around noon on our first working Sunday, Miss Sugimoto called a halt and announced that all students were to be provided with a meal at the Koa Club, across from the convent, as a reward for the day's effort. The boarders lined up with the rest of the working party for the bowl of rice and vegetables before returning to the convent.

Footsore, grubby, aching all over, we should have gone first to the bathroom to clean up and then headed for the dormitory. Instead, our feet carried us, as one, towards the refectory where we hoped we'd see our midday meals still on the table. Peeking through the closed shutters, we spied the welcome sight of our intact lunches. In a matter of seconds we had loosened a door bolt and were inside wolfing down the food. 'Sunday work isn't so bad if you can count on two lunches,' we were thinking when a tall figure appeared at the open door. The person we wanted to avoid at all costs now confronted us. 'Come out of there, you greedy children, you've already had one meal, you're not entitled to another,' she snarled.

'But these were *our* meals, not stolen from others. We've spent hours digging in the hot sun. We deserve a little extra.' Well, that's what we wanted to say, but of course nobody challenged St Finbarr. Instead, silent rage welled up inside us because we felt so powerless. If thoughts could kill, our tormentor would have died on the spot.

Not long before the double-lunch episode, Muriel, one of our number, had been caught eating some morsel provided by a day-girl. The same nun had stood her within a circle of boarders and sneered, 'This child has no shame. She collects scraps from anybody. She tells the day girls that you're all starving.'

Muriel's audience squirmed in sympathetic embarrassment. Most of us were thinking, 'There but for the grace of God go I.'

We didn't have to beg the day girls for food — they gave out of the goodness of their hearts. At a time when everything was in short supply, not just food, they attempted to help those even worse off than themselves. Two Jewish sisters, Hannah and Hilda Saul, befriended me, slipping little presents into the pocket of my school uniform. 'You have no parents to bring you anything,' they explained. Their gifts were all very welcome — a new hanky, a tube of toothpaste, a mandarin and once, a new cake of Lux soap, the genuine article, not a cheap imitation. Olga and Tessie had a small share in my bonanza — they were allowed to wash their faces a couple of times with my sweet-smelling soap.

My special treats from St James did not continue for long. Very likely, my benefactor was unable to justify singling me out for special attention when every week her sharp eye would have detected yet another lean, pale figure among her large, dependant family. Not that she carried an ounce of excess flesh herself. It's a mystery how such an emaciated frame could have radiated so much energy and courage. Unable to work the miracle of the loaves and fishes, she decided to increase the amount of rest her children received. Every afternoon during the hottest part of the day we took to our beds to sleep or read. 'When you rest,' she used to say, 'you eat a little.'

I took to the siesta period very readily. It combined two, or perhaps I should say three of the activities I most enjoyed: reading, sleeping and day-dreaming. Like Mavis Lawrence, another acknowledged bookworm, it was an excellent opportunity to indulge in reading simply for pleasure.

The supposedly banned and locked-away English books were freely available to the boarders once school was over for the day, so we made our selection from the library shelves before heading for the dormitory. And once there, to sleep, perchance to dream of foreign lands on whose vast plains countless sheep and cattle grazed, where fields of golden grain rippled by mild, eucalyptus-scented breezes, stretched to the distant horizon — before being rudely awakened to reality by the staccato 'clap, clap' signal to rise from bed and proceed to chapel for the three o'clock Rosary session.

Despite the best efforts of St James, the Angel of Death could not be turned away from all the members of her tribe. While the extra rest periods probably helped the boarders through the most difficult final months of the Occupation, the orphans, further down the food chain, received virtually no protein in their diet and slowly succumbed to the scourge of beri-beri and other starvation-related diseases.

While the boarders saw half a boiled egg a week, the orphans might have their egg ration once a month. As for the meat ration, it depended on a windfall — or more accurately, a roof-fall. Members of the musang (civet cat) family sometimes paid a roof-top visit at night, leaping off surrounding trees to retrieve the odd mango or guava from the open gutters. Occasionally, our nocturnal guest ended up in a large wire cage and would be on display next morning outside the kitchen. The furry captive would pace the confined space treadmill-fashion, exuding its distinctive pungent odour and watched by an audience of hungry children who all wished that the wee, cowering beastie were twice as large. Then the cook would appear, brandishing a large knife and end the animal's life in order to extend ours temporarily with a minute piece of stewed meat that would be sucked and rolled over and over, in the mouth until it was finally and regretfully swallowed.

The SARS scare in recent times has caused an enormous shift in perception regarding the humble musang. Where the starving boarders and orphans viewed the civet cat as a welcome addition to their meagre diet, public opinion today condemns the animal as a death-dealing feline instead of a welcome visitor!

Right until the end of the war, all convent members, except those who were seriously ill, emerged from behind the walls for the Sunday church service. As our crocodile passed the blocks of shop-houses en route, we couldn't fail to notice that beneath their awnings sat growing colonies of the destitute. At our approach, heads would turn, palms outstretched as they pleaded for something, anything, to be given them. Others squatted there staring straight ahead, seeing nothing, expecting nothing.

It's hard to say which pitiful group of human flotsam moved me more, the beggars, or the stoics. At least the orphans dying in the convent were certain they were going to heaven. That's what they told anybody who stopped to chat. No longer able to work, they sat immobile, hands resting on bloated bellies, rosary beads moving imperceptibly between their swollen fingers. Their corpses would be laid out in their Sunday best and friends would place small posies of white frangipani on either side of them as they lay still in their narrow beds. At the dormitory altar we would light a candle and ask that these formerly abandoned babies might find an eternal home.

The temporary jungle home that was to house the pioneer farmers from Singapore got under way in August 1943 when two groups left the island to establish their self-supporting agricultural communities. They comprised a Chinese group and a mixed party of Chinese, Eurasians and convent members.

The Chinese group went to Endau, a village on the east coast of Johore, while the other settlers made for Bahau. The Endau location turned out to be well suited to the project, and unlike the Bahau site, produced fairly good results.

While the desperate food situation in Singapore was the driving force behind this jungle settlement project, another equally serious matter spurred on the mass exodus. A widespread rumour was circulating the city regarding an imminent crackdown on suspected Chinese communists. Singapore's Serangoon district was the primary target. Several of the alleged 'communists' were in fact third- and fourth-generation Catholic families, members of Bishop Devals' flock. In his desire to help his people, the Bishop sought the advice and support of a long-time friend, a Japanese national who had been educated at St Joseph's and was the current Social Welfare Officer.

Until the war broke out, Shinozaki-san had been a successful business man and a popular Singapore identity. During the Occupation, many of his erstwhile friends avoided him and even his own compatriots watched him closely lest he display too much sympathy towards his former associates. Together, the Bishop and Shinozaki-san dreamed up the idea of turning the official 'Grow More Food' campaign into an escape plan for the Chinese Singaporeans under threat.

Had the supply situation not been so critical, permission for the departure of thousands from suspect Red areas might not have been forthcoming. As it was, permits and rations for one month, as well as farming implements, were issued to the intending pioneers. The Bishop actively encouraged the convent residents to join the flood of emigrants, then he himself took charge of the expedition and led his flock to what he believed would prove greener and safer pastures.

During the Bahau experiment, Seremban became a sort of rest and relaxation centre for colonists from the Infant Jesus Convent, especially the sick members. Like them, we were short of food but we did have clean tap water, a hospital nearby, some access to medicines and we were housed in solid buildings, unlike their flimsy tin or attap sheds (woven palm-frond structures).

Mary and Annie Dragon came to stay in Seremban, both suffering from malaria. They recovered after a course of quinine, but their faces bore the tell-tale yellow signature for some time afterwards.

We were all curious about life in the jungle because we'd heard that the normal convent routine had largely given way to a day-to-day existence centred around growing food and warding off insects and animals of all kinds, crawling, climbing and flying. Mosquito nets provided only minimal protection.

Mary and Annie spoke of how hard everybody worked; orphans, nuns, Christian Brothers and the Bishop — especially the Bishop! Despite his diabetic condition, he led from the front, digging wells, chopping wood, lugging sacks of grain. He would have been the last to assert that his rank gave him an excuse to avoid heavy manual work.

Occasionally he appeared in our midst. Thinner, greyer, but still an erect, commanding presence. On his town visits, he would liaise with the authorities to obtain rations, garden tools and other needs, then say Mass in the chapel, serving both the physical and spiritual needs of his parishioners.

The boarders would line up outside the chapel to obtain his blessing and exchange a few words. On one occasion, spying Olga and me in the waiting group he enquired, 'No news of your father yet?'

'No, Your Grace.'

'Don't worry, he'll turn up one day. D'you know we are old friends? I often sailed on his boat when I had business along the coast. Where's your brother John now? Several Penang Eurasians were recently interned at Sime Road Camp in Singapore. He may be amongst them … Have courage and patience, my children.'

'Yes, Your Grace.'

'No need for such titles now. Haven't you heard that I've become a coolie — a Bahau coolie!' And with a merry chuckle he moved on.

Despite the Bishop's optimism and spirited leadership, the Bahau colony did not prosper and many temporary settlers became permanent residents, leaving their earthly remains in the unproductive soil. Meanwhile, our convent ranks were depleted, mostly the very young orphans and the very old nuns. St Theodora, an elderly German nun, was buried there, her coffin an orange crate. Such were the times!

Worse was to come. In the last few months of the war, the Bishop was bitten on the leg by a venomous spider and the wound turned septic. An anxious St Anselme conveyed the news to the boarders. 'The Bishop was rushed to Seremban hospital this morning,' she told us. 'The doctors have amputated the leg hoping to save his life.'

When we next saw St Anselme, she didn't need to utter a word. Her white face and red eyes said it all. Our dear, kind Bishop Devals had died.

His body lay in state in the front parlour for a day. A round-the-clock vigil was mounted by the nuns, while voluntary visits were made by all the members of his flock who expressed their silent or not so silent grief at the side of their dead shepherd. His funeral service was a moving and solemn affair held in a packed church. People of all races and religions came to pay their final tribute, including a Japanese delegation: the Governor, his aide and one other civilian. Shinozaki-san? It might well have been him. As the coffin was carried down the aisle to the waiting hearse, the three men rose as one and saluted the corpse of a fearless soldier of Christ.

At our 'Notes' session the following Sunday, a sad and pensive St James urged us all not to lose faith and courage. 'The darkest hour heralds the dawn,' she reminded us.

15

'NOT WITH A BANG BUT A WHIMPER'

This is the Way the War ends,
This is the Way the War ends,
This is the Way the War ends,
Not with a Bang but a Whimper.
(With apologies to T.S. Eliot)

The Japanese got the bang — we got the whimper.

Even as St James encouraged us to think hopefully of the future, the tide of the war was turning in the Allies' favour, though we were largely unaware of the progress of the fighting on all the different and distant battlefronts. A trickle of good news occasionally reached us by way of unknown sources, snippets of information that fell like manna on our parched desert of ignorance and somehow kept us believing that one day the nightmare would be over.

Early in 1945, probably about the time the Burma campaign was reaching a successful conclusion, air-raid drills began to punctuate our days. In the same classroom where we're sheltered from Japanese planes, we now took cover from Allied B-29s that zoomed low over the town dropping pamphlets. We would have preferred to rush out into the open waving and cheering, but we knew better than to display any signs of jubilation at the prospect of a British return. Anybody caught picking up a pamphlet was either summarily shot or hauled into Kempeitai headquarters for questioning. Nevertheless, some people managed to collect one secretly and its information rapidly seeped into the school.

Miss Sugimoto spoke to Rose Charlie about the aerial bombardment of Japan and her fears for the safety of her family and friends. At one assembly, Mr Kawashima told of his mother dying in an air-raid over Tokyo. Behind the thick glasses, his eyes blinked a few times. Tessie whispered, 'What's he saying? He looks sad.'

'He's just lost his mother.' We exchanged glances. We knew what that felt like. But any lingering sympathy we felt for him was dispelled at the next assembly, when he warned us not to imagine the enemy planes would frighten the Japanese away. Our usually mild-mannered Headmaster was momentarily replaced by a fanatical soldier who punched his fist in the air exclaiming, 'If the British bomb this country, we will all die together because 'We Japanese will never surrender!' Picking up some chalk he wrote the characters for KAMIKAZE large and clear on the blackboard, foretelling that the Heavenly Wind that destroyed the Mongol fleet in ancient times would soon destroy the American fleet now threatening their home islands.

It is easy now to dismiss as crackpot raving his firm conviction that Divine Intervention would prevent the American armada from invading the Japanese archipelago. Yet our side had had its own share of credulous fools — those who had believed until the last minute that fortress Singapore was impregnable.

We didn't doubt his claim about the Japanese resolve to hang on to their conquered territories no matter what. The Communists (under the Malayan People's Anti-Japanese Army or MPAJA), with their British Commando officers, did their best to destabilise the Japanese forces by staging ambushes, derailments, bridge demolitions and other acts of sabotage. At first these were followed by swift and bloody reprisals but in the dying stages of the Occupation the guerrilla attacks became bolder and more frequent while the Japanese search-and-destroy missions became fewer and less effective. Another destabilising tactic was the introduction of counterfeit currency, printed for the Malayan region at the Colombo headquarters of Force 136, the British Commando group working with the MPAJA. The local people became quite adept at producing their own paper money, and some enterprising townspeople manufactured very credible notes on their own printing presses. On the first Monday of each month, pupils paid their school fees at roll call time. Staff began to notice slightly different versions of the same denominations of currency. Not being experts, they couldn't tell the genuine article from the fake, so their policy was to accept all contributions gratefully. Which brings us to the following little exchange that really did take place in our school:

Teacher: Sally Ng.
Sally: Present, Teacher.
Teacher: Have you brought your fees today?
Sally: No, Teacher, I'll pay tomorrow.
Teacher: Why not today?
Sally: Sorry, Teacher, the ink wasn't dry this morning.

One day in July 1945, we schoolchildren were pleasantly surprised to receive a gift from the Education Department: a notebook, some pencils and a dress-length each. At the same time, the local staff were given little parcels of soap, toothpaste and handkerchiefs, which may have originated from the Red Cross. The nuns were excluded from this largesse because they were classified as Foreign Aliens. However, they didn't miss out entirely; Miss Sugimoto remedied the situation by making up little gift bundles for the nuns out of her own supplies. She told Rose Charlie that it was unfair to leave them out when they worked as hard as anyone else. It was daring of her to act against the official line. According to classroom gossip, she had an influential friend (some said boyfriend) at Headquarters, so she may have felt free to act somewhat independently.

One of the pamphlets secretly retrieved from an airdrop proclaimed the successful conclusion of the Burma campaign and the scheme to liberate Malaya in the near future. We were happy to know there were definite plans to retake the peninsula but were fearful of a blood-bath before the final victory.

The second term of 1945 closed at the end of July. School had emptied itself of day-girls and most of the boarders had gone home to their families, leaving the usual handful of 'permanents' behind. The Malay student-teachers had also departed, leaving their wing vacant. The remaining boarders thought it might be a good time to revisit that building and watch from its verandah to see if anything was happening along Birch Road. In the past day or two, the streets had been unusually quiet. We'd heard rumours of Allied victories and German defeats, of plans for an American invasion of the Japanese mainland and another for the British invasion of Malaya — we didn't know what to think.

It was now the second week of August and our group was gathered in the dormitory looking through old magazines for dress patterns now that we had some fabric to make up. We were about to move on to the Malay college next door when we heard several voices below, Japanese voices, coming from the little courtyard between the two buildings. Peering through the shutters, we witnessed a strange and significant scene. All the Japanese teaching staff were present. Each in turn placed some books, bundles of paper or documents in a neat pile on the turf and then stood to attention while they ran the Hinomaru up the flagpole and solemnly saluted it. Lowering it again, they then folded it carefully over the mound of combustible matter and ignited it. Not a word was exchanged as they stared at the flames until the whole pyre was consumed. There were some tears but no sobs. It was a silent grief. The ashes were carefully raked over before they departed with shoulders bowed and eyes lowered, having completed their part in the drama.

My God, they've burnt their flag! Something terrible has hit them, we all thought. Have they surrendered? If so, why! All asking questions at once, we broke our own silence and lost no time heading for our favourite viewing platform to discover what, if anything, the street and passing parade could tell us.

The full extent of the catastrophe that had initiated the hypnotic tableau we'd just witnessed was revealed in slow stages. Several bands of urchins were running along the fence or frolicking in the middle of the road waving small Union Jacks. Amazing! When they spotted us they grinned widely and chanted over and over again: 'Nippon-go, British come! Nippon-go, Yankee come!' Amazed at their daring, we automatically glanced in the direction of the sentry-box on the corner. It was empty! There were no soldiers on the street, no military activity of any kind. No Japanese to be seen anywhere!

Later that day somebody brought in a few copies of the latest air-drop pamphlet. I cannot recall the exact wording of the text but it gave us the news everybody had most wanted to hear. The war was over.

That's what the first line of print told us. We didn't turn somersaults or shriek with joy because we were afraid to trust the good news. Could peace arrive so stealthily, without warning, without a final bloody struggle? We hoped, oh how we hoped it was so, but … anxiously we read the lines that followed.

We learned that Germany had surrendered several weeks earlier but the Japanese had fought on until the bombing of Hiroshima and Nagasaki on the 6th and 9th of August. It appeared that something called the atomic bomb had been dropped on these two cities and completely razed them. What on earth was the atomic bomb? It must have been an immensely powerful beast if just two bombs had persuaded the enemy to surrender when the earlier deluge of bombs had failed to do so. At the time, we were greatly relieved to know that the new weapon had ended the fighting before any more people, ourselves included, got killed.

To dispel any lingering doubts about the authenticity of the information, Rose Charlie was asked to consult Miss Sugimoto about the statements contained in the leaflet. We knew she would not lie, however unpalatable she found the facts. Rose returned from her visit after being assured that Japan had indeed surrendered unconditionally. The Emperor had spoken! For the first time his people, listening with heads bowed reverently, had heard his divine voice relayed to them in a radio broadcast. He had ordered all his subjects to lay down their arms immediately and almost to a man they had obeyed! For herself, Miss Sugimoto had no desire to live and was contemplating *jigai* (throat-cutting), the form of ritual suicide prescribed for Samurai or aristocratic women as opposed to *hara-kiri* (belly-cutting) for men. We had no further contact with her so we never knew whether she carried out what she considered the honourable solution to an abhorrent situation.

Sugimoto sensei, sayonara …

The day after we learned of the Japanese surrender, St James decided to get rid of all the Japanese currency she possessed because she realised it would become valueless almost instantly. Calling the half-dozen boarders up to her office, she placed $500 in each outstretched palm. 'Spend all of it. Don't bring any money back!' she instructed us.

For a normally thrifty person, this was the most extraordinary thing for the Reverend Mother to say, but then, these were not ordinary times. Within minutes Olga and I were outside the front gate heading for the shops. Not many were open, but here and there an open shop-front indicated the owner was still trading. We spied a shoe shop that offered rubber-soled leather sandals, all the same style and colour. No matter. Seeing we hadn't owned a decent pair of shoes in three years, they looked utterly desirable. Only the price shocked us. '$400,' the man said. Barely a week ago, one of the teachers had bought an identical pair for $40! But today was not a good day for haggling. We walked out of the shop wearing our new purchases, with $200 dollars left between us, wondering if we'd find anything else we could afford because of the astronomical inflation we'd just encountered. A fruit stall caught my eye. The vendor didn't boast a large selection, just a few bunches of bananas and three or four medium-sized papayas. Olga picked up a papaya. '*Berapa*?' ('How much?') — '*Seratus lima puluh*.' ($150). She handed over our $200 dollars and grandly added, 'Keep the change!' Laughing at our extravagance, we proudly bore the footwear and fruit of our shopping expedition back to the convent.

A couple of days later, on our way to church, there was tangible evidence of St James' canny ability to read a difficult situation. The monsoon drains we skirted contained the usual flotsam — rags, rotten vegetables, dead cats and dogs, but a new type of debris was clogging up the drains and blowing in the wind like confetti; literally millions of dollars of Japanese paper money! Nobody even bothered to pick any of it up.

Obviously, we hadn't spent our fortune a moment too soon!

Days after we'd been told that the war was over, some of us were still pinching ourselves every morning to ascertain that we were really awake and peace was a reality, not the stuff of dreams.

Some isolated communities were not aware of the Japanese surrender until weeks later, but all the large towns had been informed by air-drop by mid-August and people were no longer afraid to collect the pamphlets raining from the sky, while those who possessed radios openly tuned in to the BBC for the latest news.

The official signing of the Instrument of Surrender took place on the 2nd September 1945, but at the convent we celebrated the return of peace on the 15th August, the feast of the Assumption of the Virgin Mary.

It seemed extremely appropriate to celebrate Mary's reception into Heaven at the same time as we rejoiced in the long-awaited Allied victory. With joyful abandon we sang our hymn of jubilation, the *Magnificat* and afterwards got quite merry on the drop of altar wine that appeared in every glass at lunch time. The long refectory table was bare except for the lump of tapioca or sweet potato and bitter, boiled leaves on each tin plate, but such was the level of happiness around the table that every mouthful tasted wonderful. Afterwards, we trotted out the precious gramophone and danced and sang until late in the evening, then talked ourselves hoarse into the early hours of daylight, earning only a gentle chiding for tiring ourselves out unnecessarily.

Now came another waiting period for those separated by the war from their loved ones.

Like many others in my situation, I always thought about my absent family members at morning Mass and bedtime prayers but attempted to block out all thoughts of them during the day, because there could be no word until the war was over. But now the war really was over; now every day began in hope and ended in disappointment and the fear grew lest the silence from the other side became permanent.

A trickle of letters began to arrive through the Red Cross. A very welcome postcard reached us from our brother John at the end of August.

27th August 1945
Sime Road Internment Camp

My dear Olga and Maisie,

It won't be long now before we are united again. How are you both keeping? As for me, I have had quite a trying time here, but anyway, it is all over now.

The Rev. Mother in charge has been extremely kind in looking after you two in those distressing times. All I can do is to thank her very much and pray that God bestow his choicest blessings on her.

Regarding Daddy, I heard that he is interned in Sumatra. I hope it is true as we all long to see him again. All our aunties and uncles are all right. Aunty Frances and family are here too. Uncle Bertie is quite all right.

I shall be ending now, with all my love and best wishes to you and hoping to see you both soon.

Your loving brother,
John

Olga and I were surprised and delighted at the affectionate tone of his card, for our brother had never been given to overt displays of fondness for his sisters. Few brothers are!

The days came and went but there was no news of Dad and no sign of our liberators. The Japanese soldiers had vacated the streets and withdrawn to their barracks around the middle of August, but the British forces did not make their appearance until roughly a month later, so there was a hiatus in the transfer of government. During this power-vacuum, the communist fighters came out of the jungle and commandeered all the Japanese arms and equipment they could get hold of. This meant that when law and order were restored under the Union Jack, the wartime MPAJA (which was itself largely made up of members of the Malayan Communist Party) would be well equipped for its lengthy campaign against the returned British rulers. Before the guerrillas slid back into their forested terrain they took the opportunity to settle some old scores. Known or suspected collaborators were rounded up and beaten up or killed, as were members of the Japanese Army who figured in their hit list.

During this period of anarchy the civilian population stayed indoors whenever possible and waited patiently for the first British troops to arrive. Life somehow struggled on; the water supply was erratic, food was very scarce, electricity failures were frequent — then one day, one glorious day, all the uncertainty was over. Our conquering heroes finally arrived.

The events are clearly etched in my memory. It was the afternoon of 11th September, hot and humid as usual. Siesta time, all quiet on the dormitory front. Suddenly, there were shouts, cheers and traffic on Birch

Road. We raced to our special spot and watched a small convoy of trucks and jeeps (as we soon learned to call them) drive slowly past our front fence.

No photographers or camera crew were on hand to record the antics of a group of girls almost flinging themselves off the convent verandah in their excitement at the arrival of their Saviours. On either side of the street, people clapped and cheered the motorcade on its way. Several waved Union Jacks. Where had all those flags come from?

In the open car that led the modest convoy rode two officers who smiled and waved to all and sundry, including the whirling dervishes on the verandah. 'They saw us, they waved!' we shrieked at each other and raced off to spread the good news to everyone.

We never thought to ask ourselves why the liberators were so few in number; it was enough that we had witnessed a British presence in the main street of the town. Now we were safe! Later on we discovered that the two officers whose presence had filled us with such joy were on their way to the Japanese military headquarters in Seremban to take the surrender of the Japanese commander. The pair were not strictly military men at all, but Army chaplains attached to the medical unit of the British Far Eastern Forces.

In a comic-opera type bungle, the medical corps had been sent on ahead of the regular army, with the amazing result that the highest ranking members of the small British force in Seremban happened to be two Irish Catholic priests!

About an hour after the drive past, we were in the refectory drinking mugs of the coloured water we called tea when we heard booming, exultant male voices in the parlour. Peeping beneath the swinging saloon-type doors we spied leather army boots. Our warriors had called to see us! Immediately we straightened up, ready and willing — oh, how willing to greet and shake hands with Captain Malone and Lieutenant Hickey — or, if we preferred, Father Malone and Father Hickey of the Royal Army Medical Corps.

16

A SCHOOLGIRL CRUSH

'Hello, hello! It's wonderful to meet you girls. We've just driven up from Port Dickson. All those happy crowds along the route — we are delighted to be here, we saw you on the verandah — so what have you got to say for yourselves? Come on, speak! We're not ghosts!'

At this point St Anselme interposed and introduced them both, giving their military rank and then adding, 'But you may call them Father Malone and Father Hickey.'

'We know you've all been through a very grim period. Perhaps we can offer you a treat. What would you like to eat most of all? Make a wish.'

We found our voices. 'Bread!' we shouted.

'*Bread*?' they echoed, perplexed. 'Not cake, chocolate, ice-cream?'

'Well, ye-e-e-s, all of those things, but first of all white bread with a crisp crust,' we insisted.

'Very well! Then bread it will be, tomorrow. But for today, how about some chocolate?' And they produced a few bars of solid, military-ration chocolate which we divided up and chewed with relish.

Our soldier priests were as good as their word. The next afternoon they turned up bearing aloft a huge loaf of bread with a high-domed crust which they proceeded to cut up and pass around. 'We forgot the butter and jam, can you eat it like this?' By way of answer, we demolished the loaf in a few minutes, exclaiming that it tasted just like cake.

A new routine began. The pair took to visiting us two or three times a week during the gardening period in the late afternoon. With the advent of peace, no new plots were established but the crops we'd already planted had to be watered and weeded and eventually harvested. At the time, there was a critical shortage of firewood and on one occasion, Fathers Hickey and Malone came upon us sawing off the lower branches of a stand of pines in order to replenish the kitchen stocks. They marvelled at the amount of heavy manual labour such undernourished young women could accomplish.

Meanwhile, the problem of malnutrition was being tackled. With the arrival of the regular army, supplies of basic food became available to everyone and medical supplies and later clothing were also distributed. In short, the hungry were fed, the sick cured, the semi-naked clothed. No wonder the Allied troops were regarded with great warmth and esteem by the civilian population.

Our friendly twosome seemed to symbolise all that was best about the liberating forces. There was an aura about them. To the boarders in particular, they were very special. They were unlike our usual parish priests. Instead of the regulation cassocks they wore smart military uniforms; they spoke loudly and confidently and they had the air of benevolent conquerors. When they came calling they strode past the sister at the gate with a cheery smile, not bothering with the permission-to-visit routine and they'd join us in our garden patch or in the recreation hall offering muscle-power where needed plus an unending supply of yarns and jokes.

On one of these impromptu visits, the idea of a beach picnic surfaced. We were all wildly excited at the thought of a twenty-mile ride in an army truck to Port Dickson, a whole world away from the convent walls. What an adventure! But what would St James say? We knew in advance what she'd say when she was approached for the first time and the second, and the third — the fourth, the fifth ... Understandably, she had her misgivings. How could she allow two attractive young men to take charge of her boarders for a whole day? True, they were priests, but they didn't look or behave like traditional priests. They showed none of the usual deference towards her and were not maintaining a certain distance from the boarders. Besides, other military personnel would be present; non-clergy and overwhelmingly non-Catholic! Could she entrust her darlings to a band of soldiers for a few hours?

Eventually, she did. Perhaps she gave in because she wasn't used to being pestered and these determined young men wore her out. But there were conditions. Several chaperones were appointed, there was to be no swimming, and we must be back behind the gates before six p.m.

Hardly was the grudging approval wrenched from her than our two champions were amongst us, declaring that we'd be going the very next day before she had time to change her mind.

So next morning we set off in two small trucks — the priests, nuns, boarders and a few orphans in one and RAMC men and catering staff in the other. What a thrill it was, bouncing up and down on the wooden benches, leaving the familiar town behind and heading for an unknown destination. When the phrase 'beach picnic' was first spoken it was the picnic, rather than the venue, that excited me. Having lived near Katong beach as a child I visualised a similar gritty grey shoreline. The outing and most of all the company of some dashing young men, constituted the main attraction. But nobody could have been blasé about the pristine beauty of Port Dickson as it was then. A palm-fringed crescent of shimmering white sand sloped gently into water so clear, it was transparent. This was Paradise!

Having admired the setting, we removed our shoes and waded blissfully in the shallows, trapping and instantly releasing specimens of the abundant marine life that darted around our feet.

A few of the lads had a swim, well away from the convent party so as not to expose their bare torsos to the gaze of young women. Naturally, none of us attempted to defy the ban on swimming. But we didn't feel deprived and there was no resentment. Instead we were grateful at being allowed to spend several hours in the open air on those white sands alongside our heroes.

After a lunch of doorstop sandwiches, chunks of tinned fruit cake, apples (the first we'd seen in years) and slabs of chocolate, we settled down in a shady spot on the soft yielding sand to talk and sing all our favourite songs, including our whole Irish repertoire, with Fathers Malone and Hickey contributing a few items of their own.

For an impressionable fourteen-year-old, the perfect setting and attractive company were a heady combination. When Father Malone gathered his flock around him and sang "Garden Where the Praties Grow" my heart missed a beat and my knees trembled as I slumped near him, thinking, 'He is singing this just for me …' I chose to ignore the fact that several other girls were basking in the warmth of his smile and that St Vincent, St Norbert and St Matthew were also part of the happy group. As far as I was concerned, the challenging opening lines, 'Have you ever been in love, me boys? Or ever felt the thrill?' were directed solely at me. I felt deliriously happy and immensely sad at the same time, because (of course) our love was doomed. Priests might fall in love but marriage was out of the question. Like Romeo and Juliet, Father Malone and I were star-crossed lovers!

It was a very pensive Maisie Prout who rode back in the truck that evening and when she was invited to sing, she gave such an intense rendition of "Danny Boy" that a few of her fellow travellers were moved to tears. St Vincent grasped my hand. 'That was very touching, child, you've never sung it better,' she said. Father Hickey clapped loudly and asked for more, but Father Malone glanced at me quizzically and remained silent.

A few days after that eventful picnic our chaplains called again, but this time they brought unwelcome news. They had received their marching orders and were to leave for Java very soon. Their peaceful two-month interlude in Seremban had come to an end.

On this occasion, Father Malone showed me no special attention and I began to wonder if Cupid's arrow had merely glanced off him while embedding itself in my heart. But I still wanted him to know how I felt about him. How could I possibly manage this? When they visited, we were never left alone with them. Writing was out of the question; all incoming and outgoing mail was censored. So I decided to hand him a 'Thank You and Farewell' card when he came with Father Hickey to say goodbye. For some time I had been making my own Christmas and birthday cards, so I thought it would be possible to offer him one of my specials without attracting undue attention.

On the cover, I'd drawn a typical Malay kampung scene — a chequerboard of lush green paddy fields bordered by graceful coconut and banana palms framing a few attap huts — one of my better efforts, I thought.

The note inside read: *Goodbye and Thank You ever so much for all your kindness. I will never forget you! Affectionately, Maisie.* I could not afford to be more explicit, in case the card fell into the wrong hands.

I remember the morning the pair arrived to say 'adieu' to their devoted followers. I was at a piano lesson with St Anselme and after they'd seen the others, they came past the music room before departing. In a flash I was outside, proffering my humble offering.

'Oh,' said Father Malone, surprised. 'I didn't know you were an artist.' I was trembling all over as I struggled for self-control, aware that I was making a spectacle of myself. St Anselme watched me, puzzled and irritated. 'What on earth ails you, child?' she demanded. A deep blush now engulfed my neck and face, proclaiming to all who were present (as I thought) my guilty secret.

'I'm — I'm … very upset that Father Malone and Father Hickey have to leave Seremban,' I managed to blurt out.

Father Hickey attempted to calm things down. 'We'll miss all our friends here very much. We'll write to you, I promise.'

St Anselme led the way back to the music room. 'They're with the Army. They have to go where they're sent,' she said in a matter-of-fact tone. Very likely she added 'Good riddance' under her breath. As a confidante of St James she would have been aware that these young chaplains were regarded as an unsettling influence on the boarders and a threat to normal discipline. My odd behaviour on that day doubtless confirmed that opinion.

Before that pair of 'meddlesome' priests departed, they made Olga a present of a small portable stove complete with fuel tablets and several cans of tinned food. The Allied Forces that liberated us also introduced us to some of the results of several years of scientific discovery and invention spurred on by the needs of a vast war-machine. One example was synthetic rubber, created as a substitute for the unobtainable natural product usually supplied by Southeast Asia. The miniature stove that Olga received was part of a commando kit designed for a mobile fighting force whose equipment had to be light and compact for ease of movement.

A small circle of patrons was on hand for the midnight opening of Olga's secret kitchen — her wardrobe in the dormitory. The fuel tablet was ignited, the open soup can boiled over; a disaster was narrowly averted. This was an inauspicious start to her cooking venture, but all the participants had a lot of fun. She described the incident to Father Hickey in a letter posted by an obliging day-girl. From 'Somewhere in Java' he wrote back to say that Father Malone and himself had been greatly amused by the tale of our antics. He pointed out that the inventors of the stove had created it for battle-weary troops hiding in hostile terrain, not for a bunch of mischievous girls planning a midnight feast. He urged her to select a safer spot for her next cooking session.

A week later another letter came through the official channels. It was addressed to 'All our friends at the convent', and told us that fighting had broken out in Java because the local people were resisting the return of the Dutch colonials. Father Hickey remarked how peaceful Malaya had been by comparison. Their tour of duty was coming to an end and they looked forward to going home to Eire. Father Malone had not written a single line to me or anyone else. A joint signature on a Christmas card was his sole concession to written contact. He may have been warning me not to expect any replies if I were foolish enough to write to him. To all intents and purposes, that was the end of the story.

About the same time as our friends made their exit, school reopened. It was a catch-up period for all students attempting to cram nearly four years of missed lessons into three months. Everybody had an intense desire to acquire knowledge at a fast and furious pace in order to fill up that vast educational gap, so that in a year, or two, or three, we would hold in our hands that most prized possession — the Cambridge Certificate.

But we were not simply cramming our heads with facts and figures. There was a need to catch up on world events, on general knowledge, on a host of matters which had been and were currently changing post-war society.

The British Army's education unit staged a series of photographic exhibitions, documentary film shows and lectures so that schoolchildren and the general public could catch a glimpse of some of the things they'd missed during their years of seclusion behind the bamboo curtain.

A nearby school hosted a major photo exhibition that featured the war in Europe. The entrance hall was devoted to the war in Britain: people huddled in air-raid shelters, Dunkirk survivors, bombed-out areas of London and pictures of the D-Day landing, the whole collection presided over by a large portrait of Churchill, solid and reassuring.

In an alcove separated from the war zone was an arrangement of Royal Family portraits. For some years we'd not seen any pictures of the Royals, so we were pleasantly surprised to note that the little princesses had grown into lovely young women. Down the passage we went from one classroom to the next, following the progress of the Allied troops from the Normandy beaches to the ruins of Berlin.

And then, without warning, we entered a chamber of horrors. A floor-to-ceiling collage of concentration camp photographs with grim, one-line captions: 'Hitler's Jewish Solution', 'Victims of the Holocaust', 'X Concentration Camp'. For the first time we learned of some of the major atrocities of the European war. Names like Belsen, Dachau and Auschwitz entered our consciousness. This photographic confrontation was a mind-blowing experience. 'I don't believe what I am seeing' — that was my first reaction. I dared myself to look a second time, then a third, to confirm that those emaciated, tortured figures were, or had been, real live people. I asked myself the question that has pre-occupied me ever since — how could a loving God have allowed this to happen?

Nobody mentioned the chamber of horrors that evening. Too difficult. Easier to dwell on the happy faces of the liberated throngs dancing in the streets and offering flowers and kisses to the victorious Allied troops.

As the year drew to its end, Olga and I told each other that if Dad were still alive, we'd hear from him by Christmas. A trickle of family letters from Europe was reaching the nuns, so there was much celebration amongst them.

In my nightly chats with the Almighty, there was a growing hint of desperation. I'd get out of bed when I thought everyone was asleep and stay on my knees for long periods, begging, 'Give us a sign, Lord. If he's alive, let word come soon — but if he's dead, don't keep us in ignorance — either way, let us know by Christmas!'

Early in December, a card with a Batavia postmark was handed to us and we read with great excitement that Aunty May and our cousins were all alive and well. Uncle Willem had just rejoined his family after spending the war years in India. We had now heard from John, the Coules family and the Pijpes. Only a letter from Dad remained outstanding.

Meantime, preparations for Christmas were getting under way. There was much to rejoice over — peace in the world, happy reunions for many families (Olga and I tried not to envy the lucky ones), an end to food shortages. Red Cross parcels were distributed and everyone received a dress-length in good quality fabric which the sewing-mistress made up for us with the help of the best seamstresses amongst the orphans. Except for minor variations, all the dresses ended up looking very similar: softly gathered blouses and waists, rounded or pointed collars, puff or mutton-chop sleeves. The styles didn't really matter, we were thrilled to own a new frock and when we teamed them up with hats and shoes (also courtesy of the Red Cross) we felt very stylish indeed.

ENSA (a British entertainment unit) put on a concert for the general public and the boarders were allowed to attend. Red Cross ladies who visited us occasionally acted as our chaperones for the event. The best thing about the evening's entertainment was our introduction to the music of Glenn Miller and the songs of Vera Lynn. For some of us "We'll Meet Again" became a must-learn theme song. When our chaperones dropped us off at the convent gates, they handed each one of us a pot of gold — actually, a large, golden can of barley-sugar which we lost no time in burying in the depths of our wardrobes; individual treasure we could dip into whenever the urge arose.

So Christmas 1945 came and went, but still the longed-for letter did not arrive. After wallowing in a short bout of self-pity, I set a new deadline for God, begging that He might see fit to grant my plea in time for my birthday in late January.

We were barely into the second week of school when St Anselme's angular form appeared in the doorway of our classroom one morning. 'Excuse me — Reverend Mother would like to see Maisie Prout.' She smiled as I joined her and we collected Olga from her room down the corridor. For a talkative woman St Anselme was unusually quiet, merely saying, 'Reverend Mother must give you the news herself.' My heart beat wildly. *Could it be ...?*

St James stood outside her office smiling broadly and waving a letter.

'My children, your prayers have been answered.' She placed the precious document in Olga's outstretched hands. 'Read, my dear — read.' We glanced at the small neat writing on the closely-written sheets and inspected the signature at the end of the letter. It was from Dad all right, no question!

It is doubtful that we took in all the contents at the first reading. It was enough for us to know that he was alive, and back in Malaya. There was something about him escaping after the surrender of Singapore in a small boat. We were silent, attempting to take it all in.

'What a lucky escape he had!' St Anselme broke in. 'Reverend Mother always maintained he would manage to get away.'

St James placed an arm around each of us and slowly steered us in the direction of the chapel. 'Now, *mes enfants*, go inside and thank God for your father's safe return.'

Looking back, it seems incredible that Dad did not ring the Seremban convent immediately on hearing from the Singapore nuns that we were upcountry. But the age of instant communication was decades down the track. We had all been conditioned to the painfully slow process of contacting one another almost always by letter.

Our replies were in the post the next day and Dad's next letter contained something that made us jump for joy: two railway tickets to Singapore. Pacific Tin, Dad's mining company, was despatching him south to pick up some new dredging equipment, and he had decided the occasion was right for our reunion.

17

REUNION IN SINGAPORE

We took our seats in a comfortable, brightly-lit carriage — very different to the dark, smelly, overcrowded compartment of our last train journey.

Facing us were two British officers, a snooty English major and an amiable Anglo-Indian captain. The latter remarked as we sat down, 'Something tells me this is a happy occasion for you girls. A family reunion?'

'How did you guess?' we responded and lost no time telling him all the details. The captain seemed genuinely interested in our story. Perhaps he regarded our company as a welcome distraction during what might have otherwise proved a long, boring journey.

The major, on the other hand, might have preferred quieter fellow travellers. He rarely joined in the chatter, preferring to bury his head in a book most of the time.

Meanwhile I was enjoying myself hugely, keen to impress my captive audience with my conversational skills and *savoir faire*. I recall with embarrassment that at one point I was regaling them with *Readers' Digest* jokes, in particular the one that went, 'Report card on the American presence in the UK/OZ: The Yanks are over-paid, over-sexed and over here!' I wasn't certain what 'over-sexed' meant, but I thought it sounded like an adult joke and I was showing off.

The captain roared in appreciation, but the Major muttered something about most convent girls being quiet and demure. Maybe that's exactly how I used to be, but this was such an exciting occasion and I was all hyped-up. A couple of times Olga looked sideways at me, as if to ask herself whether this was the same silent shadow who usually allowed Big Sister to do all the talking.

The friendly captain gave us frequent time calls. 'Three hours to go — two hours — less than an hour — By the way, will your father recognise you when you meet? It's been a long time, hasn't it?'

'Oh, that's all right, we sent him a recent photo.'

Eventually the train pulled into Singapore station. Craning our necks out of the window we glimpsed a trim figure on the platform, standing somewhat apart from the crowds, pipe clamped firmly between his teeth, monocle in place, surveying the new arrivals.

'Daddy!' we yelled as we leapt out of the carriage and tore down the platform towards him. Hugs and kisses all round, then we stood back a little to take a closer look. 'Where's your luggage?' Dad asked. At this point, our obliging captain appeared and deposited two suitcases at our feet. Dad thanked him for his help and the captain made some complimentary remarks about his lovely travelling companions and wished us all a wonderful reunion.

To Olga, Dad remarked, 'You're the spitting image of your mother.' Turning to me, he hesitated, sucked on his pipe and pronounced, 'Don't know who you take after, dreamy Daniel — perhaps you remind me of my sister Lily.' We walked towards the carpark.

'Shall I call a taxi?' offered Olga, poised for action.

'No, no — see that Jeep? I have the use of it, so hop in!' Dad replied. 'We're going to the Van Vliets — Flora and Dick are longing to see you both.' To us they were 'Aunty Flora' and 'Uncle Dick', old family friends. Dad told us they still had their boarding-house at Tanglin.

What a thrill! Our first jeep ride — totally exhilarating. We steered our way carefully through the tide of humanity in the city: people on foot, on bicycles, in pedicabs, in old-model cars — the civilian traffic. Khaki-coloured traffic was also very much in evidence. Scores of jeeps whizzed around carrying army brass hither and thither and whenever and wherever they appeared, they seemed to attract smiles and even cheers. The local community in general still regarded the returning Allied forces as popular heroes.

On our way to the Van Vliets, as on subsequent forays into the town, we were aware of a furious rebuilding spree. The battle-scarred city was rising from the ashes and it was wonderful to be part of the hustle and bustle of a new dawn. Perhaps my own emotional state at the time coloured my surroundings. Yet I am mindful of other, more mundane visits to the Lion City, when I arrived jaded and depressed, and departed feeling rejuvenated. If I were more knowledgeable about these matters, I would make out a case for Singapore's good *feng shui*.

Leaving the city area behind we reached the leafy Tanglin district. As Dad turned into the wide avenue of majestic rainforest trees where the Van Vliets lived, he remarked in a low voice, with just a hint of bitterness, 'I lost everything I owned, but they didn't lose a thing, not even a teaspoon!'

After the British surrender, several large houses had been taken over by the Japanese, especially if the owners had fled the island. The Van Vliets had chosen to stay and in their case it was the right decision. Dick, being Dutch, was interned, but Flora was allowed to remain *in situ* with all her goods and chattels intact and continued to run their boarding-house with her usual flair, ably assisted by her efficient and loyal Chinese staff. Where previously she had catered for European civil servants and professional people, her clientele during the Occupation consisted of high-ranking Japanese officers. When the Japanese in turn surrendered, Europeans re-occupied the spacious rooms and partook of the culinary feasts prepared by her expert Hainanese cooks. Just like a game of musical chairs!

Dad parked his jeep in the pillared portico and as we alighted, an attractive, well-dressed woman in her forties called out our names and embraced us warmly, exclaiming at how we'd grown. 'Come and say hello to Uncle Dick,' she said. As a small child, I'd given Uncle Dick a wide berth because he looked so big and tough beside my small, neat father. In addition, Uncle Dick possessed a pockmarked face and bulbous nose, items not usually associated with a handsome appearance. As I approached him that evening, a cruel but funny comment made about him by Mum and Aunty May surfaced out of the dim past — 'Flora didn't marry him for his good looks, did she?'

Somehow this big bear of a man didn't terrify me any longer. He gave us both a big hug, a bear's hug, then said, 'I hope you're hungry, because the cook's been told to put on an extra special feast for our extra special guests.'

We didn't need any urging to do justice to the meal. But later on we realised we had eaten not wisely but too well; our stomachs were not accustomed to such rich fare.

Before we parted for the night, Dad spoke of his escape from Singapore.

Days after the surrender, the Japanese were still coming to terms with the enormity of the task ahead of them. Their advance down the peninsula had been speedier than their most optimistic estimates, so when Singapore fell, they were still formulating plans for how to run the city. Faced with an administrative nightmare, they were obliged to ask British officials in key posts to carry on as usual.

There weren't enough prisons to hold all the potential prisoners, civilian as well as military, so several large empty buildings served as temporary places of confinement. Dad was held in custody with a number of men in a big old house near the Sea View Hotel in Katong, familiar territory for him. Security was lax; it did not require commando-level fitness for his gang to smash a window, climb out and sprint down to the beach undetected. Before long they met up with hundreds of other panic-driven citizens attempting, lemming-like, to put to sea in virtually anything that would float — sampans, junks, yachts, launches. Not all the craft were seaworthy, and experienced sailors were in short supply.

The last of the passenger ships had sailed just before 'The Fall', so there was no vessel large enough to take all the intending evacuees. It was left to the individual to coax, beg or buy a passage on any of the craft about to weigh anchor. The skipper of a certain yacht was offering a free berth to anyone who possessed the expertise and experience to plot a reliable course to Sumatra, where most of the rag-tag fleet was heading. Dad snapped up the offer and got the boat with its thirty or so passengers safely to its destination.

En route they were nearly rammed by a small fishing vessel with a dark-skinned, sarong-clad, songkok-wearing crew. Malays? Or Japanese marines disguised as Malay seamen? The yacht was unable to outrun the smaller craft because of its full complement of passengers who waited in fear, expecting the worst.

To their immense relief, no sooner had the pursuing boat come alongside than one of the crew doffed his *songkok* to reveal a mop of ginger curls.

'Scared you, eh?' the 'fisherman' laughed. 'We're Gordon Bennett's party and we're making a run for it to Australia — got some very important business to attend to over there. Good luck, all of you!' Three pairs of hands waved in farewell and faded into the gloom.

At this point in his story, Dad paused and voiced his opinion of the General's fateful action. 'He should have stayed with his men — no question of it. He ought not to have run away.'

Out of the thousands who put to sea immediately before and after the surrender, only a small percentage survived. The Japanese Navy lay in wait all along the coastal waters, determined not to allow the British the consolation of a second Dunkirk. Luck played as big a role in survival as good seamanship.

Sumatra was still in Dutch hands when Dad's party landed and the Dutch did their utmost to help the escapees to reach safe havens. Two passenger ships had just left their main wharf for Colombo and Perth respectively. The vessels were radioed back to pick up the new arrivals. Neither ship could take all thirty of them, so half embarked for Colombo and the rest of them for Perth.

A torpedo hit the Colombo-bound vessel just after it cleared the harbour; it is believed there were no survivors. The Perth-bound ship reached Western Australia safely with its human cargo alive, but in very poor shape physically and mentally. Dad spoke of being a nervous wreck for more than a year and of being nursed back to health by Aunty Bobs, who was very relieved to see him again.

We were up early next day. It was the 26th January 1946, my fifteenth birthday. As if on cue, it was also the day I became a young woman. The event took me completely by surprise; for us convent girls the whole area of human reproduction was shrouded in mystery — 'secret women's business'. When I consulted Olga, my oracle, at the first evidence of bleeding, she replied somewhat solemnly, 'You're grown up now — you are capable of having a baby.' It was all very confusing.

'You should have warned me!' I said, slightly resentful at being kept ignorant of the most obvious and basic signpost on the path to womanhood.

'Nobody warned me either,' she countered. 'It came to me out of the blue.'

From Olga's expression, I could not tell whether my dramatic surprise was something to mourn or to celebrate. Aunty Flora was in no doubt at all that it was a joyful occasion. 'We'll drink a toast to you tonight, young lady, and wish you many happy returns for your birthday.' And then she placed a gift-wrapped parcel in my hands. 'You'll have a lot of fun with that,' she said. Indeed I did. The parcel contained a Pond's make-up kit, my first ever. Getting dressed that morning took ever so long. I applied the rouge and lipstick quite liberally, looking at my face in the mirror and thinking, 'I'm not a child any more. Today I look at least twenty — hurray!'

Dad dropped us off at our Singapore convent on his way to the wharves. Less than two years before, we'd stood outside the same gates feeling anxious and fearful about what lay in store for us on our return to Seremban. But that day it seemed as if the whole world smiled on us.

Outside on the streets and inside the walled convent alike, the mood was buoyant with an expectation of good things to come. We were received with open arms by all our 'fellow inmates' and caught up with many old friends. To our disappointment, St Madeleine had left for Europe a few weeks earlier on the *Devonshire*. Far from robust, after subsisting on a diet of little else but papaya during the final weeks of the war, she was put in charge of a group of nuns even frailer than herself who were going home for an extended period of recuperation.

The Infirmary nun, Sister Françoise, gave me a very special welcome. During my early years as a boarder, I had spent a great number of days in her domain. There had been the usual childhood diseases such as measles, mumps and chicken-pox, as well as several other undiagnosed problems — high fevers, extreme lassitude and recurring gastric complaints — through which she had nursed me successfully. Now she was thrilled to see a healthy, well-fed young adult in place of the thin, sickly-looking child she had known before. She kept on stroking and pinching my plump arms and cheeks. '*Mon Dieu*,' she exclaimed, 'look at her now — she used to be a *cicak kering*!' (dried-up skink).

No Singapore boarder who'd ever been ill was likely to forget Sister Françoise. She defended her territory fiercely against incursions from malingerers, but if she was convinced that the patient was genuinely ill, she turned into a ministering angel. Some of the nuns used to jokingly refer to the process as 'earning one's passport to the Infirmary'.

Somebody we hadn't expected to see was very much in evidence on that occasion; none other than Betty Pun, youngest daughter of the Chinese mining magnate from Kuala Lumpur. Her behaviour had always been courteous and modest, but on this occasion it was her attire that drew our attention. Betty was wearing nun's robes; she had become a novice in the Infant Jesus Order, and we wished her happiness and fulfilment in her vocation.

Both Olga and I knew we would not be going down the same path. In her chosen Order, Betty would be able to maintain a close contact with her family. 'Any time you're in Kuala Lumpur, call and see my family,' she suggested in her usual hospitable way, 'They'll be happy to see you.' We promised we would.

Sometime in the afternoon, Dad fetched us and we enjoyed cream cakes and buttered scones before going on to Sime Road to meet John. Dad had already visited John before our arrival, and he was able to tell us that father and son were now identical in size.

Many things must have been going through Dad's mind that evening as we drove towards the POW camp to attend a concert given by all the remaining internees. He had left three young children behind in 1942; now, on his return, he was confronted with three young adults — three young strangers, perhaps. Olga and I were excited about meeting John again. Would we recognise him? As a precaution we'd exchanged photos, but in the event we'd have known him anyway. There were changes, of course. He was taller, thinner and spoke with a deep voice. John looked surprisingly fit when we met him that evening and we told him so.

'You should have seen me a few months ago, just skin and bone!' he told us. He said that many of the internees might not have survived without the frequent assistance of local Chinese farmers, who used to drop food packages over the barbed-wire fences when the guards weren't looking.

He informed us that the Coules family, with whom he'd been interned, had left for Britain a few weeks earlier. It would be some time before we met them again.

The concert was about to begin, so we took our seats fully prepared to applaud anything and everything these prison survivors cared to perform. Naturally our loudest claps and cheers were directed towards those items in which John appeared. After the show, we were introduced to the camp commandant, Major Lether, who happened to be a woman. John was now working for her in the camp office, where his maths ability and neat handwriting were highly valued. Later, after the camp closed down for good, a glowing testimonial he received from his boss secured him a clerical position with Whiteaway Laidlaw, a large department store in the city.

When we presented ourselves for dinner that evening at the Van Vliets' boarding-house, a certain Mr Jenner, a rubber planter who was returning from England to Johor, made up a foursome at our table. He joined us after downing several Tigers and as a consequence he was in a merry, expansive mood. He lost no time in telling Dad how much Olga and I reminded him of his own two daughters, who were still in England. Olga and I thought he was pleasant company and we were quite happy to chat, but Dad had other ideas. No sooner had we finished our soup than a suddenly stern, authoritarian father stood up and said, 'Come, girls, I think we'll make it an early night.' Despite our obvious reluctance, he led the way out of the dining room to an upstairs lounge, remarking crossly, 'I can't stand men who aren't able to hold their drink!' Olga and I exchanged rueful glances. We hadn't been at all put out by Mr Jenner's well-lubricated conversation — we minded far more being deprived of an excellent meal!

The Van Vliets had noticed our dramatic exit and joined us later to enquire if anything had upset us. Dad didn't want to talk about it, but I blurted out, 'Mr Jenner was a bit tipsy, so Dad thought we should leave.'

'Oh, what a shame!' Aunty Flora said, 'I'll get cook to send up some dessert.' It arrived with a bottle of chilled champagne and everyone drank a birthday toast to me. After the Van Vliets had withdrawn, Olga and I were ready for bed, but Dad had another surprise for us.

'Don't go yet,' he said, 'I have something important to tell you.' We half-expected him to say, 'When we're all sorted out in Kuala Lumpur, I'll ask you to join us there.' What he actually said was: 'You have another sister — a half-sister. Her name is Patricia and she's two years old now.' From his wallet he pulled out a couple of small photos of Patricia and Aunty Bobs, then from his suitcase he produced a large colour portrait of the new Prout daughter.

We saw a bonny child with huge blue eyes, a mop of auburn curls and a wide-awake look about her. 'Isn't she beautiful?' Dad said proudly. 'Everybody who sees her thinks so.' The tone of his voice, the look in his eyes, clearly indicated that this newcomer was the centre of his universe. Which meant the older Prout offsprings were even further on the outside than before. Despite his affectionate letters and obvious pleasure at seeing us again, our status as 'virtual orphans' was confirmed; we effectively possessed no home outside the convent.

At some point, Dad noticed our discomfort. There were unshed tears in our eyes. 'Don't cry. You'll love Patricia the moment you meet her, everyone does.' We didn't doubt it either. Who could resist such a gorgeous child? Our tears were for lost dreams and abandoned hopes. He attempted to console us. 'Cheer up, girls, everything will work out, you'll see.'

The gloss had faded from the wonderful reunion but somehow we comforted ourselves and resolved to make the most of the rest of our holiday.

Singapore was still an exciting place to be. There were people to see, things to do. As much as anything, we enjoyed living outside a large institution. We appreciated the privacy of a room for just us two, a room with bedside tables, reading lamps, scatter-rugs and a dressing table — a huge improvement on a dormitory with sixty or so identical beds, primary and high-school pupils and trainee-teachers all sharing the sleeping space together.

Before our return to the convent, the Van Vliets invited a few friends over for a musical evening. We stood around the piano while Aunty Flora played and sang several of our old favourites, reviving memories of the Brooke Road days. Flora liked keeping up with the times as well, so we attempted some of the popular Vera Lynn and Glen Miller numbers too.

Dad remarked that I sang like my mother and suggested I keep on practising; I had a list of new songs to teach my boarder friends and a pile of uncensored magazines to share when I got back to Seremban.

Surprisingly, while all our correspondence was monitored, our bags were never checked after a holiday 'Outside'.

I bade a tearful farewell to the Van Vliets. Aunty Flora whispered in my ear, 'Don't cry, my sweet, I'll have you over for Christmas!'

On the way to the station, I told Dad about Aunty Flora's offer. 'Don't depend on it,' he said. 'That woman counts her pennies very carefully.' He put us on the train and promised to visit us whenever he had a free weekend. 'After all, Kuala Lumpur isn't far from Seremban, is it?' We agreed but tentatively remarked that we'd like to stay with him, if that was possible. He didn't answer at once. As usual, he was smoking a pipe and a few puffs and smoke-rings later, he replied quietly and reasonably: 'Life on the outside isn't all that it's cracked up to be. You are fortunate to have St James looking after you. That woman loves you — yes, really! You are the children she never had.'

During the long, dreary return journey to Seremban we pondered the opinions he had given of two very different women. We felt he was wrong about Aunty Flora but that he might be right in the case of St James.

Disconsolately, we stared straight ahead for most of the trip, resigned to the likelihood of remaining, for several years to come, 'on the Inside looking Out'.

18

LOVE AND MARRIAGE, CONVENT-STYLE

'Prison — convent — all same!' the Seremban Military Governor had declared on one occasion, when he decided that the Prout sisters were adequately confined and did not need to be interned in Changi or the Sime Road POW camp. He was of course exaggerating — just slightly!

However, for those 'Inside', conditions were now improving somewhat. Little puffs, if not gales, of fresh air were insinuating their way into dusty corners of convent life. The religious community welcomed new sisters into its circle, the full black habits gave way to a black and white combination, which in turn was later replaced by a full white outfit at long last, a suitable colour for the tropics. The teaching staff, contrary to pre-war practice, took in a number of non-convent educated, non-Catholic, expatriate women; the wives or daughters of planters, miners or government officials. Their inclusion had the effect of broadening the hitherto narrow convent educational focus and providing students with wider social horizons.

One of the new brigade was Mrs Eunice Scott, a geography specialist and a first-rate teacher. Her commonsense approach to work carried over into religion, politics and all other spheres of life. In time, she earned the trust and affection of St James, despite her diametrically different cultural and religious background — being a Protestant from Northern Ireland.

Passenger shipping lines and sometimes troopships were again delivering cargoes of fresh-faced recruits from temperate climes to Far Eastern outposts, to fill gaps in government departments, private enterprise and missionary fields.

In the Parish house, too, it was time for a changing of the guard. Enter Father Laurent, young, idealistic, modern in outlook; exit Father Auguin, ageing, traditional and conservative.

New boarders joined our ranks, including, surprisingly, three young members of Malay royalty. The three Malay princesses became boarders while a new palace was being built for them, and it was hoped that placing them in an English-speaking environment would enable them to become fluent in the language. Their weekends were spent at home but during the week they followed the same routine as the boarders except for chapel attendance, when they retreated to the dormitory to roll out their prayer mats facing Mecca for their own form of worship. We other boarders were warned not to disturb them; if our infidel shadows crossed their prayer mats they would have to begin their devotions all over again.

That a Catholic institution could have been considered a suitable place for Muslim royals reflects very favourably on the liberal and progressive views of the princesses' parents. Is also indicates the high level of acceptance of the Infant Jesus convents in the local communities.

The term-time ban on weekend absences was slightly relaxed for the other boarders as well, and several families enjoyed the option of spending more time together. The Prout sisters would have jumped at the chance of a weekend in Kuala Lumpur but the offer never came, though Dad did show up in Seremban once or twice to take us out for lunch and a chat.

While outings were less restricted, all correspondence was subjected to the same intense scrutiny as before. Towards the end of 1946, a letter from Aunt Flora caused a bit of a stir and I was called upon to explain a number of things. Why had Mrs Van Vliet addressed the letter to me, rather than Olga, my older sister, I was asked. In her letter, Aunty Flora had asked for the words of "*Parlez Moi d'Amour*" — 'Because she knows I'm the one who collects songs,' I explained.

Obviously, Aunt Flora hadn't anticipated Reverend Mother St James reading her letter. At the time, she was spending a week or two in hospital recovering from a minor operation. Her surgeon happened to be young and handsome. In an idle moment, she wrote to me asking for the words of the French love song because, as she jokingly put it: *Next time Professor Ransome, who is so handsome, visits me, I'll sing him "Parlez Moi d'Amour"*!

I regarded this as a piece of lighthearted fun but that is not how St

James saw it. Respectable married women did not behave in such a flirtatious and frivolous manner! Clearly, Mrs Van Vliet was not setting a good example for young impressionable girls. Chastened, I withdrew from the office and later replied to Aunty Flora's letter saying that I didn't know the song she requested and wished her a speedy recovery.

In spite of my unhelpful response, she wrote again early in December. This time directly to St James, saying she wished to invite Olga and me to spend Christmas with her husband and herself. She enclosed two first-class railway tickets to Singapore. We were summoned to the Reverend Mother' s office, where we were shown the invitation and the tickets. St James must have noticed the joyful anticipation in our faces. She moved quickly to quell our rising excitement. Picking up the tickets, she returned them to the envelope saying firmly, 'I'm sending these back, *mes enfants*. I'm sorry, but I don't believe Mrs Van Vliet would make a suitable chaperone for you.'

'And where have you young ladies been, all dolled up like that? You look quite dangerous in your war paint! If I were Reverend Mother, you wouldn't be allowed outside the gates!' In his friendly, teasing manner, Father Moran, a Jesuit priest, joked with us boarders when he visited the convent once a year for the nuns' annual Retreat; a period of lectures, prayer, meditation and strict silence.

During Retreat, the nuns did not speak to us at all, unless an emergency arose. It was an occasion when the lay teachers became our minders. Rules were relaxed somewhat and the living became easier. Wearing make-up and going to a daytime movie were permissible. How else could we have taken in films like *Gone With The Wind*? (At the time, it was on the banned list for Catholics). We thoroughly enjoyed it, maybe more so because it was forbidden fruit.

Father Moran would quiz us lightheartedly regarding boyfriends and possible engagement or marriage plans, but for the orphans, the question of marriage was very different. It was unlikely we would be prepared to accept any strange young man who had walked into the convent off the street in search of a wife. Yet where the orphans were concerned, if the suitor was single, employed and a Catholic, he stood a very good chance of success. Both the orphan who presented herself for the interview and her suitor had the right of refusal and both could ask to see somebody else, so the system allowed for a small element of choice. Chinese were matched with Chinese, Indians with Indians. Mixed unions between these two races were very rare. There were never any Malay orphans.

If the young pair liked the look of each other after their short chaperoned meeting, they would meet again to discuss wedding plans and the intending groom would bring his lady a few small gifts and give her some money to get her hair permed. Our closed community didn't need to wait for the banns to be called on Sunday to know that another orphan had found her Mr Right. Her tightly permed hair (first time ever) would shout the news to one and all and Father Auguin's sing-song, Mandarin-inflected way of publishing the wedding banns always caused considerable amusement among the boarders in the front pews. The time-span from first meeting to wedding ceremony was usually no more than a couple of months or less. This was the way the system had operated for decades.

Father Laurent, the Parish priest who succeeded Father Auguin, was horrified at the cavalier manner in which these young girls from a totally segregated environment were handed over to virtual strangers for a lifelong relationship without adequate preparation. He told some of the older boarders that newly-wed orphans had been known to run away from their new homes to the parish house. In great distress, they would complain about the sinful things their husbands were doing to them. The priest then had the unenviable task of explaining to these frightened and bewildered young women the meaning of the phrase 'conjugal rights'.

Father Laurent was determined to change things. He could not, of course, guarantee that all future weddings would be successful, but he was adamant about providing essential facts and information so that during his stewardship, any failures that occurred would not be attributed to ignorance. He must have put his arguments very forcibly to St James, because she allowed him to offer marriage guidance instruction and basic sex-education to engaged orphans, and to give lectures on the subject to the whole Senior School.

In 1946-47, this was pioneering work. Given the conservative social environment and a rigid Catholic culture only just emerging from the shroud of the Middle Ages, Father Laurent was a courageous man — a trail-blazer!

Attendance at his after-school lectures was not compulsory, but they were packed with attentive students eager to learn about the birds and the bees from an authoritative source instead of depending on rumour and innuendo.

There were, however, problems beyond the scope of this intrepid crusader. Such a case presented itself in 1946 when a twenty-year-old Chinese girl was placed in the convent by her parents, who objected to her intending marriage to an Indian gentleman, a senior teacher at the school she attended. This enforced separation was to last six months, until Kim Neo turned twenty-one. During this period, Mr Veerapen, her suitor, was denied visiting rights, and was reduced to glimpsing her once a week when she walked past him in the church-bound convent crocodile. From his vantage point on a pavement under a shop-awning, they would smile and wave to each other. This brief sighting proved sufficient to keep alive the flame of their devotion. There were no phone conversations, but perhaps a couple of *billets doux* found their way into Kim Neo's hands and kept her smiling and cheerful despite her predicament. The boarders were surprised that she showed no bitterness or resentment towards her parents. In every way, she was a model daughter — except that she was not about to break off her engagement to please them.

This Romeo and Juliet story had a happy ending. The wedding took place two days after Kim Neo was released from 'confinement', and in 1996, they celebrated their golden wedding anniversary together with their children and grandchildren.

By way of contrast, another local marriage lasted barely an hour. My art teacher and her soldier husband had exchanged their vows in Church and driven to the reception hall not far away. As they mounted the steps of the building, a burly military policeman stepped forward, tapped the groom on the shoulder and announced, ' I am arresting you on a charge of bigamy.' Shades of *Jane Eyre*! Even small communities have their dramas.

19

PENANG IDYLL

The travel-hungry sisters were sometimes permitted to accept holiday offers despite the failure of Aunty Flora's bid. Those that came from close relatives usually succeeded and occasionally people outside the family were allowed to play host if they passed St James' character test.

In August 1946, Olga and I were on our way to Penang for our first visit since our departure as infants. Uncle Peter was assuming responsibility for us during our stay. Aunties Belle, Martha and Therese shared the Vaz home with him on Kelawei Road, not far from the old family home.

The journey took several hours but the time passed quickly enough: unlike the countryside between Seremban and Singapore, this was all new territory for us. Around eight in the evening, Prai station hove into view and we gathered up our bags. A face on the platform stared up at the carriage windows, a face we'd seen in many photos, now older and greyer but still recognisable. Uncle Peter came forward to meet us, Olga in her navy-blue overcoat and me in a light fawn one, both well-equipped for the 'chilly' Malayan night.

'When last I saw you, you were that high!' he exclaimed, gesturing with his hands. Then he turned to a lithe young man at his side, whom he introduced as Welby Foley. 'I brought him along for the ride and because he volunteered to help with your luggage,' Uncle Peter said.

What an obliging young man, I thought. We shook hands. We smiled. I felt instantly at ease with him. He was about my own age, I guessed, and good-looking too. How nice!

How long did the ferry take to reach Penang that evening? I've no idea because Welby and I found we had so much to say to each other. We were on a voyage of discovery. Actually my companion already knew a fair bit about the Prout sisters. All the way across to Prai our gossipy uncle had been filling him in on our background history — our life in

Singapore, Mum's death, our convent upbringing — it seemed as though he had concentrated on that.

Was I thinking of becoming a nun? Welby was anxious to know.

'Oh, no — definitely not!' I responded. He looked relieved.

'You'll meet my mother and two of my brothers at your uncle's house,' he told me. 'We're boarding there at the moment. You won't meet my father — he died of malnutrition and disease after being imprisoned by the Japs.'

Why was he taken prisoner, I wanted to ask. And how did he die? And when? But I decided to wait. Perhaps later we would talk about that obviously painful subject. Not tonight. The air was balmy, we were young and carefree, the lights of Georgetown were winking at us just beyond the jetty, and it was time to disembark.

Two trishaws deposited us at the door. 'See you tomorrow,' said Welby, placing our suitcases in the hall and mounting the staircase to his room.

'Nice boy,' said Uncle Peter, looking after the departing figure. 'I can see you like him. They are all fine boys, all five of them. Such a shame, losing their father so young … '

'Peter, Peter, the girls must be hungry — you can tell your stories tomorrow!' Aunties Belle and Therese came to greet us with hugs and kisses and sat us down to a light supper. As we tucked in, we were aware of them watching us intently, hungrily. Very likely our visit provided a high point in their uneventful lives. Over the years, no letters, photos or phone calls had passed between us; suddenly the babies they had nursed had materialised into a pair of young women sitting before them. 'Are the nuns good to you?' they wanted to know, 'Are you planning to join the Order when you finish school?'

That question again! Everyone we met sooner or later asked it. We always replied that we had no intention of living behind convent walls permanently.

We had a question to put to them. Where was Aunty Martha? Wasn't she living with them? Belle and Therese smiled knowingly, then Therese disappeared into a back room. We could hear her urging Martha to come out and come soon, because Olga and Maisie were tired and wanted to go to bed. 'Martha takes ages to get dressed,' Belle explained. 'She's been getting ready all day for your arrival. Just tell her how wonderful she looks!'

At that moment, Martha made a dramatic appearance. She certainly was eye-catching! Her outfit would not have been out of place in an Edwardian drawing-room. Poor Martha! Opportunities for dressing up were few and far between since the tragic day she'd been widowed. But it was her face rather than her clothes that caught our attention. Where make-up was concerned, Martha subscribed to the notion that more was better than less, and much, much more was much, much better. Her eyes peered through a thick white mask. It was hard to tell whether she was smiling or frowning.

'You look lovely, Aunty Martha,' we remembered to say.

A guitar was being lightly strummed as I dropped off to sleep that night. Welby? Was he serenading me? I listened for a while then drifted off into a calm, restful slumber.

We met Mrs Foley and her boys in the hall next morning. She greeted us warmly, saying she'd heard a lot about us. Uncle Peter had been telling her that Olga had obtained a Grade I Senior Cambridge Pass, and was now a trainee-teacher while I was doing well in Standard VIII. 'You're in the same year as my Welby, perhaps he could benefit from a little coaching,' she said, turning to me.

'We can start today,' I offered, happy at the prospect of officially sanctioned time with her son. There was no reluctance on Welby's part to become my student. During my stay, we covered some poetry, play-reading and maths together, but it was a bit of a charade. We just wanted time together, even chaperoned time — for Aunty Belle was always hovering in the background, silent, unobtrusive, smiling. Perhaps she was going back in time to the Arratoon Road garden when she so often had to keep an eye on Mum and her suitors.

Our lessons gave way to song-sessions. I learnt "Lilli Marlene" and "Don't Fence Me In" (which I taught the boarders on my return). The latter became our theme song. Naturally, Welby's repertoire expanded in the exchange. I had known only organ and piano accompaniments, but now I adapted quickly and happily to his skilful guitar backing and harmonising. He possessed a pleasant, light baritone voice. With all the practising we did in the daytime, we felt game enough to perform at night. Our performances were not drawing-room concerts but open-air affairs, with a low stone wall at the gate providing seating.

Lots of Vaz cousins came visiting. Polly Vaz rode over on her bicycle to meet us. Somewhat older than Olga, she was working in an office and about to become engaged to a young widower, Richard Cornelius. She rode her bike so confidently and fearlessly that I thought it must be easy and asked Welby to teach me. He didn't hesitate about offering his machine or his time, but I was a slow learner. I may have shone in the classroom, but out on the road, astride his precious bicycle, I was a complete dunce! The only way I could keep my balance was by pedalling furiously and recklessly, but then I couldn't stop without catapulting myself over the handlebars, or falling sideways on the gravelled road. After several tumbles that resulted in grazed knees and elbows, bruised arms and legs, I gave up the idea of cycling lest I crack my skull in the attempt and wreck Welby's bicycle into the bargain.

On my last bike trial, when, as usual, I'd come to grief and was picking myself up and dusting myself down, an army jeep drove past carrying my cousin George Vaz and his boss, Lieutenant Goodbody, and they stopped to rescue rider and machine. At this time, George was riding high as official interpreter for the Military Police in Penang. Like my other Vaz cousins, he could speak all the main languages of the colony, Chinese, Tamil and Malay, so his services were sought after whenever there was a communication breakdown between the British servicemen and the locals. For the benefit of his cousins, he organised a couple of lavish Chinese dinners at city hotels to which he invited all and sundry. Who paid the piper? Not Georgie! Supposedly, the hotel managers were happy to lay on the banquets as a gesture of goodwill towards the military authorities.

He certainly impressed us with his ability to make things happen. Would we like to go dancing? No problem! A large party of us was soon twirling around the dance floor of the downtown cabaret one night. Dennis, the dance partner of my infant years, was playing in the band. He took time out to partner his cousins round the floor — a much changed Dennis whose forlorn figure moved mechanically to the music.

He had been trapped for some years in an unhappy marriage to a Malay wife nearly twenty years older than himself, from which he couldn't, or dared not escape. 'My poor Dennis' — Aunty Belle always prefaced any reference to her son with that telling phrase. 'My poor Dennis would like to give you girls a little treat. Perhaps an ice-cream at the nearest coffee shop?' Wining and dining his cousins was out of the question, alas.

By way of contrast, we had a visit from a happy and successful relative. Matty was one of Polly's older sisters. Nursing was her profession. She excelled at it — healing and comforting came naturally to her. She radiated good cheer, good humour and confidence in hospital ward and at home alike. Even my lethargic aunts would bustle around offering coffee and biscuits and tell innocuous little jokes when Sister Sunshine was around.

Yet Matty had her share of heartache. Her soldier husband of only two years, Bill Thomas, had been taken to Japan as a prisoner of war and died there in a US bombing raid. She felt his loss keenly but that didn't stop her living life to the full.

Our holiday in Penang was coming to an end. We couldn't leave without visiting two of Penang's main attractions, Batu Ferenghi Beach and Penang Hill. We left early one morning for the beach that took its name from the strange, slightly sinister rock sculptures that provide a dramatic backdrop for that stretch of coastline. Welby and I raced across the sands and splashed in the shallows, frolicking like carefree children, wringing every ounce of enjoyment out of the moment. Having a boyfriend was such fun! My companion was so attentive and gentle that I took a perverse delight in teasing him, knowing he wouldn't retaliate. Olga was not excluded from all the fun and games. She too could claim an admirer in Arnold, Welby's cousin, who joined our special trips.

Where was the Aussie larrikin I had declared that I would marry on that long-ago day when the Australian soldiers had marched past the convent? There was no sign of him on the horizon. Perhaps there never would be.

Penang Hill was the last of our excursions. In those days it was a source of wonder and delight to island visitors wanting to explore a pocket of the Malayan jungle within easy reach of Georgetown. As mountains go, 3,000 feet is a mere anthill, but when you've grown up on the plains, even 500 feet represents high land. The larger hill-stations on the mainland boasted tea plantations, fruit, vegetable and flower farms, schools, replica English villages with pubs as well as extensive golfing greens. Penang Hill was relatively untouched at this time, because access to the summit was not by road but by a funicular railway. Sadly, in the last thirty-odd years, development has caught up with this lovely hill-station; for us old-timers, its modern face is tasteless and unattractive.

We took our places in the narrow, wooden carriages with angled floors matched to the steep gradient. Passengers gripped the protective rails in front of the benches while the thick steel cable hauled its load uphill through the rock cutting. As one train-load went up another came sliding down, trailing its umbilical cord to ground level. The open sides of the carriages allowed an unimpeded view of the forested mountain slopes. The air became noticeably cooler and sweeter. From rocky clefts, jets of clear cool water sprayed rainbow-hued droplets over the surrounding vegetation. Tree ferns waved green parasols above clumps of wild orchids nodding purple bonnets. Birds sang, monkeys shrieked; at the halfway mark, members of the furry-brown tribe invaded the station platform, demanding alms with menacing gestures.

Then we were at the top! Our party had spoken very little during the ascent. Too much to look at along the way. Now we stretched arms and legs and took in great gulps of the heady mountain air. Feeling exhilarated and euphoric, I remarked to nobody in particular, 'I feel marvellous!' It must have been a touch of mountain madness.

From a number of vantage points we spied familiar landmarks down below, our lofty eyrie providing magnificent views. But Welby and I were no longer interested in the landscape, no matter how spectacular. The tension between us had been rising, keeping pace with the altitude. There were things we had to say to each other — three little words in particular. We needed a secluded spot to make that declaration. Several little paths led off the winding road at the summit. Our chaperones, Richard and Polly, advised us all to keep together and not to go off on our own. Welby and I exchanged glances. We stayed with the gang for a while, but managed to outwalk them and reach a clump of dense vegetation dominated by a massive angsana tree. Its canopy provided a circle of deep shade tapering off into a vertical screen of leaves.

Penetrating the green barrier, we reached the solid brown trunk at the centre. We paused, embraced. Our lips met; time stopped. The earth spun as I clung to my companion for support. He was trembling. What was he saying? Something about my shiny brown hair. Almost timidly he ran his fingers through my shoulder-length tresses. In the gloom, his eyes looked so large and soft. Nestling my head in the crook of his shoulder I said, 'Your heart is pounding.' He nodded, then in my ear he whispered those precious, ritual words, repeating them more loudly as we looked directly at each other. My own declaration, 'I love you,' chimed with his. We both felt a surge of joy followed by a huge sigh of relief, as if we had shed a heavy emotional burden or finally confessed to a guilty secret.

'We can't stay here much longer, you know.' Welby's voice was tinged with regret. I didn't want to leave either. Not straight away, but I liked the idea of my boyfriend behaving in a mature and responsible way, taking charge of things.

'Yes, what a shame! This is a lovely spot. Our secret spot, our special tree.'

We emerged from under the sacred umbrella and returned to the others and to the real world with a jolt.

'Where on earth have you been?' Olga's voice was shrill with anxiety.

'It's all right, don't fret.' I decided there was no point in hiding anything. She had only to glance at our radiant faces. 'We kissed, that's all!'

'That's all!' she exploded. 'I should hope so.'

'It's all right, really.' I attempted to calm her down. 'Remember, I attended Father Laurent's lectures too. I know about the birds and the bees.'

As elder statesman of the group, Richard felt he had a part to play. He looked at Welby and indicated a bench some yards away. 'Better come and have a chat with me.'

In the train going down, Welby told me he'd been advised to be very careful and not rush headlong into things. We were so young, still at school and all the rest of it. Excellent advice, and we adhered to it, more or less. Kisses, however, were still on the menu, cartloads of them. Good morning, good afternoon, goodnight kisses. And, inevitably, goodbye kisses. But none of them possessed the incandescent magic of that first kiss.

We almost missed the train ferry to Prai on the morning of our departure. From dawn, the rain that keeps this island so lush, came down with a vengeance. Not a single cruising pedicab or taxi came down our street, so Welby and Arnold were dispatched to find and deliver the required transport. They had no luck, so they delivered us to the pier astride their bicycles, gallantly handing us their raincoats. They made the crossing with us and delivered us onto the south-bound train complete with luggage. Shades of Sir Walter Raleigh!

During the long journey back to Seremban, Olga took the opportunity to lecture me on appropriate behaviour in public places. On the ferry to Prai station, Welby and I had displayed a lamentable lack of restraint. Holding hands would have been acceptable, she told me, but kissing and cuddling weren't. We had been completely oblivious to everything but the trauma of our impending separation. Olga and Arnold had been very dignified in their leave taking. Nor was Olga alone in her disapproval. She had watched with growing concern the angry glances and threatening looks of a Haji across the aisle from us — a Muslim who had made the pilgrimage to Mecca and wore a distinctive type of headgear. A subsequent event would prove to us all that it was decidedly unwise to ignore the religious and cultural sensibilities of the Malay population.

Poor Olga! It must have been tough playing mentor when she was only three years older than me. For so long, she herself had played the rebel and now her little sister was kicking over the traces and she had to turn guardian.

School had not resumed yet but a few boarders, including Tessie and Lyn, were back already, so it was a good opportunity to tell Tessie all about my Penang holiday and in the telling, to relive the thrill of my first romantic encounter. St Vincent was also taken into my confidence and she proved surprisingly broadminded about the whole affair.

Soon after our return, we dutifully wrote our thank-you letters to Uncle Peter and the Aunts. In his reply, Uncle Peter gave us lots of detailed news of the Foley family. Mary Foley, Welby's mother, had remarried and was now Mrs Augustin. Her new husband was the manager of Merah rubber estate, on the mainland in Kedah, and the family had moved into a spacious new home there. There was an item of special interest to me. Welby was about to join the army the following year. After doing his training in Johor, he would be stationed in Singapore. Uncle's letter concluded with a glowing account of his short stay on the estate and he wrote that Mary Augustin had asked him to convey an invitation to the Prout sisters to spend some time with the Foley/Augustin family on our next visit north.

I found the news about Welby somewhat unsettling. His father had been a schoolteacher and I had pictured him following suit. But it wasn't so much the prospect of a soldiering career that gave rise to my vague misgivings. It had more to do with the altered venue in which we might next meet. Our time together in the enchanted island had been so perfect that I dreaded any change in our circumstances.

Welby, I convinced myself, belonged in the quiet, tree-lined streets of suburban Penang, with the Esplanade, the beaches and Penang Hill within easy reach. A suitable alternative would have been the gardens and open green spaces of their new residence on the rubber estate. The noisy Singapore streets and crowded sitting-room of Aunty Joan's house were not a promising environment. No, in my opinion, Welby and Singapore were not a good match! Meantime I was busy telling my close friends all about my first boyfriend. They were suitably impressed. Naturally I swore them all to secrecy, unaware of the absurdity of demanding their silence while I was unable to keep my own mouth shut!

One of the girls so honoured was a new arrival at the school. Louise was one of those people who appeared to have everything — good looks, brains, a loving family and a comfortable home. She knew exactly what she wanted out of life and if self-confidence and motivation had anything to do with it, you felt sure she would achieve all her ambitions. We were often together, for our tastes in reading, films and music were similar. Academically I held my own in class but I was very conscious that my short, plump figure compared very unfavourably with her tall, slender one. Perhaps in speaking of Welby I was hoping to make her sit up and take notice of me by claiming something she didn't as yet possess — or so I assumed.

Louise listened without comment or interruption, her face betraying no surprise. At the end of my recital, she commented that there was nothing extraordinary about having a boyfriend — she'd had one for ages! She and Aubrey had been unofficially engaged from the time she was fourteen. He was presently in the United Kingdom completing his legal studies and when he got back, they'd get married. Beside my small photo of the boyish-looking Welby, she placed a large studio portrait of a man in a tweed suit who looked to be about thirty. My turn to be surprised, even amazed. Not only did Louise have a boyfriend, but someone as mature as Aubrey. (Was he too old?). She responded to my unspoken thought by stating firmly that she wasn't interested in silly young boys! I'm not certain if she actually said 'silly', but the implication was certainly there.

In the sphere of one-upmanship it was a case of game, set and match to Louise.

20

A QUESTION OF LOYALTIES

The next five or six years produced varied holiday plans for the Prout sisters. We became practised train travellers, moving up and down the peninsula and even travelling overnight occasionally. August and Penang, up north, usually went hand-in-hand; December and Singapore, down south, were another vacation pair; while April was spent at Seremban, but we were not restricted to the convent grounds as previously. Local friends such as Kim Neo (now Mrs Veerapen), the Lawrences, Louise's family and others had us over for meals and outings, and our geography teacher, Mrs Scott, often invited us to spend a few days with her family. When her husband was transferred to Kuala Lumpur and later to Johor Bahru, she continued to welcome us at her home.

I surmised that our newly acquired ability to travel freely and frequently was based on Olga's growing reputation for level-headedness and complete reliability. I guessed they weren't so sure about me, but believed Big Sister could cope with any problems.

From the time Olga faced her first group of real pupils she gave herself fully to the task, knowing she had found her niche in life. In no time, the rebel schoolgirl had become Miss Prout, a mature adult and a pillar of the boarding community.

With her first pay packet, Olga offered to start paying boarding fees for both of us, but St James suggested that she should pay for herself, and that I should do likewise when I started work. Olga and I had assumed — incorrectly, as we were to discover — that Dad had resumed paying our boarding fees once he was re-established in his mining job at Pacific Tin. When Olga told St James that she would like to pay the fees, she did it as a gesture of independence; she had no inkling that Dad had been extremely remiss in his financial obligations and St James never disclosed the true state of affairs to us. It took my form mistress to reveal the unpalatable facts in my final school year.

One of the set plays for the year was Macbeth and the whole class was advised to see the film. After the others had filed out of the classroom, I asked St Jude if I might go as well.

'Have you got the money for the ticket?' she enquired.

'No,' I replied, 'but couldn't it go on the bill for my father to pay later?'

My innocent query drew an explosive response. 'Your father has not been paying any bills or fees for ages — you act like a princess when you're really a pauper!'

This thunderbolt stunned me for a while, then I burst into tears, and mumbled incoherently that I had no idea as I slouched away, humiliated beyond belief.

As luck would have it, St Anselme came across me in this sorry state and of course wanted to know the reason for my tears. She gave me a brief hug, then said, 'Don't worry now, I'll speak to St James — everything will be all right.'

A few hours later I was in the familiar office behind our dormitory repeating the exchange for St James's benefit. She said, thinking aloud, 'I wonder how St Jude came across that piece of information. It has never been my policy to discuss the boarders' financial arrangements with anybody apart from my most trusted confidantes.' She paused, then added, 'I hope you are always polite and attentive in class.'

As if!

'Go now, my child, put it all behind you and study hard for the forthcoming exams.'

The following day, St Jude sought me out and apologised for her insulting remarks. We sobbed together, then shook hands. Emotional types, we convent members!

'Friends now, Maisie?'

'Yes, of course!' I readily agreed.

We both worked hard at avoiding clashes and the rest of the year went by smoothly.

The matter of waiving boarding fees was not uniquely beneficial to the Prouts. Beatrice Garcia's case comes to mind. Beatrice grew up in the orphanage, but St James allowed her to transfer to the boarders because she showed considerable academic ability. She went on to get a good Senior pass and justify the trust that had been placed in her. There may well have been one or two other non-fee paying boarders in our group. Why was I singled out for special mention? Possibly I lacked humility. *Mea culpa*!

And Cinderella did go to the cinema after all!

Considering our very limited budget, it's amazing how much travelling Olga and I managed to do. Naturally, our relatives did not charge for our holidays with them, so once we had the train fare and some pocket-money for essentials, we were set — have tickets will travel.

For a year or two after his return from Perth, Dad used to send us small sums of money for birthdays and Christmas. Then, sometime after Olga began her teaching career, the trickle petered out until one Christmas when not even a card or note came our way, St James took the unusual step of inviting Olga to call Pacific Tin in Kuala Lumpur and enquire if Dad was still working there.

The Manager took the call and was surprised to discover that Mr Prout had three children from his previous marriage who had never even been mentioned. He informed Olga that Dad had left Pacific Tin a few months previously to take up a position with the Central Electricity Board. He wished us luck in contacting Dad. Olga said he'd sounded very sympathetic and so we weren't surprised when the phone call was followed up a few days later by a very nice letter enclosing a cheque for $100, which the Manager offered us as a late Christmas present.

Of course Olga dashed off a thank-you note to our benefactor and another to Mr Prout, care of his new workplace, which brought a response.

Dad apologised for not writing earlier; he claimed he'd been too busy chasing up his new job, then packing and moving and getting settled into his new position and new house. From now on, he promised we'd see a lot more of him. Unlike the mining quarters, his new house was conveniently located at Bukit Nanas, on the outskirts of the city. The railway station, shops and schools were all within easy reach. He suggested that on our next trip north we might break our journey for the day at Kuala Lumpur and catch the night train to Penang. Aunty Bobs would be happy to have us spend the day and we'd get to know Patricia, our half-sister. He'd join us for high tea after work and drive us to the station in time for our train.

We gladly grasped the olive branch and agreed to meet him on his home territory, seeing as he no longer visited us in Seremban. A reluctant father, we felt, was better than no father.

There was just one thing about the daytime stopover. The early train from Seremban arrived in KL before seven a.m. and Aunty Bobs wasn't keen to see us quite so early. Could we possibly either wait at the station or fill in the time window-shopping in the town for an hour?

We had a better idea. Our good Chinese friends, the Puns, had invited us to call in whenever we happened to be in KL. The early hour was no bar to their hospitality. So it came about that on our initial try-out of the new timetable, we'd no sooner left the station platform than a sleek Jaguar pulled up and a young Chinese woman came towards us, smiling.

'Yvonne?' we said hesitatingly.

'Yes! You recognise me! I wasn't sure I'd recognise you — it's been about six years, hasn't it? Hop in! The syce will get your luggage.'

We didn't need urging. When we got to the family home the younger members were still in bed but Mrs Pun welcomed us warmly, not at all perturbed at receiving visitors so early. She didn't speak English, but she didn't need to — her message of goodwill was written all over her face. She produced the customary bowl of green tea for guests and then we shared a hearty breakfast with the rest of the family. Afterwards, where would we like to go, we were asked. The car was at our disposal. Our friends entertained us royally, and we were in no hurry to drive to Bukit Nanas. After taking us to a Chinese restaurant for a huge meal, they dropped us off at the Prout home, promising to repeat the performance whenever we were in KL.

The time spent with Aunty Bobs and Patricia passed pleasantly enough. We were invited to help with the tea-time cake-making and joined in enthusiastically. Pat was a friendly and talkative five-year-old who enjoyed the extra attention. Two of our step-siblings, Bobs' children from her first marriage, were attending school in Australia, and Barbara, the eldest, was living and working in KL not far from Dad's work premises, so he used to collect her from her office on his way home in the evening.

On our subsequent visits to Kuala Lumpur, we followed more or less the same routine, spending half the day with the Puns and the other half at the Prout home, chatting about clothes, movies and boyfriends and picking up a few cooking tips from Aunty Bobs, who was an adept pastry and sponge maker.

But on our third or fourth visit, things went horribly wrong and the *entente cordiale* with our stepmother was shattered by what started off as an ordinary tea-time conversation.

She was pouring tea as we tucked into freshly baked cream-puffs.

'Is St James still in charge of things?' she asked. The question seemed innocent enough.

'Yes, of course, she's still our Mother Superior.'

'I know her from my Penang convent days.' A note of suppressed rage crept into our stepmother's voice, then erupted into a full-blown tirade against the woman who had fed, clothed and housed us throughout the war and beyond. Dad sat in his armchair white-faced and mute, his tea at his elbow, his pipe cold in his lap, while Olga and I faced him from the couch, coiled and tense, expecting him to make some remark, no matter how mild or trivial, in defence of the Reverend Mother. The ranting and raving continued — 'narrow-minded', 'tyrannical', 'hypocritical' were just a few of the expressions we heard, while I attempted to remind myself that people are entitled to their own opinions. Glancing across at Olga, I noticed her lips drawn into a straight line — which of us would explode first? Then I heard the word 'pig'. That did it as far as I was concerned. Why that word? Perhaps because it was so inappropriate. In the estimation of some people, St James might have seemed aloof, autocratic, even harsh, but never gross, greedy or self-indulgent. NEVER!

I stood up and shouted the word back at Bobs. 'PIG! Are you calling St James a PIG? Maybe that's what you think of her, but Olga and I see her very differently. To us she is both saviour and protector. We have recently been made aware that we owe her everything, including our education.' I wanted to say more, but so much passion had gone into my declaration that I broke down into loud sobs and ran from the lounge into the kitchen.

Olga followed me. 'Don't cry, don't cry,' she comforted me, while tears ran down her own cheeks. 'Are you okay?' I nodded. 'You were right though, somebody had to stand up for St James,' she said.

'It should have been Dad,' we said in unison.

We regained our seats after a decent interval and avoided eye-contact with the enemy. Understandably, the atmosphere was decidedly cool. Dad dropped us off at the station as usual that evening, but he made no mention of the performance. Possibly, he was ashamed of his cowardly role in the drama, and so he should have been.

Back at the convent once more, we told St Anselme about the fracas at home. Perhaps we wouldn't be invited again, we surmised. However, we weren't barred from the Bukit Nanas house, though by mutual agreement, the Puns now hosted us for the whole day on our succeeding stopovers, only dropping us off after five p.m. in time for a cuppa with Dad and the family.

21

THREE QUESTS

Singapore vacations were usually very busy affairs, with movies, dances, visits to friends and relatives, and of course shopping. I spent most of my time visiting while Olga devoted more time to shopping. My purchases were usually carried out quickly, impulsively, often carelessly. Olga took her time, only making her final decision after inspecting the whole range of goods and comparing price and quality.

Occasionally, while strolling downtown, we'd bump into an old friend from pre-war days, usually a former schoolfriend who'd escaped from the doomed island with her family and had now returned to resume her education or seek employment in the bustling city. We'd spend a happy time together exchanging tales of survival and reunion.

One story that related to a returned former prisoner of the Japanese became headline news in 1950: the Maria Hertogh case. In the final desperate days before the fall of Singapore, a Dutch lady handed her young daughter, Maria, into the care of her Malay amah in the hope that the child would survive even if she herself died. But Mrs Hertogh didn't die; she outlived the privations of the prison camp and returned to Singapore in search of her daughter, now a girl in her early teens.

The child was finally located in good health, still in the care of the family amah. This should have been the occasion for great jubilation, but it wasn't. The foster-mother refused to hand the girl back to her natural mother. Mrs Hertogh immediately sought the assistance of the law to reclaim her daughter and the court decreed that Maria be handed back to her mother. The former amah refused to comply and organised a betrothal ceremony in which Maria became engaged to a young Muslim suitor. The case now went to the Supreme Court in Singapore, which decreed that Maria be taken from the Malay family and placed in the care of the Good Shepherd nuns pending the final judgement.

Placing Maria in a Catholic convent had the effect of raising the tension in an already volatile situation. What was initially seen as a Malay versus *orang puteh* (European) struggle now escalated into a racial and religious clash between Muslim and Christian values.

While this *cause célèbre* was being played out in the papers and on the radio, Olga and I arrived on the island for our December holiday. High on Olga's list of priorities was Christmas shopping. She required a number of items for her midnight mass outfit, chief among them a white hat. She happened to select the very day that the final judgement in the Maria Hertogh case was to be handed down. She caught the early bus into town and began a methodical and painstaking search for the required article.

It was early afternoon before she spied and purchased the right hat. Armed with her prize, she left Raffles Place and walked towards the North Bridge Road bus stop where she normally picked up the Katong bus. To her distress, all the buses swept by refusing to stop to pick up passengers, leaving scores of stranded travellers. A number of people in the bus queue hailed taxis and Olga did the same, feeling extremely uneasy about the whole situation.

From early morning, the Padang outside the Supreme Court had been taken over by a jostling, angry crowd of young hotheads whose emotions were further inflamed by a small group of reckless firebrands. When the verdict went in favour of Mrs Hertogh, a roar went up from the mob and chants of '*pukul, pukul!*' (attack, beat up!) filled the air. A member of a small army unit on standby outside the Court fired a warning shot over the heads of the crowd. That shot appeared to trigger a frenzied surge into the shopping-centre area. A few hours of looting, smashing and burning occurred and any fair-skinned person who happened to get in the way of the rioters was set upon, beaten up and in some instances, killed.

Olga's cab driver unwittingly chose the route through the worst trouble spot in the city, the area around Rochor Canal. The taxi slowed to a crawl because a roadblock had been set up and gangs of screaming, stick, stone and bottle-wielding youths were dragging passengers out of cars and attacking them, all the while yelling '*Pukul, pukul!*' Olga's blood ran cold and she began to panic as a group of thugs approached her cab. Just as they were about to wrench open the rear doors, a thin dark man leapt into the front passenger seat and shouted, in Malay, 'Move on! Keep moving — fast! Faster!'

After five minutes of maniacal driving, they were clear of the danger and the stranger in the front seat turned to Olga. 'I look like a Malay but I'm Eurasian,' he told her. 'Because of my dark skin, I've been able to help other people like yourself.'

My normally talkative sister was so overwhelmed at her lucky escape that she could barely find the words to thank her brave rescuer.

'You'll be all right now, I'm going back to help other victims,' he told her, and with a wave he was gone. He didn't even tell her his name. A dark-skinned angel.

A very shaken big sister pulled up at the Karikal Road house and the hair-raising events of the afternoon poured out of her. 'I wish I'd asked his name and address so that I could have thanked him properly,' she said over and over again.

By nightfall, an uneasy calm had fallen over the city but isolated, violent incidents still took place. Troops were sent in to mop up any problem areas and within a few days, law and order was restored and only those who'd been personally involved remembered the events of that December nightmare. Not surprisingly, Olga lost her taste for shopping for quite some time after that event.

'What were you thinking when you saw the mob closing in on you?' we asked her after she came home, curious to hear from someone who'd had a near-death experience.

'I thought that they were going to kill me,' she answered. 'Then I picked up the precious hat on the seat beside me and moaned, "Too bad, I'll never get to wear it!"' (But of course, she did).

'Really?' we were incredulous, 'Thinking of a hat at such a moment.'

'Really and truly,' she insisted.

Young people are resilient. The recent unsettling events in the colony did not prevent all the young cousins at Karikal Road, Katong, from attending the usual dances and parties. The Victoria Memorial Hall was packed for the New Year dinner-dance and Olga and I were among the merry crowd ushering in the new dawn.

Consequently, we didn't stir till late the next morning. It could have been nearly noon when cousin Myrtle shook me awake to announce that I had two visitors. 'One is the bloke you were dancing with last night. He says he'd like to take you to the pictures today. I've never seen the other one before, he says he's from Penang. He's called Wilbur, I think, Wilbur Foley.'

At the word 'Penang' I had leapt out of bed, and was flinging clothes hither and thither and in record time I was fully dressed and ready to meet my callers. But jeepers, creepers! Why did Welby have to pick today of all days? Descending the staircase, I glimpsed a room full of faces; my cousins and their friends as well as my two callers. I murmured an embarrassed greeting to both of them, then turned to Welby.

'I wasn't expecting you today!' I said somewhat lamely. No welcoming kiss or embrace. As I entered the room, he had come towards me smiling. Now he sat down hurt and puzzled. What a ticklish situation! At that point, the conversation turned to the Maria Hertogh riots and I was grateful for the diversion, which gave me a little time to sort things out in my head. Was there a polite way to ask last night's escort to buzz off? That's what I'd felt like doing, but I dithered. While Olga's dramatic presentation of her taxi ride through the mob held everyone's attention, my mind flashed back to the first time I'd seen Welby since our tearful farewells at Prai.

The setting was Kuala Lumpur railway station a few months earlier. We'd ended our Penang vacation and were returning south to Seremban. This was to be a quick change of trains with no time out in KL. Dad was coming to help us to our other platform and to have a brief chat. Our eyes scanned the platform for his slight figure, then Olga spotted him. Not Dad, Welby! A boyish, khaki-clad figure drooping listlessly against a pillar. He didn't notice us approaching. Just as we caught up with him, Dad caught up with us, saying, 'Come on, girls, better hurry, your train will be leaving soon.'

'Dad, this is, er, I'd like to introduce Welby Foley. We met last year in Penang.'

'Oh! Very pleased to meet you, young man — you're in the army, I see. Going home for a spell?' Dad was polite but not cordial. The time and setting were hardly conducive to a lengthy conversation. I managed to slip Welby Aunty Joan's address in Singapore before we were whisked off to find our seats in the Seremban train. Welby was heading north. What wretched timing!

And now he was sitting across the room from me with his back to the wall, looking strained and unhappy. The dear face that had become so familiar now appeared strange and alienated.

Olga's tale came to an end and no ingenious solution to my dilemma had entered my mind. So we went to the Roxy theatre together, the three of us. I have no idea what the film was about or who was in it. The movie was incidental. The main action was played out in the auditorium where we sat stiffly in our seats, the two young men gazing stonily ahead on either side of me, saying never a word to each other while I attempted to engage first one then the other in bright conversation.

We sprang to our feet willingly when the strains of "God Save the King" ended our misery. At that point, Welby declared he had to leave straight away as he was meeting some mates in the city. I don't recall us even shaking hands and he marched off without a backward glance. My other date walked me home and stayed on to sample one of Aunt Joan's tasty curries. I cannot remember his name but his presence at the time jeopardised any chance of a continuing link with Welby.

22

A PLANTER'S WIFE

Perhaps all was not lost. In August that year, Welby's mother, Mary Augustin, invited us to spend a few days on the Merah estate with her family. Strange! After that disastrous encounter in Singapore, I was surprised that mother and son still wanted to maintain the connection. Apparently Welby had written to say that he'd seen me and had spoken of me in a very complimentary way. It must have been written after the KL sighting and before the Singapore fiasco, I decided!

Olga and I were happy to experience life on a rubber estate. Even though rubber trees are as much a part of the Malayan landscape as the familiar eucalyptus in Australia, few people outside the industry get to view life from a plantation bungalow.

Robbie Augustin was an amiable and energetic person who ran his estate in a capable manner, making his rounds early in the morning, then getting to the office around eight to tackle his clerical work, ably assisted by his Indian and Chinese office staff. All sensible people completed their outdoor jobs before the sun was fully up. Only mad dogs and Englishmen …

While he ran the production side of the plantation, Mrs Augustin supervised a team of household servants drawn from the workers' quarters — gardener, cook, cleaning-woman and wash-amah, the last named being the most indispensable. In those pre-washing machine days, even families on modest incomes relied on the services of a *dhobi* or wash-amah. During unhurried afternoon teas on the verandah and somewhat formal and extensive dinners, Mary and Robbie Augustin talked about the ups and downs of a planter's life.

Their large, airy timber home was perched on a grassy knoll surrounded by lawns edged with brilliantly coloured clumps of cannas and multi-coloured hibiscus bushes. From the wide verandahs one looked through bougainvillea arches to the rubber plantation, where trees lined up row upon row like sentinels with cup-bearing waistbands of stripped bark, all the way down to the barbed-wire perimeter fence. Just inside the gates was a security post with its team of Special Constables, rostered to provide twenty-four hour surveillance. Wasn't the war over? Why the need for barbed-wire fences and armed guards?

As we sipped our tea we appeared to be part of an orderly and peaceful world, monarchs of all we surveyed, but nobody who read the papers or listened to the radio could have been ignorant of the escalating unrest in the country and of the particular vulnerability of rubber estates and tin mines. These national economic engines were enjoying a period of high demand and peak prices. That made them obvious targets for industrial sabotage. In 1947, the terrorists, ex-MPAJA members, launched over three hundred strikes on these important industries in an attempt to cripple the economy and put them in a position to dictate terms to the British Imperialists. When this strategy failed to halt production, the Communists followed up the strikes and demonstrations with more aggressive actions: arson and murder. Several of the worst atrocities were directed against hardworking, law-abiding Chinese citizens. To their fellow-countrymen, the terrorists were saying: 'Unless you help us with money, food or shelter, you will die.'

Planters and miners were high on the hit-list and they made easy targets, especially the former. While mining engineers lived in cluster-homes, six, eight or more to a compound, plantation managers tended to live in splendid isolation, their bungalows usually sited hundreds of yards from the coolie lines and workers' quarters, the main road beginning a mile or more further down where the unmetalled estate track joined it.

Structurally, the light and airy estate residences were difficult to defend, designed with a view to maximum ventilation and protection from nothing more sinister than sun and rain.

All through 1947, the planters kept agitating for protection. They also wanted a State of Emergency declared. Their requests fell on deaf ears until a spate of vicious murders in early June 1948 forced the High Commissioner, Sir Edward Gent, to reconsider the situation. On 18th June that year, he declared a State of Emergency over the whole of Malaya, but the terrorist campaign continued unabated. He was recalled to England that same year. When Sir Edward's plane reached Heathrow airport, it collided with another plane and he was killed. His successor Sir Henry Gurney also failed to bring an end to the Communist insurgency. He died in an ambush on Fraser's Hill in 1951. For both High Commissioners, directly or indirectly, their Malayan appointment turned into a fatal connection.

The war against terrorism lasted three times as long as the World War II Malayan campaign. Civil wars appear to drag on and on. When Olga and I visited the Augustines, some of the protective measures were already in place; the barbed-wire perimeters were topped with searchlights, armed guards were stationed there, hand guns had been issued to all planters and miners and armoured cars were in use for estate work and everyday trips.

As plantation managers enjoyed their sundowners on their breezy verandahs, their guns were within reach; they were well aware that at any moment their tranquillity could be shattered by a sudden raid on the property. The 1950s film *The Planter's Wife* portrayed life on a rubber estate during the Malayan Emergency. The danger factor was somewhat exaggerated in that ambushes, raids and sieges occurred almost daily — but nevertheless there were underlying truths in the film.

Mary Augustin took things in her stride. She didn't seem particularly fearful or nervous. When not involved in domestic matters, she devoted her time to her many hobbies: landscape painting, embroidery, floral art and an unusual but very practical skill for women in her situation — pistol-shooting. With her steady hand and keen eyesight she became a crack shot and wherever she went, her Baby Browning went with her, fitting snugly into her handbag.

The year 1949 was important for me, full of new beginnings. My schooldays had ended and I had to make a career choice. My exam results had been good, but not as good as I'd hoped. St James was highly gratified that I'd won the medal for French and obtained the highest marks in religious knowledge. Mrs Scott was delighted with my 'A' in geography, but I was disappointed because I'd come second, not first, in the class of '48. I had nobody but myself to blame. Boyfriends can affect one's concentration!

'There's more to life than studies and exams,' I told my image in the mirror, in an attempt at self-consolation.

St James called me to her office for a chat. She didn't waste time asking me if I wished to join the Order. I had made it abundantly clear that I wasn't cut out for the cloister. Teaching was the next best option. Office work and nursing were about the only other possibilities — not so many employment avenues were open to women.

'I expect you'd like to start the teaching course,' she began.

'But, Reverend Mother, I don't really want to teach.'

'You don't want to teach? Olga is so happy in the classroom.'

'But *ma mère*, Olga always wanted to be a teacher!'

'So, my dear, what do you want to do?'

'I'd like to become — an air hostess!' I had dared myself to say the words, knowing the reaction would not be favourable.

'*Mais, mon Dieu*! Where did you get that crazy idea? Have you ever been in a plane?'

'Yes, Dad took us up once for a joy ride over Singapore — before Mum died.'

Fleetingly my mind went back to that enthralling experience, remembering a father who'd enjoyed providing unexpected treats for his children. Now I tried to explain what I found attractive about air hostessing.

'Flying is so exciting — you can travel all around the world — you meet lots of interesting people — it's a glamourous life, such smart uniforms …' The longer I went on, the more hollow and superficial I sounded, even to myself.

Perceptive lady that she was, St James sensed it wasn't the job so much that appealed to me as the opportunity for immediate escape that it offered. She patted me on the shoulder, her voice tinged with regret and resignation.

'You young people, all you want is independence, *n'est pas*? When you are a qualified teacher, you will be able to live outside. You don't dislike teaching itself?'

I shook my head reluctantly. 'Not really. But it takes three long years to qualify.'

'The time will pass quicker than you think. Very little that is worthwhile in life is gained in a hurry.'

'Yes, Reverend Mother.'

'So you'll enroll for the Normal Course? And you will be a good teacher?'

'Yes, Reverend Mother, I'll try.' — Yes, I'd do this because I owe it to you for your devotion and generosity over the years.

Did I actually speak those words of gratitude? Unfortunately, no. But how I wish I had, and thrown in a couple of kisses for good measure.

Before leaving Merah Estate, I had written Welby a long letter in an attempt to mend bridges. The gist of it was: *If only you'd been here we could have worked things out. I've missed you!* I enclosed a recent portrait of myself in a wide-brimmed hat and asked for his photo in exchange.

A year later, I was again a guest of the Augustins. They were now living in a new domain, the Jabi Estate, and I was happy to spend a few days with them. It was a larger plantation, a bigger house, closer to the Siam border — and supposedly deeper into terrorist terrain.

During the long interval since I had last stayed with them, there had been no reply from Welby. Had I given him any special address? He knew he could not write directly to the convent. Perhaps he had not wanted to maintain the connection. Perhaps … he was going to surprise me and turn up during my stay. When I asked his mother about this possibility, she merely said her son would be coming later on in the year. I asked myself why she had invited me. If it was for Welby's sake then it seemed a little strange that such an efficient woman could not co-ordinate our comings and goings the second time around. On the face of it, it seemed more likely that she might have asked me over for her own sake — having five sons and no daughters, she relished the novelty of a young woman's company. One didn't ask Mrs A directly about her motives.

Olga had not accompanied me to Jabi Estate; she had decided to stay on with Aunty Frances and Uncle Bertie, who were hosting us during this holiday period. The Coules family had returned from England the previous year and Uncle Bertie was now running a 'White Ant' (termite extermination) agency from his office in Georgetown.

I settled into this new plantation kingdom quite happily, looking forward to several hours' undisturbed reading, letter-writing, sketching and listening to the radio — all day, if I wished, compared to one hour an evening in the staff study room of the convent. The time passed pleasantly enough for the first couple of days, then Mrs Augustin chose to liven things up by inviting a few neighbouring planters over for afternoon tea.

'You must be bored without company of your own age,' she said.

I assured her I was quite happy with my quiet pursuits. Besides, Gordon and Michael, her youngest sons, were always willing to join in a game of cards or stroll with me around the gardens. She insisted: 'There's a young planter who's only just arrived in the country — he knows nobody apart from the staff on his estate. He's in his mid-twenties, nice young fellow.'

I asked his name.

'Oh, Geoff — Geoff Beresford-Cooke.'

'Well, let's show him some Malayan hospitality.' I was never one to say 'no' to a party.

Around four p.m., our guests arrived. Mr Browning, sixtyish, and his assistant, Sandy Stewart, thirtyish, arrived together in Sandy's new red MG. Geoff Beresford-Cooke drove up a few minutes later in his secondhand Hudson. We were introduced. Mary told her guests I was a student-teacher and so they'd all better behave, or words to that effect. Geoff immediately commented that all the women teachers he'd known wore twin sets, tweed skirts and sensible shoes, so he was pleasantly surprised to meet a teacher in a light cotton frock and high-heels. The pair of us engaged in the cut-and-thrust of verbal fencing while mounds of sandwiches and scones disappeared and the afternoon turned into evening.

Having started in an educational vein, we spent a lively time discussing United Kingdom and local school systems. I caught a whiff of the old colonial attitude, of a superiority complex which rated him and the Old Country more highly than the local people and its institutions. As a product of the Malayan system, I wasn't likely to tamely accept that local was necessarily inferior and said so in a very forthright way. Actually, I found the argument very stimulating. At least we didn't have to fall back on the weather as a conversational topic. Needless to say, much of the talk among the oldies had been about the Emergency.

Our guests departed sometime after seven, giving us time for a pre-dinner drink. I told Mary I'd enjoyed myself. 'Yes, I could see that,' she replied. 'I believe you scored a few hits — Geoff seemed very impressed.'

I didn't tell her that I was attracted to this uppity young planter with the wavy blond hair and deep-blue eyes, and suspected that he was drawn to me too. We had made no plans to meet again; I was prepared to let fate take its course.

A bit of soul-searching that night. Should I write another letter to Welby and this time make certain he could reach me if he wished to? Yes! I thought that would be best. One more letter, *mañana*. But wait! One more question. Was he too young for me, 'a mere boy' as Louise had once labelled him? In the past year, I had become fixated on age. Who knows where I picked up the notion that men should ideally be about four years older than their wives, so that the couple would possess the same mental age?

No point asking Welby's mother what she thought. She took an arms-length approach to our situation. On my arrival she had, when asked, given me a recent photo of her son in uniform, stiffly posed beside a bowl of flowers on a stand. At the same time she offered me a small oil painting he'd done on his previous leave. I promised to take good care of both these offerings.

A phone call from Geoff next morning decided things for me. He rang to ask Mrs A if he could call and take me to a movie that evening.

'You'll have to ask Maisie herself,' said Mary, offering me the receiver.

'What's on?' I asked, trying not to appear too eager.

'Oh some film about a pirate captain, starring Errol Flynn and Maureen O'Hara. Interested?'

The soft Scottish burr was more noticeable over the phone. Idly, I wondered what my phone voice sounded like. 'You still there? Are you coming?'

'Yes, if it's okay with Mrs Augustin,' I answered, looking in her direction. She nodded, adding, 'Tell Geoffrey he can stay to dinner after the show.'

Had St James taken Geoff's call, she would have asked, 'What are your intentions regarding Maisie?' Unless he had stated unequivocally 'I wish to propose marriage', he would have been barred from calling again. A claim such as 'I wish to become better acquainted with her' — or worse, 'I'm not sure of my intentions' would have earned him a firm Permission Refused. But this was not a convent scenario!

Permission granted, I turned my thoughts towards the outing. And the letter I'd meant to write joined the graveyard of all good intentions. *Que sera, sera!*

Geoff turned up punctually and opened the passenger door of his car for me, warning me that I'd have to hop into the back when he picked up his special constable at the gate. If we'd expected great viewing from this swashbuckling saga of pirates and damsels in distress, we would have rated the evening a total failure. In a perverse way, we were highly entertained by the escapist nonsense, Geoff making caustic comments about the wildly improbable plot while I joined in this new game of film criticism — my erstwhile movie idol, Errol Flynn, acquiring feet of clay in the process.

Back at the estate, the special constable was dropped off at the entrance gates and I was invited to fill the space in front for the trip to the house. No sooner had I settled in than Geoff leaned across and kissed me. Then he drew back in mock surprise, exclaiming, 'What, no slap? That's what Maureen O'Hara did, remember?'

'Disappointed?' I countered, 'I can still oblige,' indicating a stiff palm at the ready. But he was unrepentant and I was not angry. 'Better check for lipstick,' I warned.

'How much longer are you here for?'

'A day or two at the most, then I'm heading back to Penang under my own steam. The Augustins are unable to take me back this time around.'

'Oh, really! Well, maybe I can help. Sandy and I were planning on driving to Penang for the weekend. We'd be happy to deliver you to your Aunt's doorstep.'

'That sounds wonderful! Ask the boss.'

Over dinner, Geoff broached the subject of my return and repeated the offer of a lift. As my temporary guardian, Mary was placed in a difficult position. She hesitated. 'Should I entrust Maisie to your care? It's quite a long trip, a few hours. You're not taking your special constable, are you?'

'Never fear, she'll be perfectly safe.' Geoff was well aware that Mary was not simply concerned with my physical well-being. There was the moral aspect as well. 'Sandy will make a good chaperone, he's very responsible! And if bandits show up, we'll blaze away at them!'

Mrs A was unimpressed by his show of bravado. She appeared to be giving the matter serious consideration. Would her son later on interpret her consent as encouragement of a rival? Perhaps the possibility crossed her mind. Meantime, we were waiting for an answer. 'Very well,' she said reluctantly. 'You will be extra careful, won't you?' Her glance included us both.

Geoff readily agreed, while I nodded and added, 'Thank you.' On the face of it I was merely accepting a lift back to the island instead of going by public transport, but we were all aware that a lot more was involved. I was leaving behind a family that had warmly welcomed me into its bosom and going away with an unknown quantity. One part of me mourned the loss of the familiar and reliable, while the other was agog with excitement about this new adventure.

Two days later the open road beckoned. We made one stop for afternoon tea and to pick up Sandy and then we were on our way again. None of my other dates were car owners; I enjoyed sitting up front with Geoff, the wind in my hair, the wheels chewing up the miles until it seemed no time at all before we reached the car-ferry at Butterworth and went across to Penang and Aunty Frances.

We got there around six, time for pre-dinner drinks. Uncle Bertie had changed from his working outfit to the sensible garb adopted by many Europeans when relaxing at home — sarong, singlet and slippers. He offered my escorts a choice of gin or whisky. They accepted the whisky but it didn't appear to loosen them up. They seemed ill at ease, spoke very little and declined a second drink. When I saw them off, Geoff muttered under his breath that he wasn't comfortable with 'white men gone native'. I just shrugged. 'I'll take you out tomorrow,' he said. 'You really will like this film — *Joan of Arc* with Ingrid Bergman.'

Aunty Frances was not overly impressed by my new boyfriend: 'Too snooty, not friendly at all,' she pronounced, while Uncle Bertie added, 'You still run into those puffed-up colonial types.'

A humble pedicab delivered Geoff to the door next day. He'd put his car in for a service. Without his Yank tank he didn't look quite as dashing. With less enthusiasm than I'd displayed the previous afternoon, I took my place beside Geoff and we pedalled off to the cinema. This time there was no chatting or dismissive remarks during the show. We were engrossed by the story and enthralled by the acting.

Afterwards we talked at length about the big questions raised by the film and discussed our own attitudes towards faith and non-belief, courage and cowardice, life and death. Geoff began to talk about his family, his father in particular. Almost as if he were talking to himself he spoke of growing up with his brother in a clergyman's household, and of being aware that his father wasn't entirely happy in his vocation. He was a doubter. He gave excellent sermons, but they often contained more questions than answers. Then one day the two boys were asked to search for their father; it was getting dark and he had not appeared for dinner. After a long search they found him in a laneway near the house with his wrists slashed.

'We found him — we found him all right,' Geoff muttered with a bitter edge to his voice, reliving a traumatic moment in his youth. Just talking about it with a sympathetic listener may have brought him a degree of comfort. This disclosure made me feel protective towards him. 'Don't judge him too harshly,' I remember telling my aunt when he delivered me back and declined her invitation to stay for dinner.

'*Banyak sombong* (very conceited), that planter, we're not good enough for him!' said Aunty Frances.

'He won't be offered any more of my good whisky!' declared Uncle Bertie.

Despite Geoff's low approval rating, I was not about to give him up. Naturally I would have liked Aunty Frances to approve of him, for I valued the opinion of this warm-hearted woman who had been a second mother to my brother John during the war years.

The Coules' home was an agreeable place, full of happy, energetic children presided over by big sister Lizzie, who seemed to possess some magical power over her five brothers. Without raising her voice, she had everyone behaving beautifully — most of the time! Lizzie's velvet control enabled her mother to concentrate on the latest baby. I was in awe of her child handling powers and wondered how I'd fare as a mother. Somehow I didn't think having lots of babies was my thing and I know lots of new mothers in our circle thought so too, because I was never offered an infant to nurse, whereas Olga was invariably called upon to hold the baby.

Matty had undergone a dramatic workplace change. Instead of being attached to the main hospital and living at the Nurses' Hostel, she now ran the Health Clinic at Bayan Lepas near the airport. Her territory comprised two matching bungalows, one the clinic, the other her residence. The houses stood on low pillars on either side of a gravelled track which eventually led across a big lawn edged with scarlet cannas to the road. It was a welcome change from her single room at the hostel. Better still, she was more or less her own boss.

Her home soon became a Mecca for visiting relatives and friends, especially for distant cousins who needed a place to stay. Olga and I occupied floor-space frequently and on many occasions Diana and Barbara Peterson rolled out their mattresses beside ours in the no-frills accommodation Matty so cheerfully provided. Barbara and Diana were the daughters of Angeline, Matty's elder sister. Their home city was Bangkok. About the same time that Matty became District Nurse of Bayan Lepas, she took delivery of a new blue Morris Minor, her pride and joy. She was probably the first member of the Vaz clan to own a car and she took to driving in a big way, never needing any urging to take Baby Morris out for a spin.

The Glugor barracks was not far from Bayan Lepas if you had wheels. As a war widow, Matty was always welcome at army functions. On one of her visits to Glugor Barracks, she met two pleasant young men, Frank and Ron, both school teachers in civvy street and she invited them over to meet her schoolteacher cousins from Seremban over lunch. Curry and spice and everything nice! History repeats itself.

Ron, the elder, was an amicable, brotherly figure who was my constant companion when we went out as a group. Friend and companion but not suitor. He made it clear from the outset that he had a girl at home. It's a pity that so many male expats were less than truthful about their marital status or intentions. Frank and Olga paired off straight away and appeared to be an ideal couple. No doubt they spent ninety per cent of their time together discussing teaching strategies! Well, maybe eighty-five per cent. Frank was a very personable young man and few young women could have found fault with him.

Normally, on our return to Seremban, we would have shared our experiences with St Vincent, recounting our latest exploits in great detail. However, St Vincent was no longer at Seremban. In 1948 she had been transferred to Kuala Lumpur before taking up her position as principal of the convent in Kajang, a branch school.

I was torn between sadness at losing such a dear friend and elation at her elevation to a higher rank in the Order. 'You see, the people at the top appreciate your worth,' I remember saying, 'unlike certain mean-spirited types who treat you with scorn and sarcasm.' I was referring, of course, to St Finbarr, who considered the younger nun far too soft and gentle in her handling of the boarders. I had on several occasions watched with dismay as the senior nun vented her displeasure on her meek subordinate. Now the tables were turned. 'Just think,' I gloated, 'whenever you bump into each other, St Finbarr will have to show you due respect!'

Far from appreciating my partisanship, St Vincent gently chided me. 'My dear child, I have long ago forgiven and forgotten all slights, real or imagined, that came from that or any other quarter and I beg you to do likewise in your life. Do not make a practice of harbouring bitter, hurtful thoughts, because eventually they will corrode your soul. Only cherish what is good, beautiful and joyful — nothing else is worth remembering.' Who could quarrel with a saint?

St Vincent had gone, but Tessie was around and always an avid listener to my discourses. To her I confided the tale of Olga's apparent discovery of Mr Right and of my own new romantic lead and the possibility that I might soon become a pistol-packing planter's wife.

The year 1949 ended on a high note with the return of Aunty May and the girls from the Netherlands. Uncle Willem had come back the previous year to take up a desk job with his old firm, KPM. Although his seafaring days were over, he was glad to be back in Singapore.

After a gap of eight years we looked forward to our reunion with the Pijpes with a great deal of excitement and a small measure of trepidation. Mary and Cora had been so much a part of our lives; we wondered how easily we would be able to bridge the long separation. Circumstances had altered greatly on both sides.

At first sight, we locals were struck by their European chic and felt somewhat shabby and parochial by comparison. However, any awkwardness passed very quickly because our ultra-smart cousins behaved in a natural, unaffected way avoiding any display of airs and graces. What's more, nobody hearing Aunty May's earthy chuckle could have felt anything but comfortable and at ease. In no time at all we were up to our old capers together — Mary and Olga out-shouting each other with comic anecdotes drawn from the abundant supply of family foibles while Cora and I, the less rowdy pair, joined in the mirth.

The Pijpes rented a large semi-detached bungalow in a newly developed area of Katong, not far from the Bruces. It boasted flush toilets and a phone next door to which they had access. Modern times were catching up with the suburbs. This Goodman Road home became our holiday base whenever we stayed in the Lion City. To John this was good news because it meant he didn't have to vacate his small upstairs room in the Bruce home every time his sisters hit the island.

Cousin Willy had remained in Holland to complete his education but his sisters had arrived ready to start work as bilingual stenographers equipped with Dutch and English qualifications.

Now that Uncle Willem spent most evenings at home, Olga and I were able to spend a lot of time in his company and we began to appreciate the sterling qualities of this soft-spoken, self-effacing man with his quiet sense of humour and his rock-solid devotion to his family. We grew very fond of our Dutch uncle.

No sooner was the last suitcase unpacked at the new abode and the upright piano installed in its alcove, than the welcome mat was unrolled and the serious business of open-house hospitality began, in the tradition of Grandpa Vaz's home in Penang. Both situations had one very significant similarity; there were daughters and nieces to be married off. Aunty May threw herself into matchmaking mode with considerable enthusiasm. Up the garden path at Goodman Road strolled seamen, young and not-so-young, Uncle Willem's connections. City types came as well, colleagues of our cousins. Weekend evenings were lively occasions with laughter, song and dancing. The tiled dining-room floor got a good workout from couples eager to try out the latest dance craze. Victor Sylvester's genteel music had given way to Glenn Miller's more upbeat sound and other post-war big band names.

Perhaps the most significant difference between the old scenario and the new was the status of the women being courted. The young ladies at Goodman Road had all received a good education, were currently employed and so could afford to be more choosey. They could indulge in the luxury of refusing suitors who didn't measure up to their expectations.

During these days, I got to know my aunt a lot better and through her, my long-dead mother. Frequently, I was alone all day with Aunty May while uncle and cousins were at work and Olga was out visiting — or, more likely, shopping. Usually I followed my aunt around the house, doing a little dusting, a little flower arranging, a bit of cooking. The heavy work was done by the amah. A lot of the time we sat and talked. Usually this actually meant that I listened while Aunty May talked, passing on to me chunks of family history, especially as it related to Mum and herself as young Penang girls in the 1920s and later on as married women in the Singapore of the 1930s.

Uncle Peter Vaz had tried to pass on to me anecdotes from the good old days, but I hadn't been interested. Aunty May was far more successful in engaging my attention, for she was a born storyteller. Her presentation was highly dramatic; she imitated voices, included gestures, interpreted feelings. I had not imagined family history could be so entertaining. Who needed movies?

About the war years she was far more reticent. The story of the Pijpes' getaway from the doomed island and their semi-imprisonment in Java (Indonesia) had to come from Mary and Cora. I was appalled to discover that Aunty May had nearly been beheaded because a certain bloody-minded guard at her prison compound believed she did not display sufficient respect whenever she bowed — meaning that she did not bow down low enough.

One fateful day, the soldier flew into a rage over Aunty's usual nod and, making her kneel before him, reached for his sword with serious intent.

A more humane officer, summoned by a frantic Mary, arrived at the scene just in time to stop the execution.

23

COLOUR BAR

The 1950s began on a bright note for the Prout sisters. Cards, letters and gifts arrived through the post from attentive beaux. Geoff sent affectionate greetings and a Parker pen that was supposed to help me write him numerous letters.

We took several vacations outside the convent walls that year. The Scotts had been transferred to the neighbouring state of Selangor, where Mr Scott now managed the newly established cocoa plantation at the Agricultural Station outside Kuala Lumpur. We spent a very pleasant long weekend during the Chinese New Year with them and appreciated being regarded as part of their extended family; two elder sisters for their two young daughters.

In Penang the two-year stint of the schoolteacher-soldiers was coming to an end and Matty's home provided a suitable venue and ample opportunity for Frank and Olga to discuss their situation. They seemed serious about making a future together, and in every aspect but one they seemed entirely compatible. The problem area was religion, not in general terms but in the specific region of mixed marriages between Catholic and non-Catholic partners. The Vatican decreed that the non-Catholic party had to promise all children of the union would be baptised and raised as Roman Catholics, and sign a document to that effect. No other species of Christian baptism and upbringing was acceptable.

The Vatican's authoritarian attitude was the sticking point for Frank. However, he did not rule out his eventual compliance in the marital pre-conditions. He asked to meet both Dad and St James on his way to Singapore in September, to catch the boat home, so that he could make himself known to both father and guardian — the Protestant and Catholic sides of the equation.

There was talk of his return to Malaya after he was demobbed from the British Army, to take up a teaching position in the colony. The air was thick with plans and good intentions between Olga and Frank.

Naturally, the holiday provided more than just a talk-fest. The traditional attractions of Penang remained undimmed by modern development; we were still able to enjoy the near-pristine beaches and re-visit the island's lovely green mountain. Penang Hill was virtually unchanged in appearance from my first visit. Predictably, however, the magic was missing. I have a vague recollection of wandering from one clump of forest to another, scrutinising every spreading giant in the crazy hope that one of them would whisper to me in jungle-talk: 'Psst! It's me, your special tree!' That other who wasn't present on this occasion should have had the foresight to bring along a penknife so that positive identification could have been made! Then what? Very likely I would have embraced the gnarled brown trunk to reassure myself that something tangible remained of my first romantic encounter. An early tree-hugger in action.

Towards the end of our holiday, Geoff arranged to drive over from the mainland and take me out to dinner. He mentioned an expensive open-air restaurant. That surprised me. Expensive dining-out was definitely not his style. Was he about to propose, I wondered. On his arrival he chatted amiably with Matty but with the others he was stiff and distant. With me he was always very natural and agreeable, but this time there was a certain *je ne sais quoi* that had not been present before. He's nervous, I thought. Big step for a man to put the question. Dinner over, we sat under the stars and exchanged a kiss or three.

'You know I'm in love with you,' Geoff murmured, 'but …' He started again. 'I'd marry you like a shot if — if you weren't Eurasian.' A big pause followed this pronouncement. Crushed, I waited for him to finish. 'If I follow my heart, my career will suffer. I nearly cancelled this outing because I asked myself if I should be seeing you at all, if I can't marry you …'

Can't or won't, I wondered.

'If we keep on spending time together things could get out of hand. I'm sure you realise what I'm saying,' he concluded.

I was too bruised for words, but I was thinking furiously too. The moral issue was always present with any man, but the racial issue had never been raised before, and this is what I focussed on.

A pertinent phrase came to mind: 'colour bar'. It was a phrase frequently used in both pre-war and post-war colonial Malaya, but easily disregarded if it was never applied to you personally. Now it had smacked me in the face. Colour bar really did exist; it was touching me in my intimate life.

Having taken the zing out of the evening, Geoff attempted to console me by offering a few crumbs of hope. 'I haven't made a final decision — I'm still weighing things up — there could still be a happy outcome for the two of us. Please don't stop writing to me. I keep all your letters in a special drawer and read them over and over — *oh, say something!*'

Thanks a million for nothing! my mind was yelling, but I remained mute, winded and wounded by his remarks. Soon afterwards he dropped me off at Matty's. He didn't linger. Frank was there. 'I don't like your planter,' he muttered. 'He's a real snob.'

'He's not *my* planter,' I was about to retort, but stopped myself. The fight had gone out of me.

Matty had noticed Geoff's quick getaway and overheard Frank's comment. She drew me aside. 'Anything upsetting you? Come on, you can tell me.' So I did. Everything that had taken place. Matty's response was indignant. 'If Geoff thinks his job should come before you, just drop him. Who the hell does he imagine he is, anyway? You're not twenty yet. Time's on your side. There'll be many more offers, far better ones, you'll see!'

Boarding the south-bound train with two escorts, Frank and Ron, was a new experience. Ron was travelling straight through to Singapore to join their ship bound for the United Kingdom, while Frank was to stop off at Kuala Lumpur to meet Dad and then at Seremban to meet St James. Our compartment wasn't crowded so we occupied two alcoves across the aisle from each other. This gave Ron the opportunity to talk to me privately about Olga and Frank.

As we approached Kuala Lumpur, I looked across at them and remarked how happy Olga looked. Ron agreed, then added, 'I only hope Frank doesn't let her down.'

'What on earth do you mean? Isn't he coming back for her?'

Ron hesitated. 'Well, he certainly gives that impression, seeing that he's anxious to meet your father and the Mother Superior.'

'So, what's amiss? Something he hasn't told Olga?'

'Well, yes. Like me, he has a fiancée back home. I wonder if he's mentioned her. It's not my place to say anything and he does appear to be all set to return to Malaya. But I'm a bit concerned for Olga's sake. What if he doesn't reappear? Very upsetting for her.'

Upsetting! That was an understatement. 'Shouldn't I tell Olga straight away so that if he hasn't told her about his fiancée she can confront him and find out if he's deceiving her?'

'No, please don't do that. Not right now. I could be wrong about Frank. He hasn't been discussing things with me recently. It's possible that he's broken off with his English girlfriend. He's certainly behaving as if he's quite serious about your sister. Wait till we're sailing home. First chance there is I'll corner him and get to the bottom of the matter. I promise to write to you from our first port of call.'

The train pulled into Kuala Lumpur. Ron carried on to Singapore while Frank alighted with us and was introduced to Dad. Later, when we stopped in Seremban, he duly met St James. Both our connections were impressed by this polite, articulate, personable young man whom Olga introduced to them. Both pronounced him most suitable.

About a fortnight later, I received the promised letter from Ron. With some trepidation I slit open the envelope. *Dear Maisie,* it read, *I'm sorry to have to tell you that my suspicions about Frank have been confirmed. He is planning to marry his English girlfriend on his arrival. He should be telling Olga this himself, but is too ashamed to contact her directly right now. He asks her to try not to think too badly of him. He promises to write later when he gets up the courage.*

Frank did write an explanatory letter some time later. In extenuation of his strange conduct, he claimed not to have made up his mind until he actually began the voyage home. Then he weighed up the pros and cons of living in England or emigrating to Malaya — and finally it came down to the vexed question of signing on the dotted line for a Catholic marriage, an insurmountable obstacle for him. Would Olga ever forgive him?

Yes, she did. In her own way.

Britain was at the time still suffering severe food shortages. My dear sister sent a huge food parcel to his address, avenging herself by being magnanimous. A truly Christian response!

The French have a saying, *'partir est mourir un peu'* ('to part is to die a little'). 1951 was full of little and not so little deaths. Early in the year I heard from Matty that Geoff had been fired at and wounded by the communist terrorists and he had been sent home to England for treatment and recuperation. He had not written to me since that dinner together when my racial origins were cited as the stumbling block to our union. Christmas had come and gone without any greeting from him. Rather than wait around for a letter that would never come, I decided to act decisively and put a definite end to the relationship. I wrote to him asking for the return of all my letters, and when I received them I retired to a secluded corner of the schoolyard, lit a small bonfire and burnt his letters along with mine. Dust to dust, ashes to ashes. Did I stop thinking about him? Not immediately.

A little later there was another parting when St James was transferred to Johor Bahru, a much smaller convent with a lighter workload. She had been in poor health for many years. In 1947 she had flown to Paris for specialist treatment for her neuralgia, and there was the suggestion of brain surgery. She was accompanied by her younger brother, an admiral in the French Navy no less, according to St Anselme.

The operation she underwent had not alleviated her suffering but that did not prevent her from taking charge again on her return, despite continuing bouts of intense pain. The slightest puff of air across her right cheek could set off a spasm and she was never seen without a large white handkerchief held against her face. I once witnessed one of her attacks. Her already pale face turned ashen, she didn't make a sound, but her eyes told the story. 'Reverend Mother, are you in pain?' I enquired. I knew I was speaking out of turn.

'Do not be concerned, my dear child — it will pass very soon. Every day my health is improving.' Of course she was lying, but she would not give in and admit her suffering. St James had a reputation for being tough on her religious community. She was even tougher on herself.

Before she left, I spent a few minutes alone with her to express my sadness over her transfer. 'I must go willingly wherever God sends me — pray for me and I will do the same for you,' she said. Naturally, I promised. She said she had a little keepsake for me — not so little, as it turned out. She placed a volume of the complete works of Shakespeare in my hands. A precious gift still in my possession.

Tessie had joined the student-teacher fraternity a year after me, at a time when the teacher training system was about to change dramatically.

That year behind put her in an advantageous position with regard to the teaching scholarships on offer to a number of first and second year students. Third year students like Louise and myself were not included in the intake for Kirkby College, England, because we were so close to completing our Normal course. My double promotion (from Grade V to Grade VII) way back in 1946, which had pleased me so much then was the cause of depriving me of a UK scholarship and parting me from my closest friend and confidante. I would have given anything to join Tessie and the others on the slow boat to England, making whoopee all the way!

For a while I felt very sorry for myself. Then I was made aware that others in my vicinity were also beset with problems, one of them being Louise. Her longtime long-distance fiancé, Aubrey, had written to tell her he would not be returning to Malaya to marry her. She was far too young for him, he said. He had met a Welsh girl his own age and they had become engaged. So sorry, and all that! Louise had comforted me after Geoff's defection — now I comforted her.

Men! How inventive they were when sliding out of a relationship. The girlfriend acquired a myriad of serious afflictions: wrong race, wrong religion, wrong age — the problem was seldom of their making.

Olga and I holidayed with the Pijpes at year's end. A vacation in Singapore always lifted my spirits and this year was no exception. Besides, we had a lot of catching up to do with Mary and Cora. There were several untold stories about the war years. We also spent a few days with the Scotts who had now, like St James, been posted to Johore Bahru. Their new home overlooked the Straits of Johor; all along its southern aspect one could enjoy pleasant water views.

'Do you remember our house in Seremban?' Mrs Scott asked. 'We overlooked the cemetery. A daily *memento mori*. This view is definitely an improvement!'

Before going on to Singapore, we were invited to spend the coming Easter holidays with them as well and we cheerfully accepted.

24

I'M TWENTY-ONE TODAY!

In January 1952, I turned twenty-one. Straight after Mass that morning, I walked down the aisle towards the exit, stopped at the Mother Superior's chair, just inside the door and announced to St John Baptist: 'Reverend Mother, I am twenty-one today!'

'Yes, my child. Congratulations!'

I waited silently and made no move to leave.

'Would you like permission to go out this afternoon?' St John was quite liberal about such things.

'No, Reverend Mother, I would like to receive my mail unopened now that I've come of age.'

'Oh, you haven't wasted any time! Well, yes, it is your right now that you're an adult.'

Right then my request was something of an empty gesture. Nobody — well, nobody special — was corresponding with me, but just in case a certain somebody turned up, all the communication channels would now be open and there would be no impediments.

Fast-forward to Easter. We took up Eunice Scott's offer and settled into their comfortable home once again, enjoying the culinary skills of their two devoted servants. Of course we took the opportunity to visit the Johor Bahru convent and spend some time with St James and St Anselme, who had accompanied her Superior south. If anything, St James was thinner and frailer than before. Only her fierce, indomitable spirit kept her going.

Olga and I were looking forward to a very quiet, relaxed holiday dividing our time between the Scott's house and the convent, when everything changed. A phone call from one of Eunice's close friends altered everything. The caller had just undergone a major operation and wondered if she could spend a week convalescing with her old friend.

Unhesitatingly, Eunice told her, 'You're most welcome, come whenever you like.' Then she turned to us. 'I have to ask a special favour. As you know, this house only has two bedrooms, so I'll have to offer your room to my friend. If she were fit and healthy, I'd ask her to postpone her visit until your departure, but the way things are —'

'Don't worry, Mrs Scott, I'm sure Aunty May will have us,' Olga said at once. 'Let's ring her now and find out.'

Aunty May responded as we'd predicted and we arranged to holiday with her while Eunice had her friend to stay and to return after she left. All very simple!

At Goodman Road, we picked up our usual routine. I shadowed my aunt around the place, while Olga was out shopping and visiting. Aunty May told us we had picked a good time to stay. She was expecting a special visitor that week, an Australian marine engineer who for some time had been delivering parcels from one Vaz relative to another up and down the west coast. In Bangkok he'd pick up durians (the notoriously pungent tropical fruit) and some Siamese delicacies and hand them over to Aunty Frances in Penang, who in turn would give the messenger some salt-fish pickle or other speciality for Aunty May in Singapore. She, of course, would have a few bundles ready for him to take to her niece in Bangkok and her sister in Penang.

'He's so obliging, he never seems to mind acting as our postman, and he enjoys Asian food, so we always have him over for a meal when his ship calls here.' On and on she went, describing this big Australian — not bad-looking, she said, always joking …

Could this be my Aussie larrikin, I wondered. 'How old is he?' I asked.

'About thirty — he says he'd like to settle down and get married. I think he had his eye on Cora for a while, but she wasn't interested, silly girl. Uncle Willem and I think he's a fine catch. If I were a young girl, I'd have him!'

She'd certainly whetted my appetite. 'Could I meet him?'

'Well, I'm never sure when he's coming — he just appears when his ship's in port.' She smiled. 'Supposing he arrives this evening while you're at the Bruces, I'll send a taxi for you with a message — how about it? Any sensible young woman would like Bob!'

Olga and I were sitting in Aunty Joan's lounge that evening when the taxi arrived as promised. Olga stayed at the Bruces' house, but I got into the cab and headed back to Goodman Road.

If he's half as kind and good-natured as Aunty claims, I'll have him! I decided. After all, I'm twenty-one now — that's the right age for a woman to marry, isn't it?

I got out of the cab, walked in and noticed the solidly-built occupant of one of the armchairs. I smiled. He smiled back. What a roguish grin he had! And large hazel eyes, probably his best feature. He had been entertaining his hosts with a funny story, one of his fund of amusing tales and I was soon an attentive listener. When he asked me if I'd like to go out with him the following evening I agreed.

Aunty May beamed approval when I said I liked Bob and told her we'd be going out together. 'A pity my Cora didn't care for him — maybe she thinks he's too old.'

I was inclined to back my Aunt's judgement. Hadn't she picked the very best of husbands for herself?

Olga, however, didn't share Aunty May's enthusiasm for this Aussie seaman when she returned later that evening. 'He's not your type, you wouldn't have much to talk about.' Her disapproval was not about to make me change my mind.

Next evening, after an early dinner, Bob called for me and we drove off. We stopped at a roadside fruit stall. 'Like some grypes, Myzie?' he asked me.

Occasionally it took me a few seconds to work out what he was saying. His broad Australian accent got in the way of instant comprehension. Back he came with a huge cascade of grapes. Where to now? Nowhere in particular, just an open stretch of coastline. Lots of Singaporean couples seemed to find that particular spot attractive. We parked and got out to sit on the sand. In a sense we were alone, but we had lots of company. It was something like dining in a crowded restaurant when you concentrate on your own conversation and ignore everybody else.

'You look lovely, very desirable,' Bob said. Nowadays he might have used the word 'sexy'.

This man is pretty direct, I was thinking. I decided not to beat around the bush with him. 'Are you still sweet on Cora?' I asked.

'I was, but she didn't offer me any encouragement. But I still visit the Pijpes because your aunt and uncle always make me so welcome. I really enjoy calling on them whenever my ship brings me to Singapore.' He changed tack. 'Tell me about your life in the convent. You're not thinking of becoming a nun, are you?' Then, in answer to my negative response he said, 'I didn't think so, but I had to ask.'

By the time I'd sketched in my life prior to Mum's death, the war years and the post-war period, all the grapes had vanished. Yet we still had so much to talk about, so many gaps to fill.

Bob told me he was between ships, looking for a berth on a coastal vessel. He could be sailing again in a matter of days. He'd look for a shore job if he had a good reason to give up going to sea — like getting married. He looked me squarely in the eye. 'Will you give me that reason?' he asked. No answer. 'Will you marry me?' Still no answer. I had hoped he'd pop the question but now that he'd done so I got cold feet.

'I know, I know — I've only just met you and sailors have a bad reputation. A girl in every port! I'll admit it's mostly true. I've had my share of girls in various ports, but all that would be in the past if we got married. This sailor would sail no more. There'd be no other woman in my life — just you. What do you say?' He'd gone through half a pack of cigarettes pleading his cause. Now he sat mute, hardly moving.

There was no doubting his sincerity. His lack of artifice and pretence appealed to me. If I said 'Maybe' I might just as well say 'No'. I knew this bloke didn't deal in 'perhaps' and 'maybe'. It had to be 'yes' or 'no', and if I refused him, he'd sail out of my life for ever. Somehow I had the feeling I could not let that happen.

'Give me a few minutes to think it over,' I said.

He made one more attempt at persuasion. 'I like your family a lot. They're kind and gentle people and I feel at home with them. Yesterday I was paying my usual shore-leave visit when my life changed very suddenly. One minute I was sitting in that armchair, the next thing a cab pulled up and a young woman entered the room. She flashed me such a dazzling smile, I thought all my Christmases had come together — say "yes", Myzie.'

Very softly I answered, 'Yes, Bob.'

'Oh, my darling …'

The house was in darkness when we returned. I had to wait till the next morning to announce our engagement.

I was awake long before anyone else. In fact, I'd slept very little. Had I done something utterly crazy? Crazy Maisie — that rhymed! The lines 'marry in haste, repent at leisure' kept running through my mind and my head throbbed as a drumbeat took up the doleful mantra.

Yet it wasn't entirely a mood of gloom and doom. Simultaneously, I felt an intoxicating surge of power and well-being. Why wasn't the whole household up at the crack of dawn to hear my dramatic news? I was bursting to tell them — perhaps to shock them!

Olga was certainly amazed and dismayed. 'My God, have you any idea what you're doing? What do you know about Bob? Don't marry him just to escape from the convent.'

Cora was surprised but happy for me. Then she remembered something. 'Oh, but he can't dance — and you enjoy it so much.'

'He can't sing, either,' Mary chimed in, 'and you love singing.'

'Thanks a million, all of you, for your vote of confidence.' Somewhat deflated, I awaited Aunty May's verdict. She was thrilled and told Uncle Willem the news. He kissed me on the forehead and said he hoped I'd be very happy.

Bob called after lunch to take me to a jeweller's to select a ring. He steered me towards a one-carat diamond solitaire.

'You can't afford that, can you?' I protested.

'Not right now, but I'll put a deposit on it and once I'm working again it'll be paid off in no time.' He seemed unconcerned about taking on a big debt. 'You have to pay for quality — don't worry, it'll be okay.'

On the way back to the Pijpes we stopped off at his boarding-house. Another seaman lived there with his wife and two young children. As soon as Bob appeared, both children raced up to him with arms outstretched, hoping for a piggyback. They weren't disappointed. A carved Chinese chest stood in the hallway. When the lid was raised a treasure-trove of souvenirs from exotic places was revealed: brass Benares bowls and candelabra, carved wooden statuettes, lacquer trays and boxes, rainbow-hued saris.

'Help yourself,' he invited. When I hesitated, he grabbed a couple of vases and half-a-dozen saris and placed them on the back seat of the car. 'These should go into your glory box,' he said.

'Glory box?' I queried.

'Don't all girls collect things in a special chest in preparation for their marriage?'

'Oh, you mean my trousseau.'

'Yeah — if you have to use French words — same difference.'

There would be many occasions when not just the Australian accent but words and phrases would trip me up. And if his taste in colour was anything to go by, it would be wise never to let him choose my clothes!

When Bob delivered me to the Pijpe's door he offered to drive Olga and me back to the Scotts at the end of our Singapore visit. I rang Eunice Scott with my big news, slightly anxious about the way she'd react. She was very calm, naturally surprised, but untroubled. She said she was eager to meet Bob and she knew St James would want to meet him as well. After the call I remembered that Mrs Scott had spent the war years in Western Australia as an evacuee from Malaya. She was quite used to Australians, at a time when they were an unknown quantity to many Europeans.

As for me, I found their direct, even blunt approach confronting at times, but I got used to it. In my opinion, they made up in honesty for what they lacked in subtlety. You always knew where you stood with them.

When we got to the Scotts' house, Bob was invited to stay to lunch and encouraged to talk about his family, his job, the countries he'd visited and his future plans, while all the time Eunice watched him carefully, interviewing him for the benefit of St James and naturally on my behalf as well. After he'd left, she gave me her candid opinion.

'He's no film star, neither is he the artistic, academic type. But he is a kind, sincere person and I believe he genuinely cares for you. You could do a lot worse! I shall tell St James exactly what I've told you. I don't know about the religious aspect, seeing as you're Catholic and he's not.' Then she smiled as she recalled an incident in her own life. 'When I brought my Bill home to meet my parents for the first time, they were anxious to know only one thing — was he or wasn't he a Catholic? When I told them he wasn't, they were delighted and accepted him immediately. Strange? Well, maybe not. We're talking about Northern Ireland!'

Bob duly presented himself to St James one afternoon. Poor lady! She must have been dismayed and disbelieving. How could I have chosen somebody so unsuitable? I haven't mentioned Bob's tattoos. He had three on each arm. However, if I remember correctly, he wore a long-sleeved shirt for the occasion, though he did turn up in short sleeves at the Seremban convent later on, much to the consternation of St John. Even without the tattoos on show, I can appreciate the shock the tiny, aristocratic St James felt when big, burly Bob stood before her, and after shaking hands announced in broad Strine, 'Myzie has told me a whole lot aboucha.'

St James then sent me away on some pretext and quizzed him about his background, his taste in music and reading, his hobbies, all the while, no doubt, asking herself what I saw in him. A greater contrast to Frank Fisher could not have been imagined. Bob Duncan, she must have concluded, was neither a scholar nor a gentleman. But then, if she had to make comparisons with Frank, she'd have to concede that one may be taken in by appearances. Olga's suitor had certainly not lived up to his outward gloss.

She gave me her considered opinion. 'He doesn't share your interests, your love of literature and intellectual debate, your flair for languages. Have you thought about all those things?'

I didn't meet her gaze. My mind was made up and I didn't want to be swayed from the path I'd chosen. Wearily my mentor continued, forcing herself to be fair and balanced. 'Mrs Scott has told me she believes Bob to be kind and sincere and devoted to you — I hope she is right. Pray for guidance, my child. I shall do likewise.'

Within three days of our return to Seremban, I received my first letter from Bob — sealed. His letters came regularly, seldom more than a week apart. Amongst other things, they informed me of job applications, interviews, offers of work from shipping companies, all of which he refused in his pursuit of a shore job. In May he got a firm offer from Osborne & Chappel, an English mining company with mines scattered over the western side of the peninsula. The mine Bob was sent to was located just over half-an-hour's drive from Kuala Lumpur. At the end of his probation period, an upgrading to a permanent position was likely, with a house to himself if he got married. Meantime he shared a three-bedroom house with two other bachelors.

Bob's immediate boss, his Dredge-master, was Eric Morris. Most of the European staff were Brits but Eric was one of the few Aussies in that crowd and he turned out to be a true friend to us both.

A couple of months down the track, Bob had paid off the diamond ring and we were officially engaged. There was no lavish party, just a dinner at the Lakeside Rest House with Olga and Dad. If Dad was expecting somebody like Frank, he was certainly disappointed. He didn't believe Bob and I were compatible. 'He's very rough around the edges,' he remarked. He also wondered if Bob had been married before — at thirty-one I suppose this seemed highly probable. Another thing he feared was that like many sailors, my fiancé might be over-fond of the bottle. The only aspect of the engagement that Dad fully endorsed was the expensive ring. However, he avoided condemning Bob outright. 'In time, maybe you'll be able to smooth out those edges and give him some polish,' he said hopefully.

My last holiday as a boarder was spent not in Penang or Singapore but at Port Dickson with the other boarder-teachers, in a seaside bungalow normally used by holidaying military personnel. On this occasion it was offered to us rent-free by a certain Malay Regiment officer as a token of goodwill towards the convent where his daughters were pupils.

For the duration of our stay we were expected to do our own cooking and cleaning. None of us had kept house before. The cleaning presented no problems but the cooking did. Here we were, five young qualified or nearly qualified teachers knowing next to nothing about the elements of basic cookery. Of course we could whip up marvellous sponges, trifles, and scones, but anything beyond teatime cooking was out of our range. We could not produce any meat, fish or vegetable dishes, not even soups, unless they came out of a can! That's how we planned to solve the tricky situation: we'd open cans for every meal — we had a good collection of them on the kitchen shelves. We were quite pleased with our solution to the culinary question and felt confident enough to invite all the current boyfriends over to spend the day. They were KL types, accountants and salesmen from the large department stores — Whiteaways, Littles and Robinsons. Chief among them was Brian Grant, Olga's beau, a clever and sprightly Irishman she'd met sometime earlier. It is a source of considerable irritation to me that I cannot recall exactly how and when they met, but it must have been a felicitous occasion for they were seeing each other on a regular basis and the situation looked promising.

Picture the scene. Four young men, five young women around the dining-table, Olga carving the Spam and Fray Bentos corned beef with great aplomb, Betty Garcia and Lynette Newman handing around the bowls of asparagus and corn; Ivy Fernandez slicing bread and me handing around the plates and cutlery, thinking: 'Bob's late, wonder what is keeping him?' Then up the garden path comes trouble in the shape of one big Australian, a large fresh fish under one arm, a sizeable roast beef under the other. He sticks his head in the door and asks 'Where do I put these things? We can have the fish tonight and the roast tomorrow.'

Did Bob mean we would actually have to cook these raw products? The dismay on our faces was clearly visible. Disbelief crept into Bob's voice. 'You mean not one of you five sheilas can cook? What on earth did you propose to eat during your stay?' We pointed to the array of tinned food neatly stacked on the shelves. 'We open a few of these every day.'

'Bloody hell! That's a convent education for you!' growled my fiancé.

With that, he whipped off his shirt and set about preparing a 'proper' meal for us. 'I'll show youse what good Ozzie tucker is like,' he declared, and aside to me he added, 'You'd better learn to cook — you can't feed me sponges and trifles all the time!'

Bob's presence certainly improved the quality of our meals, but he didn't quite fit in and he wasn't his usual, easy-going self. It may have been because he felt he didn't belong to this Kuala Lumpur 'gentlemen's club', that he took offence when one of the town types paid me a few compliments and my jealous fiancé pulled a gun on him. Surprisingly, the other man showed no fear, saying instead, 'Go ahead, shoot!' The situation looked pretty nasty until Brian, Olga's friend, stepped in and played peacemaker.

I called Bob a jealous fool and offered to return his ring. 'No, you keep it — throw it into the drain if you want,' he yelled, struggling to control his tears. I realised that the spark that fuelled his rage was his fear of losing me. Silly man!

My KL admirer was told very firmly to turn his gaze elsewhere because my fiancé had a very short fuse.

That night as we girls were settling down after all the excitement, Beatrice came close and whispered, 'Don't break off your engagement with Bob — I'd stick with him if I were you. He really cares about you … and don't forget something very important. He can COOK!'

Possession of a ring entitled me to unchaperoned outings with Bob. Olga sometimes joined us for lunch or dinner and gradually grew to like and accept him, though she advised me to wait another year before taking the final step.

'Don't marry merely to leave the Convent. Once you've got your certificate, we can leave together and live in Singapore or Penang.' Sage advice, but contrary to Bob's wishes.

Wait another year? Definitely not! We would be eligible for married quarters in October and he wanted us to move in right away. However, there was a hitch. My final exams were due in October and I wanted to sit for them and complete my course.

Bob insisted that I wouldn't need to get a job anyway; he could easily support me on his salary. I sought the advice of Mr Reece, the Inspector of Schools. Was it possible for me to withdraw from the course at this late stage?

'Possible, yes — but advisable, definitely NO,' he said. In the kindest way he warned me that I might regret my decision if I walked away at this juncture. 'You may be financially comfortable right now, but in future years you may need that qualification should circumstances alter. Please consider very carefully before you act.' His concern for me was evident. He had nothing to gain personally whether I stayed on or quit.

I decided to take the exams and made Bob wait the extra month. He wasn't happy about that and we had our second quarrel.

'You're doing exactly what the convent wants,' he complained. 'I thought you'd begun to think for yourself.'

'Well,' I countered, 'I owe the convent something for giving me a home and an education, but I'm also doing something for myself. Having started something I feel obliged to finish it.'

So it was decided that the wedding would take place in November, after the exams. But St John wanted to know why I couldn't wait till mid-December, the end of the school year. The convent viewpoint was being argued very persistently and I had to admit that it seemed a reasonable enough request. Could I risk another argument with Bob? This time it would be a major battle!

I said 'No' to the convent, but I felt bad about it. It was a difficult decision. Where did my duty lie now — to the convent or to Bob?

When a teacher leaves at the busiest time of the school year, she causes considerable disruption. I suffered a pang of regret, several in fact, when I announced my impending departure to my girls. There was such a spontaneous outpouring of dismay and disappointment that I would not be with them till December. Calm was restored after I assured them that an extremely kind and competent teacher would be taking my place and they would not be disadvantaged. I'd glad to say that my replacement lived up to the promises I'd made about her.

25

THE FINAL STRETCH

One fine Saturday afternoon in September, Bob took me to the races. It was a dress-up occasion: women in hats and gloves, high-heels and silk stockings, men in suits and well polished leather shoes. Altogether a well-dressed, prosperous looking crowd.

Near the betting area Bob noticed Mr Cooper, the Osborne & Chappel Manager. Bob introduced me as Miss Prout, his fiancé. In my formal attire I must have looked like an expat, because Mr Cooper asked if I'd arrived recently from England and what I thought of life in the colonies. Without hesitation I replied that I was born and raised in Malaya. He looked surprised and after some fatuous comment to the effect that I wouldn't mind the humid weather in that case, he walked away. My truthful reply sealed Bob's fate regarding his chance of obtaining a married contract with the firm. A few weeks later, his trial period over, he was offered a permanent position with Osborne & Chappel, but on a single basis, not a married contract. I had inadvertently told the manager I was a local girl and company policy did not consider locals acceptable spouses for their European staff. A number of Eurasian women were married to O&C staff, having successfully passed themselves off as Europeans after lying about their origins. I might have done the same — then again, I don't know. Anyway, it was too late to change things now.

Eric Morris told Bob not to worry. There were other mining companies that were less exclusive and racist in outlook and offered even better conditions — Anglo-Oriental, for instance. Their staff were mostly Australian and many were married to local girls; in fact one of the big bosses had a Chinese wife. Bob lost no time contacting Anglo-Oriental. He went for an interview and was offered a job on the spot. They wanted to know why he was leaving O&C just after he'd been offered a permanent position. He explained. 'They weren't offering me a married contract because I plan to marry a Eurasian girl.' A-O then indicated that it wasn't in the business of restricting marriage choices, which was good news indeed.

It was arranged that Bob would start work with Anglo-Oriental in mid-November, when they'd have a house ready for us. The wedding date was fixed for 8th November. We planned to honeymoon at Cameron Highlands, north of Kuala Lumpur, then go on to Perak where the mine was situated.

With the job and accommodation sorted out it was time to organise the wedding. The venue? We thought of Singapore at first, then ruled it out because of the extra travelling and cost involved. Bob and I discovered we did have something in common — almost nothing in the way of savings. We'd always spent our money as fast as we received it. Now we'd have to manage our income better.

Mother St John offered to have the reception at the Seremban convent — a truly generous offer in view of the fact that I had caused such difficulties for her, but I declined and settled on KL instead, where I would be staying with Eric and Ann Morris before the wedding. Eric would be giving me away.

Dad had said he'd be available to lead me to the altar provided the wedding was in Singapore. Then I need not invite Aunt Bobs if I didn't want to. He could tell her that one airfare was all they could reasonably afford. However, if Kuala Lumpur was the venue, he said, I couldn't invite him without including her. I pointed out to him that when Barbara, his eldest stepdaughter, had been married in KL that same year, Olga and I hadn't figured on the invitation list. 'I'm not having *her* at my wedding and if that means you can't come either, so be it!' I told him angrily. 'Olga and I are used to being ignored, even virtually abandoned.'

Olga was listening silently to my outburst and now intervened.

'Enough, Maisie, enough. No need to say any more.'

It was true — tears were running down Dad's cheeks while I was accusing him of neglect and indifference. During a quiet interval, he handed me a cheque for $300, which he told me was the amount they'd spent on Barbara's wedding. Even in those days it was no fortune, but it just about covered the cost of the reception.

Olga accompanied me to Singapore on a lightning trip to buy the wedding dress. I got something off-the-peg from Hilda's, a boutique we'd patronised whenever we'd holidayed on the island. Olga chose her bridesmaid's gown from Robinsons. John was a little apprehensive about the whole affair. 'Sure you're doing the right thing?' he asked. 'We're in no hurry to get rid of you!'

A lovely thing for a brother to say.

My sister, brother and Matty were booking into the Railway Hotel in KL the weekend of the event, together with close friends from the convent. Tessie, of course, was unable to attend but she sent her good wishes. The best man should have been Brian Grant, Olga's accountant friend in KL. He was squiring her around at the time, so he would have been the logical choice. However, John Lucas, Assistant Manager at Osborne & Chappel, had approached Bob when he heard the reason why he was leaving the firm. Maybe he wished to demonstrate that he did not subscribe to the company's racist views. So Bob took him on board for the ceremony.

Time was running out. During Bob's days off, he was expected to attend special religious classes with Father Maury, the parish priest of the church where we were to be married, to learn about the Catholic religion and be prepared for a Catholic marriage. Like Frank before him, Bob was asked to sign the document pertaining to mixed-marriages. He signed, but under protest, declaring to Father Maury that the contract turned him into a stallion for the Catholic church! After that he attended no further classes.

Father Maury contacted Reverend Mother to deplore Bob's irreverent attitude and to see whether I couldn't be persuaded to drop this uncooperative, uncouth Australian. So I had another session with St John, who gently and hesitatingly asked me to reconsider my decision. Wasn't I rushing into things? Perhaps Bob was too worldly for me. He seemed to be totally lacking in religious feeling. What sort of a life had he led before meeting me? Seamen had rather unsavoury reputations (that old potato!) and he could be a divorced man (Dad's argument). It was extremely hard to check up on his past. 'Be careful my dear,' she said, 'be very, very careful. Change your mind now, before it's too late!'

It's impossible to say how long I stood facing St John in a state of utter turmoil. Surely Aunty May couldn't have been so wrong about Bob! Mrs Scott hadn't given him a bad reference either. In my estimation, Eunice Scott was an astute judge of character. But they were only two voices among the many who were prepared to think the worst of my fiancé. I'd been over every negative aspect of the intended union during several sleepless nights — I didn't need Mother John to parade them before me yet again. Somehow I believed there was something about Bob that was worth hanging on to. I stood firm. I said to myself, 'Come hell or high water, I will keep that date in November.'

To this kind, troubled Mother Superior regarding me so intently I finally said, 'I'm not giving him up and my marriage will last, because I'll try my hardest to make it work. However, if despite my best efforts it fails, then I'll go back to the classroom and stand on my own two feet.'

For a while Olga had done her best to dissuade me from the course I was taking, but she didn't like the idea of the Church exerting undue pressure on me; now she supported me in my stand. A few days after my talk with St John, Father Maury played his final card. He said he could not recommend our marriage and he would withhold permission because it was abundantly clear that Bob was the wrong type of husband for a Catholic wife. Bob's response was: 'They've got my signature. I will honour the promise about the children. If we can't marry in the Catholic Church we'll have the ceremony in a Protestant church, or even in a Registry Office.'

Once again I was seated in St John's office. 'What will you do now?' a very sad and distraught figure inquired.

'Please tell Father Maury that I would prefer to marry in our Church, but if permission is refused, I'll marry outside it.'

When Olga heard of the latest development in our on-going saga, she said without hesitation, 'Catholic church, Protestant church or Registry office, I'll stand beside you as your bridesmaid.'

A week later, permission was given for the marriage to go ahead as planned.

All this was going on at the same time as I was studying for my final exams. It's surprising I got through without failing any subject. What a relief! Thanks to Mr Reece's sound advice, I'd now acquired a form of marriage insurance!

When my departure from convent life was imminent, back came the old doubts and a number of new ones, mainly concerning my flight from the old and familiar and my entry into unknown new territory. I'd often said I wanted my independence. Was I ready to leave the cocoon that had enveloped me for fourteen years and take the big leap outside?

For the last time I slept in my narrow iron bed in the dormitory, thinking back to my first night as a boarder, to the introspective and lonely eight-year-old missing the goodnight kisses and cuddles she was accustomed to, the soft toys on the bed, with the winking red flame of the Capitol cinema across the road offering the only friendly and familiar gesture. Goodbye to all of that …

Bob parked his car in the porch and started to fill it with my belongings while I circulated the familiar territory saying my farewells to people and places and realising somewhat belatedly how dear to me certain people were and how much I would miss them.

'We'll miss your cheerful face around here,' said one.

'We'll miss your voice in the choir,' said another.

Olga and Mother John were waiting for me near the car.

'You'll take good care of my sister, won't you?' At Olga's earnest entreaty Bob gripped her hands and gave her his promise. I merely hugged my always steadfast sister. My heart was too full for words. I would miss the protection of her safety net.

Mother John put her arms around me and said, 'My dear, if he doesn't treat you well, you can always come back.' My tears must have told her that I was touched by her generous spirit. I'd put her through a very torrid time. I promised to return and visit whenever I could.

The car headed north towards Kuala Lumpur. All my worldly goods fitted quite easily into the car boot. The more fragile wedding gifts were spread on the back seat, secured with ribbons and twine — the staff dinner-service, for instance, a very handsome gift.

Bob glanced across at me. 'You're crying! How strange! I thought you couldn't wait to leave.'

I just shook my head. Impossible to explain so many conflicting emotions.

Eric and Ann Morris were the perfect hosts. After more than twenty years of marriage they remained a happy couple, childless but contented with their lot. Their home provided an ideal staging-post for my own marriage.

On the morning of the wedding I bathed, dressed, quickly applied my make-up and got Ann Morris, my sole bridal assistant, to help me pin on my floral tiara and veil. I was ready. I'd taken less time to dress for my wedding than I normally took getting ready for an evening out.

I heard Bob's voice below as I was about to descend the staircase, so I waited until he'd left the house. On the day of the wedding the groom is not supposed to see his bride until she comes up the aisle towards him. Otherwise — bad luck!

Eric came upstairs to tell me the coast was clear. 'Maisie, you look absolutely radiant! I feel so privileged to be giving you away.' I returned his smile and thanked him and Ann for the supportive role they'd played at a crucial time in Bob's life and mine and declared they'd always be very welcome guests at the Duncan home.

A little band of relatives and friends were waiting for me outside the church. Olga clicked away with her box-camera, then looked at her watch. 'You're only ten minutes late!' she said. Eric took my arm and we began to proceed sedately up the aisle while the organ played. In a dreamlike state I reached Bob's side. He looked subdued, misty-eyed. Grasping my hand he gave it a reassuring little squeeze. I recall being immensely grateful for that spontaneous gesture. All my doubts fell away and a surge of confidence and joyful anticipation replaced them as I faced the altar and the wedding service commenced. The fateful words were spoken, rings exchanged and then my Australian larrikin and I were walking arm-in-arm down the aisle while the wedding march echoed around us and bounced off the walls.

Outside in the bright sunshine everything was a blur — so many faces wreathed in smiles, so many hands reaching out to touch us, so many voices raised in greeting:

'Congratulations, Maisie! Congratulations, Bob! 'Congratulations, Mrs Duncan!'

That sounded odd — 'Mrs Duncan', was that really me? I'd have to get used to that name as I took on my new role in life — that of a miner's wife.

envoi

Before emigrating with Bob to Australia in 1959, I applied for Permanent Resident status. The usual health clearance was required as well as a character reference from a Justice of the Peace, vouching for my suitability on the grounds that I was a law-abiding citizen.

To quote the matchless prose of the document:

Maisie Alice Duncan is … not a dangerous character likely to overthrow the Government.

An official declaration that I was not a terrorist!

Bibliography

Barber, Noel. 1968. *Sinister Twilight: The Fall of Singapore*. London: Collins.

Barber, Noel. 1981. *Tanamera: A Novel of Singapore.* Hodder & Stoughton: London.

Bradden, Russell. 1952. *The Naked Island.* Werner Laurie: London.

Chapman, F. Spencer. 1949. *The Jungle is Neutral.* Chatto & Windus: London.

Goodwin, Robert. 1995. *Mates & Memories*. Boolarong Press: Brisbane.

Maisie Duncan is a retired school teacher who now lives in the small town of Helensvale, south of Brisbane, Australia. Her memoir began to take shape after she left the classroom permanently. Although retired she enjoys an active life, closely involved in the family affairs of her children and grandchildren (nine in all) and maintains close contacts with her numerous friends, young and old.

Notes

Notes

Notes

Notes

Notes